P9-ARE-865

Widespread Acclaim for the Book Every Woman Should Read!

"[Budoff's] information is up-to-date, authoritative and clearly presented. With this book in hand, women over forty can fully understand not only what is happening to their bodies, but how and why."

—*Publishers Weekly*

"Surveys the latest word on several gynecological fronts: hormone therapy, mastectomies, osteoporosis, hysterectomies, cystitis, ovarian cancer, contraception, and laboratory tests . . . practical medical advice in a clear, interesting style."

—*The Plain Dealer*, Cleveland

"Budoff is a sympathetic exponent: even those who differ with her on specific points will find the book useful for her warnings and her advice on finding sound medical care."

—*Kirkus Reviews*

"Budoff explodes a lot of myths with the latest information . . . a handy reference in any home."

—*Star-News*, Pasadena

"Informative, well-documented, and readable. A book that should be required reading for women over thirty-five."

—*Library Journal*

NO
MORE
HOT
FLASHES

AND OTHER GOOD NEWS

PENNY WISE BUDOFF, M.D.

WARNER BOOKS

A Warner Communications Company

The author gratefully acknowledges permission from the following sources to quote from material in their control:

W B Saunders Co. for a ''Calcium Equivalency Chart'' reprinted from *Food, Nutrition, and Diet Therapy* by M. V. Krause and L. K. Mahan. Copyright © 1979 by W B Saunders Co.

Science for an excerpt from the article ''A New Marker for Diabetes,'' written by T. H. Maugh II, appearing in *Science*, vol. 215, page 651, March 1982. Copyright © 1982 by the American Association for the Advancement of Science.

Parke-Davis Division of Warner-Lambert Company for the use of drawings of the female reproductive system.

Youngs Drug Products Corporation for the use of photographs from the Koromex and Koroflex Patient's Introduction Booklets. Sole Distributor of Koromex and Koroflex Products.

WARNER BOOKS EDITION

This Warner Books Edition is published by arrangement with G. P. Putnam's Sons.

Cover photograph by Joel Brodsky

Warner Books, Inc.
666 Fifth Avenue
New York, N. Y. 10103

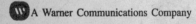 A Warner Communications Company

Printed in the United States of America

First Warner Books Printing: November, 1984

10 9 8 7 6 5 4 3 2

To the mature woman:

May the years ahead be the best we can make them.

Acknowledgments

There are a number of thank-yous I would like to make. The first and foremost is to Leslie Botnick, M.D., whom I first knew as the head of the Radiation Therapy Department at Beth Israel Hospital, part of the Harvard Medical School Joint Radiation Center complex in Boston. He is presently at Valley Radiotherapy Associates, St. Joseph Medical Center, Burbank, California. His dedication to radiation therapy as the primary means of treating early breast cancer provided me with a firm ground for the chapter No More Mastectomies. Furthermore, he contributed material, time and effort to the manuscript and answered innumerable questions as my writing progressed. At Beth Israel, I was most impressed by the teamlike attitude and cooperation between surgeons and radiotherapists. I am convinced that, in time, breast-cancer patients will no longer be torn between the opposing views of competing surgeons and radiotherapists.

Hugh Barber, M.D., director of the Department of Obstetrics and Gynecology at Lenox Hill Hospital in New York City and professor and chairman of the Department of Obstetrics and Gynecology at New York Medical College, most graciously supplied his expertise and advice on the ovarian cancer chapter. He is well known throughout the world for his knowledge of the subject. I am indebted to him for his continuing kindness.

Thanks again to Sheldon C. Sommers, M.D., consultant in pathology at Lenox Hill Hospital in New York and clinical professor of pathology at Columbia University College of Physicians and Surgeons in New York and at the University of Southern California School of Medicine in Los Angeles. My dear friend was there to answer trivia questions and to proof pages where his renowned pathology expertise was needed.

Mark Funt, M.D., coordinator of resident education in the department of Obstetrics and Gynecology at the State University of New York at Stony Brook, provided invaluable help with the chapter on urinary incontinence. His training and interest in the subject is somewhat rare among gynecologists. Arthur D. Smith, M.D., Head of the Department of Urology at Long Island Jewish Hospital in New Hyde Park, New York kindly agreed to proof read the chapter and added valuable information.

Professor Janet Haynes of the Department of Medical Technology, State University of New York at Stony Brook, contributed to the chapter on laboratory medicine. Dr. Harold Bates of Metpath Laboratories also kindly contributed research materials.

Peggy Tsukahira edited and doctored phrases that went astray and participles that were dangling.

To my office staff, Elizabeth Strom, Lois Schultz, Lynn Lazar, my appreciation and thanks for typing and retyping. Lesley Rechter, M.D., my lovely new associate, was able to take over part of my patient load when my editor threatened that deadlines were drawing near. All in all, we have a lot of fun as we see patients, do research, and get manuscripts in order. At least, we never get bored. Patients usually pick up on our close working relationship and are able to relax in this friendly, smiling atmosphere.

Last but not least, thanks to my kids, Jeff and Cindy, and my husband, Sy. They are very special people, and I am proud that they are mine and I am theirs.

Contents

Introduction

It would not be proper for me to tell you my mother's age. Indeed, if I did, I am quite certain a lightning bolt would strike me dead on the spot. I never really learned her age until a few years ago, when she decided that it would be appropriate for her to have a birthday party. But there were many years when she stayed thirty-nine and I continued aging, until I finally became older than she! And she has gotten away with it all. With her green eyes and pug nose and lovely skin, subtracting fifteen years from her age has hardly raised an eyebrow.

But times are changing. I feel that respect for the "mature woman" is increasing, and being forty is no longer synonymous with being over the hill. In fact, I had a party to announce my fortieth. I somehow finally felt respectable and mature enough to be listened to seriously. Finally *I* could pull some of that "listen to your elders" stuff!

Those of us who are over forty are not over the hill. I just have to look at Raquel Welch or Jane Fonda to know that's true. In fact, the twenty years from forty to sixty are documented to be among the most productive years of life. (That means you still have lots of work to do.)

I think that the years beyond forty are years of opportunity. Usually it is a stable time in life. Partners have been chosen, and money worries are probably less than they will be at any other time. If you have children, they're out of the terrible twos and threes and most likely they are adult in stature and are hopefully approaching maturity and independence in their thinking processes. (As you well know, the two do not necessarily go hand in hand!)

And so it is a nice time in life. It may be the first

opportunity you have to do something for yourself—work, a hobby, going back to school. Take advantage of this time to better yourself and your life. Do what you didn't or couldn't do previously. There are many doors open and many joys for those who pursue their goals.

Besides fulfilling your ego needs, you also have another obligation, and that is to your health. Your body has probably been good to you. Now is the time to be good to it and to do a little reevaluation of your own personal health situation. The next few decades of your life may be very much influenced by the care that you give your body now, and that is why I write this book—to give you the background to do exactly that.

As you age, preventive medical care becomes important to your well-being. This book is all about how to get it. It has been written especially for the woman over thirty-five and her specific questions. It is also about what to do when you have a problem, and even in some cases where to get help. For example, Chapter 4, No More Mastectomies, will take you step by step through what I believe is the easiest approach to a breast lump, both mentally and physically. Should the lump turn out to be malignant and if I have convinced you to preserve your breast, there is a list of radiation-therapy centers in the United States that you may turn to. These centers should also be able to guide you to a surgeon who has experience doing lumpectomies.

The chapter on hormone-replacement therapy was written to counteract the scare stories about menopausal therapy that have been appearing in the media for the past decade. They were wrong because they were based on bad therapy. Read the evidence. *Proper* hormone replacement therapy will be the norm of the future; now it can be given correctly. Furthermore, such therapy will save lives as well as vastly improve the lives of women who avail themselves of it.

Chapter 6 on ovarian cancer was written to warn you that danger may lurk in subtle undiagnosed abdominal complaints. Just being aware can save your life.

Urinary-tract infection and urinary incontinence are subjects that most women would like to ignore. These problems can become particularly troublesome as you age. Inadequate treatment of bladder infections can lead to chronic infection, and sometimes surgery is the worst of all possible therapies for incontinence. Yours may be another case where a little pill is better than a knife.

Contraception is one thing for the teenager, another for the mature woman. Be honest with yourself, read Chapter 9, and you will finally have an idea of the best kind or kinds of contraception for you. Or maybe *he* should be doing his part. (Well, it's worth a try, anyway.)

It took forever to write the chapter on laboratory medicine; there were so many things to cover, so many tests that are really important. And the lab becomes even more important as you age, for it can diagnose disease before it is apparent or guide your therapy and make sure you are improving. Understanding a little about lab work is fun, because it really gives you a better sense of medicine today and what it can accomplish. Once you have a little basic knowledge, you may be interested in looking at your own lab results. This could be a step that is important to your health, for if you can follow your progress, it may help you adhere to treatment plans and feel that your efforts are worth it. In my office, lab testing truly equals preventive medicine.

I wrote my first book, *No More Menstrual Cramps and Other Good News*, because I wanted to teach women as much as I could about their own bodies and how best to manage their own specific health problems. I have spent lots of time educating women via television and radio, but a book offers the best possibility of getting in-depth information out to the women.

Many who read that book found that they were as up to date on some topics as their own physicians. Others went to their doctors book in hand, requesting treatment for their cramps or hot flashes or demanding to see their pathology reports from their D and Cs and compare them with the information in the book. And so, little by little, a rustle of change, a small revolution has been stirred. I know it is happening because I get calls every day from women who are really thinking about their health care and beginning to question treatments that are suggested by their physicians.

Women are beginning to speak out—not all, not as many as should, but there is a forward movement and I am encouraged. Women must be part of the medical and surgical decision-making process, for it affects their lives and bodies, sometimes forever. It is only possible to make informed decisions when you have a basic understanding of what the problem is and what the range of alternative therapies is.

It is my hope that this book will provide the information for you to ensure that you are getting the best that modern medicine has to offer. Menopause does not signal the beginning of the end but rather the end of the beginning. The years after forty should truly be the best that are yet to be. All the groundwork has been done, your life has stability and substance, and best of all, you are beginning to have a little more free time to enjoy the fruits of your labors.

Please use this book to find out what your options are, to help choose your therapy, and above all else to understand and be an active participant in the major decisions about your health care, which in the final analysis affect the quality of your life.

NO
MORE
HOT
FLASHES

1

Natural Hormone Replacement Therapy, or No More Scare Stories About Menopausal Therapy

In the 1400's women lived to the mean age of 33. In 1900, women's life expectancy had increased to 48 years. Like small animals, women died when their ovaries stopped functioning. However, a woman born today can expect to live more than 77 years and outlive her ovaries by one-third of her lifetime.

Perhaps we have improved our life span too suddenly. Evolution cannot possibly adjust in such a short period of time. Is it normal to live without hormonal support for 25 to 35 years? Should evolution have provided for a lifetime of hormonal output? Should women be supported by replacement therapy?

"If women were universally supported with the administration of exogenous estrogen, not only through the menopause and the postmenopausal period, but throughout the rest of their lives, they would take over the world." So said Dr. M. Edward Davis, professor emeritus of obstetrics and gynecology at the University of Chicago.[1] In response to Dr. Davis, another eminent physician, Robert W. Kistner, associate professor of obstetrics and gynecology at Harvard Medical School, stated, "Not only is Davis's statement surprising, but also it may engender apprehension and fear in the majority of males. It might even invoke in male physicians a negative reaction leading to almost complete therapeutic nihilism for the premenopausal and postmenopausal female."[2]

Maybe there *is* something to fear. Women now make up

1

half of the work force in this country. We control many of its purse strings. Furthermore, we outlive men, are generally healthier, and are more self-sufficient and better able to cope in our later years, especially comparing men and women who live alone.

In general (and there are always exceptions), women's personalities are better suited for long-term survival. Women cook, clean, garden, shop, work; and take care of husbands, children, and family pets (which everyone else had *promised* to take care of). Most men are content with their work, television, and then maybe a hobby. Somehow that combination doesn't weather as well when one is retired, living alone, and fending for oneself. A woman may have health problems or suffer the death of a spouse and other personal tragedies, but as age advances, she is better able to cope, because for her, coping means simply continuing to do what she has been trained and accustomed to doing. Her male counterpart with similar problems has to assume new, unaccustomed roles which may be frustrating as well as difficult for him.

There are now some 40 million women in the United States who are postmenopausal. Each of them has a life expectancy of twenty-eight years beyond her last menstrual period. If only because of her numbers, the postmenopausal woman has become an important part of our society.

Menopause, for the most part, has been neglected by the medical community. Today it is no longer acceptable for physicians to gloss over a woman's menopausal complaints with a glib remark. They should, instead, be in tune with the latest research and thinking about the physiology of menopause and its consequences. Women, too, must begin to understand menopause, what the changes mean, why they happen, and the choices we have in order to live the next thirty years in the best way possible, both mentally and physically.

In the final analysis, it is we who are responsible for our own well-being. Fortunately, as we shall see in this chapter, the most recent work in the field of menopause brings a great deal of good news.

What is Menopause?

The word "menopause" is frequently used somewhat improperly to signify a range of time. It actually refers to a single point in time—namely the last menstrual period. "Perimenopause" refers to the time before and following the menopause. This is a transitional phase when ovarian function and its hormone production are declining. The "climacteric" is the years from the onset of premenopausal ovarian decline to the time after menopause, when its symptoms stop. The decline of ovarian function goes on for years, but the cessation of menses is an unmistakable biologic marker for the loss of reproductive function. The average age at menopause in the United States is approximately 51.4 years.

Since women's life span is increasing, the postmenopausal period has lengthened because the average age at the occurrence of menopause has remained stable. Progressive physiologic changes occur during a woman's climacteric that affect nearly every organ in the body. Some women experience nothing more than the cessation of menses, while others have disabling problems. The two most important factors in determining how a woman will fare are probably the rate of decline of her female hormones—estrogen and progesterone—and the final degree of hormone depletion.

Many other factors contribute to the overall picture, such as genetic background, general health, lifetime quality of diet, level of activity, and psychological aspects of accepting aging. The most severe symptoms occur in women who lost their ovaries through surgery or radiation when they were premenopausal. Because of the complete and sudden loss of female hormones, their bodies had no time to make the normal, gradual transition. Women who undergo a natural menopause tend to have somewhat milder symptoms.

What Happens Before Menopause

We tend to think of our monthly cycles beginning the day we start to bleed. Actually this is the end of the cycle. The bleeding marks the culmination of an approximately twenty-eight-day process, the sole purpose of which is to produce a fertilized egg and a uterine milieu in which it can grow. No sooner has the menstrual flow stopped than the monthly process begins again.

At a signal from the hypothalamus, a glandular control center in the brain, the pituitary gland releases FSH (follicle stimulating hormone) into the bloodstream. When the hormone reaches the ovaries, an egg begins to develop, gathering a thick layer of surrounding cells which secrete estrogen (in a form called estradiol) as well as protect it by bathing it in fluid and nourishing it. These cells create a layered follicle which, under the influence of FSH, swells and pushes its way up toward the surface of the ovary. The process takes the follicle from microscopic size to 1.0 to 1.5 centimeters in diameter. The surface of the ovary becomes thin and stretched over the follicle.

The estrogen circulating in the blood, meanwhile, is acting on the uterus and fallopian tubes in preparation for the arrival of the egg and the act of fertilization. The uterine lining, or endometrium, begins to thicken as the estrogen causes the cells to multiply and increases the endometrial blood supply. The opening of the cervix dilates and the mucus surrounding it becomes copious and capable of supporting the movement of sperm. Estrogen enhances the capacity of the uterine musculature to contract rhythmically—another aid to the sperm— and it also increases the motility of the fallopian tubes, readying them to receive the egg.

The powerful influence of estrogen isn't confined to the menstrual cycle. Because it and all the other hormones I've mentioned are secreted by glands directly into the bloodstream, they bathe all the tissues throughout the body. Depending on different conditions, they can affect these tissues to varying degrees. For example, besides taking part in the development of your breasts, genitals, fat deposits, and other secondary female sex characteristics at puberty, estrogen has a continuing influence on your blood chemistry, vascular system, and bones. As we shall see, this has serious significance at menopause.

The estrogen or follicular (follicle-building) phase of the menstrual cycle goes on for about nine to ten days. At that time, the estrogen level in the blood peaks, triggering the hypothalamus to signal the pituitary to decrease its secretion of FSH and start releasing LH (luteinizing hormone).

The surge of LH stimulates the follicle further and it ruptures. The egg is propelled through the surface of the ovary with its follicular fluid to a point where it can be picked up by the delicate open ends of the fallopian tubes, which will guide it on its way into the uterus. The ruptured follicle is now filled with blood. Under the continuing influence of LH, this blood rapidly dissipates, and the follicle matures into a bright yellow spot on the ovary known as the corpus luteum (yellow body). Although the corpus luteum still secretes estrogen, it also secretes the second major ovarian hormone, progesterone.

Progesterone governs the second or luteal phase of the cycle. It further develops and matures the thickened endometrium in preparation for pregnancy. It inhibits or reverses the effects of estrogen. It stops the multiplication of endometrial cells, matures the cells so that they are capable of nourishing the egg, reduces and thickens cervical mucus, and exerts a quieting effect on the uterine muscles and fallopian tubes. Progesterone also inhibits the hypothalamus from sending out instructions for more FSH, which would start a new cycle.

Should pregnancy occur, the corpus luteum will continue to produce the progesterone that is necessary to maintain the pregnancy for the first ten weeks following fertilization. After that time, the placenta normally takes over this function. If pregnancy does not occur, LH declines, the corpus luteum begins to degenerate, and progesterone production falls. As the levels of progesterone and estrogen fall, the matured endometrium breaks cleanly away from the urine wall and flows out as menstruation. The fall of progesterone also releases the inhibiting effect on the FSH-stimulating signals of the hypothalamus. Therefore, the pituitary again gets the message to secrete FSH and a new cycle begins.

And so you see that the hypothalamus, pituitary, and ovaries have functions that directly interrelate and depend upon each other. The relationship works through feedback. Changing hormonal levels from one site travel through the bloodstream and turn hormonal secretion on or off from the second site, and vice versa.

What Happens at Menopause

During the perimenopausal period, ovarian function declines. The process begins with a reduction in the number of follicles in the ovary. This reduction decreases fertility and renders the ovaries incapable of producing normal monthly cycling. As the ovaries fail, the usual amount of estrogen and progesterone that would normally flow back through the bloodstream and shut off the pituitary are missing. Because the pituitary is not getting the normal levels of feedback, it pumps more FSH and LH into the blood, as if to prod the ovary into normal production. With the continuing failure of the ovaries to respond, the FSH secretions keep rising, reaching levels thirteen times that of normal cycles, while LH levels rise approximately threefold. As her hormone levels are altered, the woman notices that her menstrual cycle is beginning to change. Women over forty often have short follicular phases to their menstrual cycles, because the high levels of FSH tend to mature the follicles rapidly. This may or may not be followed by the formation of a corpus luteum, and even if it forms, it may be deficient in its production of progesterone. Therefore, with shortening first occurring in the follicular phase (first half) of the cycle, then next in the luteal phase (second half), the woman often finds her cycles reduced to twenty-four days or less. Actually, if menopause occurs early, a woman may have only one or two cycles that are out of the ordinary. On the other hand, the woman whose menopause is late may have several years of marked menstrual irregularity.

As time passes and menopause approaches, the follicles no longer mature fully. Ovulation ceases, and no progesterone is produced. Without progesterone, the endometrial lining of the uterus is constantly stimulated by estrogen. The lining grows and grows, and finally the thickened lining outgrows its blood supply. Then it begins to disintegrate haphazardly, a little from one spot, then a little from another. Because the lining is too thick to begin with, the flow is heavy. The flow is sporadic, too, and occurs over an extended period of time as one section after another sloughs off. This overgrowth of the lining, stimulated by estrogen, is similar to the hyperplasia, or cell overcrowding, which is sometimes thought to be an early precursor of endometrial cancer. In other women, relatively low levels of estrogen resulting from poor follicular formation will persist for long periods of time without relief of progesterone. This will lead to intermittent spotting, which may be prolonged but scant. As follicular estrogen production decreases due to the loss of ovarian follicles and to the reduced sensitivity of the remaining follicles to pituitary stimulation, estrogen finally drops to a level too low to cause the uterine lining to grow, and menstruation stops.

What Happens After Menopause

Even though menopause has occurred, estrogens are still present. Which ones and how much, however, depend on several factors. Besides estradiol, the human female has two other estrogenic hormones—estrone and estriol. Estradiol is the most important and most powerful and is the major female hormone of the premenopausal woman. Estrone is the principal estrogen of the postmenopausal woman.

Estrone is made from weak, male-type hormone precursors secreted by the ovary and the adrenal gland. It is mainly produced in the body fat by conversion of these precursors to estrone. This conversion process increases with age and obesity, and therefore obese women tend to have higher postmenopausal concentrations of estrone than their thinner sisters. The third female hormone, estriol, is made from estrone. It is not, therefore, directly secreted by the ovary, and it may have less effect on the endometrium.

In the early postmenopausal time, estrogen levels (primarily estrone) may be significant. This is partly because both the adrenal gland and ovaries secrete androstenedione, one of the weak male hormones that can be converted into estrone directly or by the mechanisms within fat tissue.

Estradiol   Estrone   Estriol

Later in the postmenopausal period, the outer portion of the ovary no longer produces female hormone, but its core retains its ability to produce androstenedione. While it is functioning, the ovary accounts for approximately 20 percent of the circulating androstenedione; 80 percent comes from the adrenal gland. The core of the ovary also continues to produce another male hormone, testosterone. In the premenopausal woman, the ovaries' female hormones dominate. But after menopause, the female hormonal output of the ovary is markedly curtailed, while the output of male hormone remains relatively static or may even increase due to the stimulation of high levels of pituitary hormones. This then creates a change in the relative proportions of male to female hormones, often tipping a delicate balance and causing the growth of dark, coarse facial hairs on the chin, as well as increased amounts of fuzzy facial hair that can sometimes be noticed on older women. Finally, however, all ovarian function is lost. This leaves the adrenal as the sole producer of estrone precursors.

I think it is fascinating to see from the following diagrams of male and female hormones how little difference there is between what we hold to be the sacred distinction between male and female. Once you have seen these structures, it is easy to understand how readily they can be converted into one another. And they are constantly being interconverted. Progesterone is often the precursor for either male or female hormones; estradiol can be converted to estrone and vice versa; and testosterone can be converted into female hormone and vice versa. Male and female physiologies are not all that exclusive.

As the complex menstrual cycle ceases and the hormones that have been saturating the body for more than forty years are withdrawn, a woman can suffer conditions ranging from

Testosterone   Estradiol

mild to nearly incapacitating. These are the most common and troubling symptoms of the climacteric:

- hot flushes (or flashes) that bring a sudden, unpredictable wave of heat and drenching sweat over the upper body

- painful vaginal dryness and a general atrophy of vaginal and genital tissue

- urinary incontinence

- psychological effects such as depression, anxiety, and nervousness

- insomnia.

In addition, women face other particularly serious conditions after menopause:

- increased risk of heart attack

- progressive bone loss.

We will explore the newest research in the treatment of each of these conditions in the next chapter. But first I must let you in on a critical piece of good news.

No More Dangerous Hormone Replacement Therapy

All the conditions just listed can arise from the postmenopausal lack of female hormones. These problems may be helped by taking estrogen to replace what the body no longer produces. So, many years ago, doctors began administering estrogen, and for a while, it seemed like a miraculous treatment that improved health and staved off certain effects of aging.

Then came the bad news: a number of well-researched studies documented that estrogen-replacement therapy increased the risk of uterine cancer in women. That news made media headlines in the mid-seventies, and women everywhere stopped taking estrogen. Sometimes, with even more fervor than their patients, physicians refused to write prescriptions for estrogen because they feared that they would be sued.

Estrogen Replacement and Endometrial Cancer

What happens to the uterus during estrogen-replacement therapy? As we saw in the description of what happens at menopause, estrogen, a cell multiplier, when it is unopposed by progesterone, stimulates the uterine lining to keep growing until it resembles hyperplasia. Although the exact mechanism by which a cell becomes cancerous is not known, the basis of endometrial cancer may lie in the progression from endometrial hyperplasia to cystic hyperplasia to adenomatous hyperplasia to adenocarcinoma (the most usual form of uterine cancer; see pp. 137-140). Using estrogen alone, the chances of the endometrium entering these stages is increased.

Why not, then, administer progesterone also? This would complete the natural cycle that starts with estrogen. This is precisely the question that the medical community has failed to address responsibly until recently. Since Mother Nature found it necessary to provide two female hormones, one to balance the other, it seems to be plain common sense that if we replace one of them, we should replace the other as well. I feel that even posthysterectomy patients who have no uterus need progesterone to rest and protect their breast tissue with its antiestrogen effect. Therefore, since 1964, my patients have received *hormone-replacement therapy* (HRT) consisting of both estrogen and progesterone.

In 1976, when I gave a speech to a conference on working women, the media were just beginning an exposé of estrogen-replacement therapy as a cause of uterine cancer. I knew that estrogen-replacement therapy without progesterone was bound to cause problems, and, in fact, women who were on estrogen-replacement therapy without progesterone might well be better off without their therapy. So when I gave my speech, I argued that estrogen should not be given alone.

I feel it is the misuse of estrogen, and not the estrogen per se, that is the culprit and the cause of the prevailing controversy. If the basis of endometrial carcinoma lies in progression from endometrial hyperplasia to adenocarcinoma, then the physician who misuses estrogen is at fault. He is not providing natural ovarian replacement because he is leaving out progesterone, which would not permit even the first step in the sequence, i.e., hyperplasia to occur.

The male-dominated OB/GYN ranks have for the most part never bothered to add progesterone to the woman's regimen because adding progesterone causes a menstrual flow each month, and he feels that this is too much fuss for the doctor or the patient to deal with. Because of this attitude estrogen has been used alone. The uterine lining, therefore, is continuously stimulated by the estrogen without the relief afforded by the antiestrogen effect of progesterone. By adding progesterone, the cells lining the uterine cavity are sloughed off each month. They are not allowed to sit around, get old, and into trouble. The woman gets a clean bill of health each month as fresh new cells replace the old.

Estrogen should not be given without progesterone. If we are truly doing replacement therapy, then we must replace both hormones produced by the ovary, not just the estrogen alone.

Today the old headlines are still influencing the treatment of women. I for one am tired of hearing about research that proves that estrogen increases the risk of uterine cancer. Yes, estrogen does increase the risk, but no woman should ever have been treated with estrogen alone in the first place!

It is difficult to make physicians rethink what they have assumed is an open-and-shut case. Nearly all doctors still warn their patients about the potential cancer-causing effects of estrogen-replacement therapy. Nearly all doctors still treat with estrogen alone. How can one make a dent in such a vicious cycle?

In May 1981, I was determined to try. The American Cancer Society had invited me to speak about menopause at the Medical College in Albany, New York. My audience consisted of some 250 gynecologists. As I stepped to the podium, I warned that that they were going to hear not the results of a multimillion-dollar research project but some thoughts from a family doctor from Long Island.

I stated directly, "The increase in uterine cancer resulting from estrogen replacement therapy is a physician-caused problem." I told them, "If you treat your patients incorrectly, with estrogen alone, of course they are going to wind up with problems. Estrogen without the addition of progesterone is wrong."

The eminent epidemiologist who had delivered the lecture just before me had reported that estrogen therapy most certainly caused a 3 to 6 percent increased risk of uterine cancer. As my eye skimmed the names of the doctors whose studies she used for her data base, I noted that she had not included researchers who had used progesterone. Without them, to my mind, all of her conclusions were meaningless. As I spoke, I added some remarks on statistical results that were based on studies that used incorrect means of therapy. To me, I said, such data produced "garbage-in garbage-out" statistical conclusions.

There were some ear-to-ear grins in the audience and a lot of whispering. In fact, the buzz was so loud, I decided that I had better end my talk and sit down.

I was wondering what might happen next when suddenly a tall gray-haired man approached from the audience, grabbed the microphone, turned and looked directly at me, and said, "Penny Budoff, I love you." He paused and smiled. "You have said everything that I have always believed and written about, but you have said it ever so much more eloquently."

I don't think that I have ever been more astounded. Here I was waiting to be drawn and quartered by this gathering of gynecologists, but instead I received an accolade. My new-found friend turned out to be none other than Professor Emeritus Dr. Robert Greenblatt of the Medical College of Georgia in Augusta, who had come to give the keynote luncheon address.

Later on during lunch, the epidemiologist turned to the physician sitting next to her and made a kind remark about my talk. I was especially pleased, because all of us who are interested in HRT need to understand what the important factors are. None of the disagreements are personal. The important thing is that we find the correct solution and not create red herrings that result in needless fear.

If nothing else, being in the vanguard of any change in medical therapy teaches one patience. And if colleagues begin to agree with you while you are still alive, it is something of an accomplishment. Therefore, I was pleased when the American College of Obstetrics and Gynecology issued a bulletin in June 1983 which stated that "the addition of progestin for 10 to 13 days each cycle has been shown to reduce the risk of endometrial hyperplasia to near zero, and this should be accompanied by a significant reduction in the risk of developing endometrial carcinomas."

Progesterone and Hormone-Replacement Therapy (HRT)

Although there are tremendous amounts of data on the clinical effects of estrogen in women, trying to dig out data on the clinical effects of natural or synthetic progesterone is nearly impossible. The problem is that the progesterone data are always mixed up with the data from estrogen, because the information comes from studies on birth-control pills that contain both hormones. I have spoken to pharmaceutical manufacturers as well as to the Food and Drug Administration, and they agree that true data, that is, data that refer only to progestational agents, are almost impossible to come by.

Consequently there is a lot of confusion as to just which side effects are caused by estrogen and which are caused by progesterone. There is an urgent need to understand the specific effects of progesterone, as it is clear that estrogen given alone increases the chance of endometrial cancer in women who have a uterus.

Because progesterone acts to balance the cell-multiplying effect of estrogen, its decrease or absence in the perimenopausal phase of a woman's life often leads to unusual bleeding patterns. Abnormal menstrual cycles that occur in the perimenopause are called dysfunctional uterine bleeding. Heavy flow, prolonged flow, or menses that come with only short intervals between may occur when estrogen is present without the control of progesterone.

As you remember, after menopause, the direct production of ovarian estrogen ceases, but estrone is still being made from androstenedione, secreted from the ovary and the adrenal gland and later from the adrenal gland alone. Estrone that comes from this conversion in the body fat is not under the normal pituitary-ovarian negative feedback control, so the normal shutoff mechanisms that guard the younger woman's health are absent. In obese women, the production of estrone may be considerable. The levels usually are not high enough to cause enough growth of the uterine lining to produce a reappearance of menstruation. However, should postmenopausal bleeding occur, a thorough investigation must be done.

For many of these perimenopausal complaints of increased flow, prolonged flow, and flow/spotting between regular menses, progesterone may be all that is necessary to cure the condition. This is true for dysfunctional bleeding as well as for hyperplasias. In fact, in my entire practice, I have never had a case of hyperplasia, adenomatous hyperplasia or atypical adenomatous hyperplasia (a step closer to the development of cancer in the endometrium) that was not totally reversed by progesterone alone. Acting as the housecleaner, progesterone causes shedding of the endometrium and permits the normal formation of new tissue each month on a clean new base. Of course, proper diagnosis must be done prior to therapy with progesterone, and careful follow-up must be maintained.

Progesterone will not cure *all* bleeding problems. Women who have uterine cancer obviously will not be cured by progesterone, although some work on early cancers seems to suggest a beneficial effect from it. Also, women who have a nonfunctioning, thin, and inactive uterine lining may have bleeding problems that won't be corrected by progesterone.

After I had written the first section of this chapter and just when it seemed that I would never find a good source of information on progesterone, *The Journal of Reproductive Medicine* published a supplement on progesterone and the menopausal woman. Apparently others who are interested in the subject shared my frustration. The supplement proved to be an invaluable source of the latest information, and it reported on several studies that have been done on estrogen-progesterone hormone-replacement therapy and the risk of endometrial cancer. The results are good news indeed: *women on estrogen-progesterone therapy were safer and developed less endometrial cancer than women who took no therapy or took estrogen alone.*

Because there are side effects from all medication, whether it is natural or synthetic, there is a need to establish correct dosages as well as the number of days of therapy that will give optimal results. If the dosages of progesterone are too high, side effects similar to those experienced by the premenstrual women may be noted. These include fluid retention, irritability, depression, and feelings of being bloated and lower abdominal pressure.

On the other hand, postmenopausal women on hormone-replacement therapy need a dose of progesterone sufficient to balance the effect of estrogen. Maintaining this balance is what keeps the endometrium protected from hyperplasia as well as cancer. In order, then, to provide the most effective therapy, it is critical to establish the minimum effective dose of progesterone.

Since it takes about ten days for the progesterone phase of endometrial development to fully mature, ten days is now the accepted length of time for giving progesterone in HRT.

Whitehead's research in London supports ten days of progesterone therapy each month, using smaller doses than are usually given in this country. Gambrell, at the Medical College of Georgia, also supports therapy with progesterone for ten days in order to prevent cancer of the endometrium. My study,[3] published in 1979, and others have come to similar conclusions.[4]

There are several forms of synthetic progesterone available to treat menopausal symptoms. There are two types of synthetics: progestins, which are derived from natural progesterone, and progestogens, which are derived from testosterone. That a substance arising from a male hormone would have pregnancy-hormonelike activity seems incredible until you see the diagrams of the molecules. At a glance, they seem to be very much alike.

Natural progesterone, a 21-carbon compound, is broken down rapidly by stomach acids, so it is not ordinarily suitable for oral use. Therefore, progestins have been created from it that can be used orally. These are known as medroxyprogesterone acetate (MPA) and megestrol acetate. MPA is most commonly used in HRT.

Testosterone is a 19-carbon compound. A slight change in the molecule produces compounds with progestational activity. These are known as progestogens or 19-nortestosterone compounds, and many of their names begin with the prefix "nor" (norethindrone, norgestrel, norethindrone acetate, northynodrel).

The functions and side effects of these compounds reflect their differences and sources. For example, the 19-nor compounds have male-type activity, especially if they are given in large doses, whereas the progesterone derivatives have little. Both compounds, however, are capable of inhibiting or reversing the effects of estrogen. They do this through three mechanisms. The first is by competing with estrogen for binding sites in the cells; the second is by decreasing the manufacture of these estrogen receptors (if estrogen receptors are not available for estrogen to bind to, then estrogen cannot affect the cell). The third is by increasing the activity of the enzyme that converts the potent estradiol into estrone. To sum up, progestins and progestogens make it more difficult for estrogen to enter the cell, and even when it has entered the cell, they increase its conversion to a weaker form.

For the estrogen phase of HRT, both natural and synthetic

forms exist. The natural forms are the most commonly used.

As little as there is in the scientific literature about progesterone and progestogen comparison, there is probably less information comparing the various estrogens currently available. How should you judge which one to take? If you want to go by sales figures, Premarin (conjugated estrogen), which was introduced to this country by Ayerst in 1942, has sales figures of about $40 million yearly. Ogen (estropipate), introduced in 1968 by Abbott, has yearly sales of $3.5 million, and Estrace (micronized estradiol), introduced in 1976 by Mead-Johnson, has $1.7 million in yearly sales.

One recent study compared these three natural estrogens with each other and also with Estinyl, the synthetic estrogen used in hormone replacement and all birth control pills.[5] Twenty-three post-menopausal women were given short courses of the various estrogens and their liver functions and hormonal levels were measured. On a milligram-for-milligram basis, the three natural estrogens produced similar estrogen levels, which meant that all were absorbed equally. Premarin, however, had a slight adverse effect on liver function, which may be due to the fact that Premarin contains 20 to 30 percent equine equilin sulfate, or horse estrogen. Like most biological products, Premarin, which is made from the urine of pregnant mares, contains a mixture of ingredients including horse estrogens, rather than the single estrogen of the other manufactured products.

The authors of the study felt that Premarin's effect on the liver (albeit small) was due to the presence of horse estrogens. Little is known about the effect of equilin except that it seems to remain in the body for some weeks until it is slowly excreted. Billions of doses of Premarin have been used without any unusual effects over the past few decades. Yet the equine element could probably be removed during the manufacture of the product, or perhaps new research would show that these estrogens are beneficial and should remain in the product. Either way, an answer should be pursued.

On the other hand, synthetic Estinyl had a markedly exaggerated effect on liver function, with large increases in protein production, which makes this product less desirable for post-menopausal replacement therapy. The study concluded that "the three natural compounds would be preferable [to Estinyl] because of their decreased hepatic effects."[6]

The following table gives the trade names of the estrogen and progesterone compounds to make it easier for you to know which compounds you might be using.

Natural	*Trade Name*	*Manufacturer*
ESTROGENS		
(extracted from the urine of pregnant horses)	Premarin	Ayerst
estropipate	Ogen	Abbott
micronized estradiol	Estrace	Mead-Johnson
esterified natural estrogen plus Librium (a tranquilizer)	Menrium	Roche
Synthetic		
ethinyl estradiol (the estrogen used in birth control pills)	Estinyl	Schering
quinestrol (broken down by the body into ethinyl estradiol)	Estrovis	Parke-Davis
PROGESTERONES		
Progestins (progesterone derivatives)		
medroxyprogesterone acetate*	Provera	Upjohn
	Amen	Carnrick
	Curretab	Reid-Provident
megestrol acetate	Megace	Mead-Johnson
Progestogens (19-nortestosterone derivatives)		
norethindrone	Norlutin	Warner-Lambert
norethindrone acetate	Norlutate	Warner-Lambert
	Aygestin	Ayerst
norgestrel	Overette	Wyeth
	(actually marketed as a progestogen birth control pill)	

*Can be obtained generically at one third the cost.

Starting HRT

Whether a woman will use HRT for a few months or for several years, hormone-replacement therapy is a long-term commitment. Before starting a patient on it, I follow a strict procedure to make sure that her health is normal aside from the menopausal symptoms and to establish a baseline health profile. Frankly, I am convinced that poor screening by doctors who administered HRT to some patients who already had cancer led to estrogen being blamed for the preexisting condition and has helped create scare stories about HRT.

My patients go through the following steps:

Initial Examination

1. Complete physical exam.
2. Complete blood analysis, including data on liver function, cholesterol, blood sugar, triglycerides, thyroid function. (These are standard tests and cost my patients less than $25.)
3. Breast exam.
4. Pap smear.
5. Vaginal smear taken from the inner third of the lateral vaginal wall to determine the woman's current estrogen status. The vaginal lining is one of the most sensitive indicators of the presence of estrogen in the body. However, drugs may shift the estrogen level, so an accurate medication history is necessary.
6. Mammography. This is a must, to be sure that the breasts are normal. I have seen no evidence that estrogen causes breast cancer (we'll examine the latest research on HRT and breast cancer in the next chapter). But if a tumor already exists, estrogen might promote its growth.
7. Intrauterine aspiration (biopsy) performed in the office, to rule out hyperplasia or cancer. (Patients who have had a hysterectomy do not need this step, of course.)

Once I know what my patient's baseline is, I determine starting dosages of each hormone for her, depending on her age, current condition, and symptoms.

Estrogen. The usual dose of conjugated estrogen is 0.3 to 0.625 milligrams per day for twenty-five days a month or its equivalent in the other estrogen preparations. I would probably prescribe 0.625 milligrams for a woman in her late forties suffering from the common symptoms of hot flushes or vaginal dryness. But if the woman is fifty to fifty-two or older, I would start her on 0.3 milligrams of estrogen. Depending upon her response, dosage might be altered.

Progestin or progestogen. The usual dose for my patients on 0.625 milligrams of conjugated estrogen is 5 milligrams of Provera or a generic equivalent (half a 10-mg tablet) per day for *ten* days a month. (However, as little as 2.5 mg for ten days will suffice, especially if 0.3 mg of conjugated estrogen is used.) Likewise, the usual 5-milligram doses of Norlutate or Aygestin might be halved and given for ten days. (Ten mg of Provera is thought to be equivalent to 5 mg of Norlutate.)

One regimen for HRT is simply to take estrogen on the first twenty-five days of each month. The progesterone is added on days 16 through 25. Then both hormones are discontinued for the remainder of the month. A new cycle begins with a new month.

Two- to Four-Week Checkup

Although a complete cycle has not yet finished, I may see my patients at this point to find out how they feel and, if necessary, to reassure them. Some postmenopausal women have many questions about their therapy. I also recheck their blood pressure and the progress of the hot flushes and ask whether they've noted any breast tenderness. If they have, they may need reassuring that because their breast tissue has had no estrogen for a long time, a little tenderness is not unusual.

Six-Week Checkup

Here I do a complete physical examination and check vaginal lubrication and estrogen level with another vaginal smear. Equally important are the patient's subjective reactions. Does she feel well? Is she happy with the therapy?

If the woman reports side effects, I may adjust the doses of the hormones up or down. Too much estrogen can make the breasts tender, and the dose should be lowered if breast complaints are more than minimal. (It is well known that women who develop breast tenderness on estrogen will often get relief when they take the progesterone.) On the other hand, too much progesterone can bring on "premenstrual" symptoms.

It's important for the patient to report her symptoms and for the doctor to listen carefully. Optimum doses vary with the individual, and only through careful trials can you and your doctor find the appropriate level for you. Sometimes, for example, alternating 0.3 milligrams and 0.625 milligrams of estrogen works best. One of the most noticeable effects of HRT in women who have a uterus is, of course, the reappearance of the "menstrual" flow, as progesterone completes the maturation of the endometrium and causes it to break down and flow out after it and estrogen are stopped on day 25 of each month. (I hasten to assure you that bringing back the menstrual flow won't make you start ovulating again, so you can't get pregnant.) Depending on the dosage of hormones, however, the flow may take a few months to appear or it may not appear at all. The flow is usually light to moderate and not accompanied by cramps.

Repeat Visit Six Months Later

At this session, the patient is given a complete physical and I check her vaginal estrogen level again. Once in a while, there is a rare woman who has persistent flushes or vaginal dryness. Her estrogen level remains low because she doesn't absorb oral estrogen well. Such a patient might be switched to another oral estrogen preparation to see if this will improve her absorption. If not, vaginal creams can be used, or a once-a-month injection of estrogen will provide relief.

Unfortunately, because of a number of factors, there are still no combined estrogen/progesterone packages available for sale in this country as there are in many other countries around the world. Because of the lack of such combined packaging and the natural laziness of some of us (doctors and patients alike), it will take a while longer to establish a combined two-drug therapy in this country.

In the near future, oral preparations of estrogen may not be used. Instead, implants placed under the skin that will slowly release estrogen and vaginal creams may assume a larger share of the market. The newest method of estrogen delivery is a Band-Aid-type delivery system. The estrogen (estradiol) is contained in a patch which is worn on the upper arm or an inconspicuous spot on the torso. The estrogen is released from the patch at a controlled rate and absorbed through the skin, directly into the blood stream. The patch is thereafter changed twice a week. A multicenter research study using this transdermal approach to hormonal therapy will soon be completed.

All these methods for taking estrogen bypass the stomach, intestines, and liver and put estrogen directly into the bloodstream. Because the liver does not have to break down large quantities of hormone, unnecessary metabolic steps are avoided, and therefore such therapy may prove to be superior to oral administration.

When Not to Use HRT

I am sure that by now some of you reading this book are thinking, Is that all there is? Do I just have a choice of estrogen and progesterone for my menopausal symptoms? I have told you about HRT in detail because it deserves finally to be understood. There is little written for the general public that counteracts the scare stories headlined by the news media back in the seventies. This book is the first serious attempt to do so. At least, if nothing else has been accomplished by all of our work—your reading and my writing—you will know that, properly cycled with progesterone, estrogen does not cause endometrial cancer.

There are other remedies that work for certain of the menopausal symptoms—some tried and true, some brand new. I have included descriptions of these in the next chapter. You should also know the circumstances under which HRT should *not* be used. Although estrogens are the most effective agents known for treating menopausal symptoms, they are contraindicated or potentially harmful for women with any of the following conditions:

1. known or suspected cancer of the breast, except in appropriately selected patients being treated for metastatic disease
2. known or suspected estrogen-dependent tumors
3. known or suspected pregnancy
4. undiagnosed vaginal bleeding
5. active thrombophlebitis (blood clots in the veins) or thromboembolic disorders
6. a past history of thrombophlebitis, thrombosis, or thromboembolic disorders associated with previous estrogen use

With the following conditions, women on HRT should be extremely cautious. They may take estrogen but must be closely watched:

1. Fibroid uterus. Some fibroids may enlarge with estrogen.
2. Gall-bladder disease. Women on estrogen have been thought to have an increased incidence of gall-bladder problems. However, a recent English study by the College of General Practitioners on 23,000 women found no such association.
3. Epilepsy, asthma, migraine, heart disease, or kidney disease. Because estrogen may cause fluid retention, it might make these conditions worse.
4. Severe liver disease, or a history of jaundice associated with the taking of oral contraceptives.
5. Hypertension. Unless this is severe, it has not been a problem in my experience. Interestingly, a 1983 study from Australia published by Wren and Routledge demonstrated a decrease in blood pressure in women taking Ogen. Furthermore, there is no association with stroke and replacement therapy.
6. Diabetes is often listed as a relative contraindication to HRT (that is, it requires cautious use). However, I feel

that because of the beneficial effect estrogen may have on the blood vessels, diabetes that begins in adulthood may actually be helped by estrogen. (One of the major problems in diabetes is adverse blood vessel changes.)

7. Fibrocystic breast disease. If fibrocystic disease is a result of poor estrogen/progesterone ratios, then providing a patient with the correct hormonal balance may again be beneficial (see p. 43). However, no studies have been done to back up this suggestion.

Now that you know the best and the worst about HRT, let us go on to examine how it can help you with each of the major symptoms of menopause.

2

No More Hot Flashes—Good News!

The primary symptoms and side effects of menopause, other than the termination of menstruation, are hot flushes ("hot flash" is the popular term for this phenomenon, but as "hot flush" is the more technically accurate term, I will use it throughout the book), vaginal atrophy and dryness, urinary tract problems, psychological problems, and insomnia. The good news is that HRT is an extremely effective treatment for all these conditions. In addition, it has advantages for cardiovascular health and osteoporosis.

The decline of estrogen and the absence of progesterone result in hot flushes that more than two thirds of women undergoing a surgical or natural menopause will experience. Eighty percent of these women will be disturbed by hot flushes for more than one year, and 25 to 50 percent will have the problem for more than five years. Some continue to flush for ten years or longer. The term "flush" denotes the facial blushing that occurs.

Women describe a vague aura preceding the flush that signals that it is about to begin. Less than a minute later, there is a sudden onset of warmth in the face and neck that may spread to the chest. This wave of heat generally lasts several minutes, and the sudden dilation of the blood vessels causes an increased blood flow resulting in redness. The episode can be very annoying, for it may be associated with dizziness, headache, palpitations, and a drenching sweat over the upper body that is not easy to hide. Worse, an emotion-charged situation, such as addressing the chairman of the board, may bring it on. Women often complain that flushes always seem to creep up at the worst of all possible times. One patient exclaimed, "It's hard to appear calm, cool, collected, and sophisticated when suddenly you turn red and break out in large drops of perspiration all over your face. It always throws me when it happens."

Flushes can last anywhere from a few seconds to a half-hour. Five minutes is average. Some women experience them several times a day, others only one or two times a week. A hot drink such as coffee or tea or an unusually hot day may increase their occurrence. Emotional crises, stress, an alcoholic drink, or certain sounds may also provide an unwelcome stimulus. Severe flushes are always accompanied by profuse perspiration, but not all flushes are severe; some are barely noticeable. The only advantage of the hot flush, as I see it, may be to those women who are forever cold and who wear socks to bed even in summer.

In a study of 115 women with hot flushes, A.M. Voda asked women what they did in order to alleviate the symptoms. Thirty percent of the women fanned themselves, went swimming, or took a cool shower; 1 percent drank cold liquids; 27 percent did nothing; and 40 percent refused to give any information.[1]

One of my patients told me that she can no longer tolerate wearing long sleeves or turtleneck sweaters. She works in an office where she often sneaks over to turn on the air conditioner. Her colleagues, she says, are forever freezing and wondering why the office is so cold. They discover the air conditioning on and turn it off. It stays off only until she is alone and can turn it on again.

Another menopausal patient is in business with a younger female partner. My patient is always hot. Business is great, but she says they constantly fight about the room temperature and the air conditioning.

Such anecdotal information is interesting, but too often it is all the physician has to go on. Very little research has focused on this female problem. Until recently, there was little evidence that hot flushes were more than a figment of the older woman's imagination due to sadness about her empty nest.

However, hot flushes are very real. Recent studies have proved not only that they exist but that they are physiologically complicated. The woman's awareness of the hot flush has to do with sweating and a rise in skin temperature. Each hot flush is related directly to a pulsatile surge in LH production by the pituitary. Hot flushes are not directly caused by the LH but by the hypothalamic factors which regulate its release. This ties in hot flushes with hormonal disturbances in the hypothalamus, the heat-regulatory center of the brain.

In a study on the details of flushing episodes, women described the preflush period as lasting up to 4 minutes. During this time, they were able to sense the oncoming flush, but the researchers were unable to record any physiological changes. The first change that could be recorded was a decrease in skin resistance, or the beginning of perspiration, which began an average of 45 seconds after women first sensed the hot flush. It reached a maximum by 4 minutes, but took 18 minutes to subside. A rise in skin temperature, indicating blood-vessel dilation, followed. This occurred at 90 seconds, reached a maximum at 9 minutes, and returned to normal after 40 minutes. As heat was lost from the body due to the sweating, the body temperature fell about 0.2 degrees Centigrade, then returned to normal in about 30 minutes.

It is apparent that although the flush and the perspiration are short-lived, it takes the body nearly a half-hour to regain "normality." If flushes occur many times per day, this temperature-regulating dysfunction is constantly overheating and recooling the body for many hours of the day. If the brain is spending large blocks of time processing such abnormalities, this may well influence the well-being of the woman with incessant hot flushes.

Furthermore, hot flushes are probably more complicated than we realize. Release of prostaglandins (hormonelike substances) may contribute to the dilation of the blood vessels. Substances in the brain that transmit nerve impulses may also be involved, which directly links estrogen activity to central nervous system dysfunction. It should be fairly obvious that much more research is needed to understand why flushing occurs as well as the mechanism for treating it.

Menopausal women are often hung up over their hot flushes. They feel guilty for having such complaints or in some cases totally bewildered by what is *not* an abnormal occurrence. I had any number of patients tell me, "I never thought that hot flushes would ever happen to me. I'm intelligent, educated, and satisfied with my life. I really thought that they were mental. They're awful. They happen six or seven times a day. But the nights with the sweats are the worst. I can almost time them. Ten minutes after I fall asleep, I wake up in a pool of sweat. I used to get up to change my bedclothes—I don't bother anymore. I finally fall asleep again. It may take me an hour or so. Ten minutes later I'm up again. It's exhausting because I'm up half the night, and then I'm grouchy all day. I may not survive until they go away. I'm here because I really need help."

Sleep deprivation can have a devastating effect on anyone. It can affect your personality—even your sexuality. It may be one of the prime factors in the emotional changes in menopausal women. It certainly can leave you chronically fatigued, tired, and unable to function, as well as depressed. Sleep deprivation is often used as a method of torture. If it disorients and breaks down the defenses of prisoners of war, women who are kept awake night after night by their sweats will also finally succumb.

We don't know the exact mechanisms by which HRT relieves hot flushes, but we do know that it works in nearly all cases. Current theory is that it stabilizes the vascular system. Women who begin HRT stop having the hot flushes completely within a week or two.

Alternative Treatments

For women who can't or don't wish to use HRT, three other remedies are available for hot flushes.

Bellergal tablets have been used for many years for relief of hot flushes. They are still commonly used, especially by women who have contraindications to estrogen use, for example, an abnormal mammography, or the presence of breast cancer. Bellergal contains phenobarbital, a barbiturate sedative; ergotamine tartrate, which inhibits sympathetic nervous system activity; and a belladonnalike substance that inhibits parasympathetic nervous system activity. According to the manufacturer, it relieves symptoms of hot flushes because these disorders often involve overactivity of both the sympathetic and parasympathetic nervous systems. The drug is designed to correct imbalance of the autonomic nervous system.

Women who have peripheral vascular disease, hypertension, coronary artery disease, liver or kidney problems, or glaucoma should not use the drug; neither should patients who take dopamine for Parkinson's disease.

The pills are normally taken two to four times a day, depending on the dose.

Clonidine is an antihypertensive medication that has recently been approved in Canada for the treatment of hot flushes. In the United States at present, the use of the medication is confined to hypertension. However, a study in the *Canadian Medical Journal* demonstrated that used in small doses—0.05 milligrams twice daily—the drug reduced the frequency, duration, and severity of the flushes to a modest degree, by virtue of its ability to control blood vessel dilation and constriction. The study reported that although there was only a modest decrease in the frequency of flushing, the severity and length of attacks are also decreased, and most patients consider the treatment helpful.

Although the drug is an antihypertensive, there were no significant changes in blood pressure over the study period. Side effects include dry mouth, sedation, and, less frequently, constipation, dizziness, headache, and fatigue. One problem with Clonidine in larger doses in hypertensive patients has been that if the drug is discontinued abruptly, there can be a sharp rise in blood pressure. The drug can also enhance the effect of alcohol or sedatives.

I am currently doing a study using Clonidine for hot flushes. The drug will be used transdermally, i.e., in a skin patch that releases the medication directly through the skin.

Because of this new way of administering Clonidine, dosages much smaller than those given orally should be effective.

Oral medroxyprogesterone in a dosage of 20 milligrams per day has also been suggested as a nonestrogenic way to treat severe hot flushes in women where estrogen use is undesirable. A study published in the September 26, 1980 *Journal of the American Medical Association* showed a significant decrease in flushing. The authors add, however, that medroxyprogesterone will not improve vaginal atrophy.

Some women are convinced that vitamins, especially vitamin E, decrease symptoms. No scientific studies have been completed based on this premise, but several of my patients have remarked that their vaginal tissues were better since starting *Vitamins for Women,** which contains 200 mgs of dry vitamin E, among other ingredients.

No More Vaginal Dryness

One of the earliest changes that a woman and her husband may notice after menopause is lack of vaginal lubrication during intercourse. This can easily be overcome with some excellent over-the-counter lubricants such as Transi-Lube (Young's Drug Products Corporation), Personal Lubricant (Ortho Pharmaceuticals), plain Surgilube, or K-Y jelly. Vaseline should not be used for lubricating purposes because it is a petroleum product and many women are sensitive to it. Also, because it does not mix with water, it is difficult to remove. For some women, the use of a little prescription cream containing estrogen near the opening of the vagina will allow the penis to enter the vagina comfortably. Lubricants may also be needed for women who bathe immediately before intercourse, as their tissues will be dry from the recent washing and toweling.

Simply using lubricants will ease the burden on both partners. However, the subject may be more complicated than this. Some women feel sexually inadequate if they are unable to lubricate normally. Unfortunately, they feel that they have

*See page 66 and back of this book for information about *Vitamins for Women.*

failed if they have to use a lubricant. A husband, for his part, might feel that his wife's lack of lubrication is somehow related to his failure to arouse her effectively. This may make *him* anxious and might contribute to erectile difficulties.

The capacity for vaginal lubrication persists throughout a woman's life. Lubrication begins during the excitement stage of sexual arousal, in response to tactile and psychological stimuli. During her adolescent years and twenties, it occurs within ten to thirty seconds of foreplay. As she approaches menopause, it may require one to three minutes. The capacity to lubricate in the perimenopausal years is directly related to the level of circulating estrogens.

Because there are no glands in the vaginal walls, the lubrication comes from a "sweating" phenomenon caused by increased blood flow to the tissues immediately surrounding the vagina. The glands at the entry of the vagina, such as the Bartholin's glands, provide only small amounts of lubrication, and this occurs later in the act.

Inadequate lubrication can occur at other times in a woman's life as well. Immediately postpartum, the response of the vagina decreases due to the sudden drop in estrogen. The same basis for complaint may occur in a woman who is nursing her child. After vaginal repairs for a dropped uterus or bladder, lubrication will also be a problem for a while. In these operations, surgical undermining of the vaginal tissues decreases nerve and blood supply, especially to the lower third of the vagina. Diabetes, multiple sclerosis, and spinal cord injuries decrease the capacity to lubricate. Many drugs, such as those for ulcers and high blood pressure, have a similar effect, as do narcotics, sedatives, tranquilizers, and alcohol.

One other aspect must be considered—that is, psychological causes of inadequate lubrication. Women who experience repeated painful intercourse do not lubricate well because anticipation of pain inhibits the congestive response in the lower third of the vagina. I empathize with such a patient, for it's difficult to relax and look forward eagerly to sexual intercourse when, for the past four months, each intercourse has caused pain and resulted in tenderness that lasted for hours or even days afterward. I am never surprised that these women do not lubricate well. It may be part of a vicious cycle: lubrication falls due to a decrease in estrogen levels, discomfort follows during intercourse, at the next intercourse there is some apprehension so that lubrication is less adequate, and so the cycle goes. Interestingly, diminished lubrication is more of a problem for women who do not have regular intercourse, regardless of their age. Lubrication seems to improve when intercourse is maintained with regularity. As with Pavlov's dogs, this, too, is a learned response.

Postmenopausal vaginal changes tend to progress with time. The vagina becomes small and less expansible and loses the pliable soft folds that are present during the premenopausal years. It shortens and may, as years go by, become a rigid, tubelike structure. In fact, it is not rare to see the vaginal opening shrink to a size too small to permit intercourse. The labia majora also become smaller and flatter as well as pale and fragile. The paleness is due to the lack of adequate blood flow, as is the dryness of the tissues. The normal younger vagina has some thirty cell layers and is a strong, well-lubricated organ. In late menopause, it may thin to as few as a fragile six layers because of estrogen deprivation.

I have many patients who have come to me long after their hot flushes were gone—they had managed to get through them on their own. But the day had come when they (or maybe it was their husbands) decided that life without sex was lousy. And that was why they came for help.

When the vagina shrinks or atrophies in this way, it is prone to dryness, soreness, and itching—a condition called atrophic vaginitis. Such a vagina is also susceptible to infection, because its thin walls lack the normal secretions that cleanse the vaginal tissues. The production of normal vaginal acidity occurs when the protective superficial lining cells slough off the vaginal wall. These cells contain glycogen, which the normal bacteria (Doderlein's bacteria) break down into lactic acid to maintain the normal acidity of the vagina. With age and the loss of these superficial cells, lactic acid production decreases, and the vaginal pH rises (becomes more alkaline). At the same time, other bacteria often replace the normal bacteria and may cause symptoms of vaginitis. Antibiotics may help, but recent studies show that often the best way to cure this type of vaginitis is with estrogen, taken either vaginally or orally.

Studies have been done on vaginal function in women younger than forty, but it was not until recently that researchers focused on post-menopausal vaginal tissues to determine the effect of aging on vaginal physiology. In one such study, investigators examined fourteen women ranging in age from fifty-one to seventy before and after receiving conjugated estrogen and compared the finding with those of younger women.[2]

First they measured vaginal blood flow and found a rapid increase in the first month of therapy. The improved blood flow allowed for an increase in the quantity of vaginal fluid, which soon approached that reported for younger women in the twenty to forty age range. Interestingly, the results were similar whether the women had received 1.25 milligrams of conjugated estrogen daily or 0.625 milligrams. The women also regained their vaginal acidity with therapy. In summary, estrogen therapy reversed the changes caused by estrogen deprivation.

One additional note: some women have been led to believe that the use of estrogen creams do not carry the same risk as the use of oral estrogens. A recent study published in the *Journal of the American Medical Association* shows this is not so.[3]

This study showed that two vaginal estrogen creams (Premarin and Estrace) not only had local effects in the vagina but were also well absorbed into the blood. With daily use, estrogen levels in the blood approach those obtained with oral medication. The long-term use of vaginal creams, therefore, carries the same risks as taking oral estrogen; therefore an attempt should be made to establish a balanced estrogen-progestogen therapy. The author observed that "Delivery of estrogen into the . . . circulation following vaginal application appears to be direct and anatomically similar to secretion of estrogen into the circulation by the ovary." He added that this direct delivery into the blood, bypassing the digestive system and the liver, which break down the oral preparations, may be advantageous and physiologically superior.

Women who begin HRT are usually aware of changes in their vaginas within two weeks. Actually, microscopic changes can be noted in the vaginal cells within thirty-six hours. The increased blood flow multiplies the cells, the vagina becomes more acid, and lubricating fluids become noticeable. The urethra, clitoris, and labia majora all show changes as well.

I often kid my patients who return for their six-week examination after starting HRT. Sitting at the lower end of the table, I see so profound a change in their vaginal tissue that I have sometimes exclaimed from beneath the draped sheet, "I almost didn't recognize you!" After some laughs, the patients usually relate that they are much more comfortable and functional. They are also very gratified to have found help for a problem that was so distressing and yet so difficult to talk about.

It always amazes me how easily the vaginal problems can be reversed. Women whose vaginas bled just from the introduction of a small speculum or from taking their Pap smears return for a six-week checkup with a moist, pink, youthful vagina. Not all cases can be completely reversed in just six weeks, however. In those women with profound atrophy, the process may take a few months. The prognosis then depends on how great the loss of estrogen was and for how long.

Urinary Tract Problems

Because the lower urinary tract outlet is so closely associated with the vagina physically, it, too, is dependent on estrogen. With loss of estrogen, irritation and burning on urination may occur, as may frequent bladder infections. Inflammation of the urethra also becomes common. It may be necessary to treat the infection with estrogen as well as an antibiotic in order to build up these structures so that they can resist infection.

Postmenopausal women may also lose a degree of pelvic muscle support, which contributes to the development of a dropped bladder or rectum or uterus. Some of this is due, of course, to the process of aging and tears from childbirth, but some is also due to the loss of estrogen.

Women with poor bladder support sometimes complain that they lose urine when they cough, sneeze, or run and have to wear a sanitary pad continuously to keep from soiling themselves. Doctors often offer surgery as a cure, but HRT— perhaps simply using estrogen creams—and Kegel exercises (see page 187) should be tried before resorting to surgery. If you don't get good results from hormonal therapy and Kegel exercises, then surgery can always be done.

Advantages for Your Heart

Heart attack kills more men under the age of fifty than women. After menopause, however, a woman's chance of heart attack increases to a point equal to that of a man. Several studies on this phenomenon have led physicians to believe that estrogen has some protective effect against aging of the arteries in general, and against atherosclerosis, the major cause of heart attack, in particular. Rosenberg reported study results showing that premature loss of estrogen increases the risk of having a nonfatal heart attack.[4] He studied 279 women who were hospitalized for heart attacks and 5,580 women who were not. These control women were nurses who were matched to the hospitalized women and selected from among 121,964 registered nurses who responded to a mail questionnaire. He found that women who had had surgery to remove their uterus and both ovaries before age thirty-five had a risk of heart attack 7.2 times that of the controls who had had no surgery. On the other hand, hysterectomy without the removal of both ovaries was only weakly associated with an increased risk.

You can see that whether or not to remove ovaries during hysterectomy surgery becomes an important decision that should not be taken lightly. A patient should discuss such an operation thoroughly before signing her preoperative consent form. Unfortunately, at present one fourth of women undergoing hysterectomy before forty years of age have both ovaries removed. In the United States, the rate of menopause caused by surgery among young women has increased in recent years. Rosenberg stated, "Between 1965 and 1973, the hysterectomy rate almost doubled for women twenty-five to thirty-four years old, from an estimated 7 per thousand to 12 per thousand. For women thirty-five to forty-four years of age, the rate increased from 14 per thousand to 20 per thousand. The cardiac health consequences of this trend may not become fully apparent for years to come."

Whether HRT affects atherosclerosis is of great concern to the medical community. Doctors pay a lot of attention to risk factors that affect the development of coronary artery disease. Determining the protective effect of estrogen in HRT is complicated by the fact that birth control pills, which also contain estrogen and progestogen, have been shown to have a deleterious effect on the cardiovascular system. They have been implicated in venous thrombosis, which can lead to stroke, and in increased risk of heart attack and hypertension. These effects are noted in all women but become more than just a passing threat to the woman over thirty-five, especially if she smokes and takes oral contraceptives concurrently.

Many people compare birth control pills to HRT and think that just because both therapies involve a form of estrogen and progesterone, they are basically the same. However, there are major differences in the compounds and in the dosages used that make it impossible to equate one with the other. The effects on the body are quite different—in fact, in many instances, they are opposite.

Christensen, in a study of 87 women treated with HRT, found that blood pressure did not change.[5] Furthermore, he found a small but significant fall in blood pressure during two years of HRT with high hormone doses. He concluded that hypertension may occur in young women on contraceptive pills, but no evidence links hypertension and postmenopausal HRT.[6]

The first major difference between HRT and the pill is that for the most part, natural estrogens are used for HRT, whereas synthetic estrogens are used in birth control pills. These two estrogens used in birth control pills are ethinyl estradiol (only infrequently used in HRT—see table, page 18 and mestranol. Mestranol is broken down by the body into estinyl estradiol.

Second, the dosages of the natural estrogens are very different from the dosages of synthetics used in the birth control pills. The synthetic estrogens are, by a variety of estimates, ten to a hundred times more powerful than the natural preparations. Thus, even the touted low-dose birth control pills contain potent doses of estrogen. Birth control pills contain between 30 and 80 micrograms of ethinyl estradiol. They would only need 6 micrograms of ethinyl estradiol to have a dose equivalent in potency to 0.625 milligrams of conjugated estrogen, the usual HRT dose.

But birth control pills need to have sufficient estrogenic effect to turn off the entire female hormonal reproductive system. That's what stops ovulation from occurring and ensures excellent birth control. HRT is used only to replace estrogen, and at levels that are low and appropriate for older women.

The third major difference between birth control pills and HRT is in the progesterone. All birth control pills contain the progesterone form derived from the 19 nortestosterone configuration, whereas HRT more commonly uses a progesterone derivative. As we shall see in a moment, the differences between the two progesterones can be significant in considering heart disease risk factors.

In a nutshell, birth control pills exert a powerful estrogenic effect because of the potency of their synthetic estrogens and because of the high doses relative to the doses of natural estrogens used in HRT. This plus the testosterone-derived progestogen that is taken as a daily part of the oral contraceptive creates chemical changes in the body that promote the development of atherosclerosis and clotting problems.

Of course, the process of atherosclerosis probably depends upon a multitude of factors. Age, diet, genetics, and smoking and drinking habits all play a large role in determining the final outcome for any individual. But now there are lots of physiological measurements which can be made in the laboratory and which provide biochemical information about the development of this problem.

Everyone is acquainted with cholesterol levels. Everyone wants to have a low cholesterol value, for that is supposed to reduce the risk of coronary artery disease. Unfortunately, it's not as simple as that. Now there are other blood fats that we routinely measure that also seem to be indicators of cardiovascular health. These newer measurements include the protein molecules known as lipoproteins that carry fat particles through the blood stream. *Lipo* refers to the fat particles they carry. You may already be acquainted with high-density lipoproteins and low-density lipoproteins.

(Can you believe it? I'm trying to make you into a doctor. If you have managed to struggle through this book so far, you will probably be more knowledgeable than most doctors as far as HRT is concerned. That's okay. Someone has to know what's really going on.)

High-density lipoproteins are the good lipoproteins. They serve to remove cholesterol from the tissues. Researchers believe that through this mechanism they decrease atherosclerosis. On the other hand, low-density lipoproteins are associated with bad news. They take fat out of the blood and place it in arteries and other tissues. Therefore, ideally, high-density lipoproteins (HDLs) should be high, and low-density lipoproteins (LDLs) should be low.

We have gone through all this information in order to better understand the effect of HRT on the process of atherosclerosis. You see, the estrogen portion of replacement therapy in the postmenopausal woman causes a fall in cholesterol, slightly lowers the LDLs, and significantly raises HDLs. That is just what we want to protect our arteries.

Ross, studying estrogen replacement alone, researched the medical records of women who died from heart attack in a Los Angeles retirement community to find out the association between such deaths and estrogen-replacement therapy. Women treated with estrogen were contrasted with nontreated women over a five-year period. The results suggested that estrogen did protect against death from heart attack.

Ross then stated, "Age-adjusted death rates from ischemic heart disease in white females in the U.S. are over four times the combined death rates of breast cancer and endometrial cancer. If the protective effect of estrogen replacement therapy on risk of fatal ischemic heart disease is real, this benefit would far outweight the carcinogenic effects of estrogen.''[7]

And we now know that there are no carcinogenic effects if progesterone is added to the estrogen-replacement therapy. Another study of 2,269 white women aged forty to sixty-nine who were followed for an average of 5.6 years in a Lipid Research Clinics Program revealed that women on estrogen-replacement therapy had significantly lower death rates than nonusers.[8] Women were categorized into three hysterectomy status groups: gynecologically intact; uterus removed, or uterus and one ovary removed; or uterus and both ovaries removed. In each category, estrogen users had lower death rates than nonusers. Women who had their uterus and both ovaries removed and took no estrogen had the highest death rate. This group showed the greatest decrease in death rate with estrogen-replacement therapy. The researchers postulate that the protective effect of estrogen was associated with an increase in HDL levels, which are associated with a reduced risk of coronary disease, although they felt that other factors also contributed to the lower death rate in estrogen users.

However, we must consider what, if any, effect the addition of progesterone might have on cholesterol and lipoprotein levels. Could it undo all the good that estrogen has done? Are the various progesterones different in their effects on blood fat? If so, which should we pick to use?

To determine whether progesterones cancel the protective effect of estrogen on coronary artery disease, a group of obstetrician/gynecologists in Finland evaluated the effects of three progesterones on fat metabolism.[9] After three weeks of treatment with estrogen alone, total cholesterol and LDL levels decreased and HDL levels increased. Then they added one of the three progesterones. They found that both 19-nortestosterone derivatives *reversed* the beneficial HDL-increasing effects of the estrogen. Medroxyprogesterone acetate (Provera, Amen, Curretab) did not. The investigators concluded that the progesterone-derived compound might offer some advantage over the 19-nor compounds.

It is a vital piece of news that the 19-nortestosterone

compounds may reverse some of the good effects of estrogen, while medroxyprogesterone acetate may not. It is possible, however, that by decreasing the doses of progesterone much of this difference can be canceled. Nonetheless, it is important to preserve the beneficial effects of estrogen on the process of atherosclerosis by choosing your progesterone wisely and keeping its dose to a minimum effective level.

No More Postmenopausal Blues

There are many differing opinions as to whether the hormonal changes in menopause contribute to emotional problems and whether estrogen affects mental outlook and mood swings in menopausal women. Some doctors believe that such an association exists, whereas others believe that women get upset, nervous, and anxious about aging and their loss of youth.

Yet it is commonly understood and accepted that hormonal changes may influence a woman's mental state during other periods of her life. Postpartum blues are well known and are tied in with the rapid plunge of hormone levels after giving birth. Premenstrual syndrome is now being recognized, and the accompanying mood changes are also being blamed on hormonal variations. Therefore, why not implicate the menopausal woman's sudden loss of hormones in *her* mental complaints?

De Lignieres found that depressive symptoms in postmenopausal women, including sleep disturbance, loss of energy, pessimism, and fatigue, are often correlated with a drop in blood levels of estrogen or its precursors (androstenedione). He also found that these symptoms were reversed with HRT.

I am persuaded that women who have been depressed, anxious, and nervous all their lives will *not* be relieved of their depression when they become postmenopausal simply by the addition of estrogen to their daily vitamins. On the other hand, if a woman has been slightly depressed for years and her depression significantly deepened with menopause, I would not be averse to trying estrogen for two to four months to see if she improves. One such patient had seen a psychiatrist for many years and was on handfuls of tranquilizers and antidepressants. I suggested that we add estrogen. To date, she has been able to cut her drug intake to small bedtime doses. Furthermore, she is much more functional than when she was so heavily sedated. She also is forever grateful that her mouth is no longer dry from the antidepressants.

If there is a real place for estrogen in psychiatric treatments, I believe that it is for those women who have been stable all their lives but who became depressed, anxious, and nervous with menopause. In my experience, these women do extremely well on HRT. Of course, my experience is only clinical, but scientists have accumulated biochemical evidence that estrogen has a direct effect on brain function.

Utian performed a double-blind cross-over study of fifty women using estrogen versus placebo.* He concluded that estrogens have a "tonic mental effect."[10] Why this should be may have been identified by Aylward. In depression, the blood levels of 5-hydroxytryptamine (5-HT) and 5-hydroxyindoleacetic acid are low. He felt that estrogen indirectly has a beneficial effect on depression because it increases the availability of free tryptophan, which then can be converted finally to 5-HT. He found that during the perimenopause, free tryptophan levels were lower in women who were depressed than in women who were not depressed. His study demonstrated that HRT increased estrogen levels and free tryptophan levels and ameliorated mental depression,[11] thus linking estrogen deficiency to perimenopausal depression as well as to disturbed tryptophan metabolism. In the light of such data, tranquilizers seem to have little place in the treatment of depression in menopausal women. At least, it would seem unreasonable to shrug off complaints of depression and important to do a short trial of HRT.

That hot flushes awaken women from sleep has already been discussed. Insomnia is reported by 46 percent of postmenopausal women; fatigue by 37 percent. HRT has been shown to improve sleep patterns and increase the length of REM sleep. Women on estrogen fall asleep faster and also

*"Double-blind" means that neither doctor nor patient knows whether the patient is receiving the medication or a placebo. "Cross-over" means that the medication and placebo are switched during the study, again unbeknownst to the doctor and patient.

have more normal REM sleep patterns. This should result in better rested, more energetic, and more tranquil women.

Headaches in postmenopausal women are often regarded as psychosomatic. In a study in which headache was the primary complaint, headaches were relieved by HRT but not by placebo.

In another study of eighty-five patients receiving HRT for reasons other than headache, but in whom headache was a secondary complaint, Greenblatt observed that 93 percent of women got relief from headache when they were on HRT and that the severity, frequency, and duration of their headaches decreased.[12]

And so while many of my colleagues continue to prescribe endless quantities of tranquilizers and antidepressants to menopausal women reporting depression, I have had fairly strong feelings against doing this for some time. Most of my patients do not like to go about in a stupor, dazed to the point that they scarcely know what they are doing. We all know about the dangers of addiction and the side effects of tranquilizers and the toll they take every day on the lives of women. We should not dismiss HRT for mental complaints, only to become hooked on tranquilizers instead. I feel that, in the long run, HRT is much safer.

No Higher Risk of Breast Disease

Conjecture as to the effect of HRT on the subsequent development of breast cancer has caused many physicians to hesitate about starting their patients on it. Breast cancer is the most frequent cancer in women, accounting for 26 percent of all women's cancers, and it is responsible for the greatest number of cancer deaths among women. In 1981, approximately 110,000 cases were diagnosed, with approximately 37,000 deaths anticipated. This is more than ten times the number of deaths per year for endometrial cancer. Furthermore, as one study observed, "The mortality rate from breast cancer (23 per 100,000 women) has not changed during the past forty-five years, while death from endometrial cancer has declined from 27 per 100,000 in 1930 to 7 per 100,000 in 1975.''[13]

Because breast cancer is so prevalent in our society and so serious a disease, even a slight increase in its incidence would be cause for alarm, as it would mean a large increase in the number of deaths in this country. Therefore, any change in breast cancer incidence that might be caused by the administration of estrogen or of estrogen and progesterone must be regarded as being of paramount importance.

A few studies have shown increases in cancer rates in animals when they are given estrogen. Estrogen alone can also cause cystic breast development in mice whose ovaries are removed, whereas when progesterone is also given, proper breast development occurs.[14]

Hormonal research in 1979 suggested that an insufficiency of progesterone is the main problem in the development of benign breast disease in women.[15] The researchers measured estrogen and progesterone levels in women with fibrocystic breast disease and compared them to levels for normal women. They found that in women with breast disease, progesterone levels were significantly lower, while the estrogen levels were normal or elevated.

In another study, women with breast disease were treated with progesterone-containing gels applied to their breasts, or with oral progesterone. Many of these women found relief of pain and a decrease in nodularity of their breasts.

Another study further confirmed the importance of progesterone. (Remember, that if you do not ovulate, you do not produce progesterone.) Chronic anovulation (lack of ovulation, and therefore lack of progesterone) was shown to increase the chances of getting cancer of the breast or uterus. The Mayo Clinic studied 1,135 women with chronic anovulation and found that women with histories of irregular (or anovulatory) menses were 3.6 times more likely to have subsequent postmenopausal breast cancer; the same women had a five-fold increase in the incidence of endometrial cancer. The conclusion of the study was that the woman with chronic anovulation should be treated with progesterone, for irregular cycles (without the protection of progesterone production) placed her in a higher risk group. The authors suggested that such a woman should have very regular breast and gynecological checkups and receive therapy with progesterone.

We also know that birth control pills which contain daily doses of estrogen and progesterone decrease the incidence of benign breast disease. What effect, if any, this may have on subsequent breast cancer rates is unknown at this time.

Studies on the effect of estrogen on human breast cancer are very limited, and the results are confusing. The only studies to date have not found any significant increased risk of breast cancer from estrogen therapy. An increased risk was found in only a portion of one study population, and it is possible that there may have been statistical error "induced by excessive subgrouping of the sample population."[16] Also, these women were on estrogen-only replacement therapy.

An epidemiological study that appeared in July, 1982, found no statistically significant increase in breast cancer among women who took oral estrogen therapy, but noted an increased incidence in women who received injectable estrogen.[17] This group was small, and the statisticians who did the study warn that the statistics are therefore less reliable.

Researchers have further noted the simple fact that the incidence of breast cancer has not increased along with the accelerated usage of estrogen replacement. "Indeed, some reports have actually indicated a decrease in the risk of breast cancer in patients taking estrogen therapy in the menopausal period."[18] The most recent study published on hormones and breast cancer was done by one of the leading epidemiologists in the U.S., Ralph I. Horwitz, M. D., of the Yale University School of Medicine. Published in the February, 1984 *American Journal of Medicine*, the article reviewed previous studies and also analyzed new data, concluding that there was no association between estrogen and breast cancer.

Most studies never tried to separate women who took estrogen from those who took estrogen and progesterone. Now let us look at a few that did.

Prospective studies at Wilford Hall USAF Medical Center

found no evidence that estrogen-replacement therapy increased the risk of breast cancer and concluded that "estrogens may even provide some protection from [breast cancer] particularly when administered in conjunction with a progestogen."[19] Of the 5,563 postmenopausal women followed for 24,559 patient years of observation, 43 were found to have breast malignancy, equaling an overall incidence of 174.8 per 100,000 women per year. Among the estrogen-progestin users, there were only 7 breast cancers, an incidence of 95.6 per 100,000. In the group taking estrogens only, there were 15 breast cancers for an annual incidence of 137.3 per 100,000. The difference in incidence between the estrogen-progestin users and the estrogen users was not statistically significant but did indicate a trend. Certainly the following chart clearly shows that in the Wilford Hall study, women who took estrogen alone or with progestin had a significantly lower incidence of breast cancer than those women who took no therapy, whose breast cancer rate was 500 per 100,000!

INCIDENCE OF BREAST CANCER AT WILFORD HALL USAF
MEDICAL CENTER, 1975–79, BY THERAPY GROUP

	Patient-years of observation	Patients with cancer	Incidence (per 100,000)
Estrogen-progestin users	7,322	7	95.6
Estrogen users	10,928	15	137.3
Estrogen vaginal cream users	1,811	1	55.2
Progestin or androgen users	739	1	135.3
Untreated women	3,799	19	500.1
Total	24,599	43	174.8

In another prospective study (designed to follow subjects entered for a specific purpose), Nachtigall followed 84 women who were treated with estrogen and progesterone for ten years and 84 women who were not treated. There were 4 breast cancers in the nontreated group and none in the treated group. This difference was statistically significant.

There is another area to consider: Women who develop breast cancer while on estrogen replacement therapy seem to have better survival rates. In the Wilford Hall study, death rates were much lower in women who had taken hormonal therapy than in women who took no hormonal therapy.

This difference may be partly due to earlier detection in women who are on HRT. However, it is now widely accepted that women who have been on oral contraceptives have a lesser incidence of benign breast disease and a better prognosis with increased survival rates if they develop breast cancer. The better course of breast cancer in hormone-treated women may parallel the better prognosis of endometrial cancer in estrogen-treated women. The reasons, however, are not clearly understood to date. Earlier detection in hormone-treated women might lead to early diagnosis and better prognosis, or it may be possible that a less aggressive tumor may develop in women on HRT. There is need for much more research in this vital area of women's health.

The decision as to whether you want to follow any of the regimens discussed in these chapters is yours alone to make. However, it is important that you know that several therapies are available and are probably quite safe. It is even more important that you now can make your choice from a position of knowledge.

The decisions you make do not have to be permanent. You may begin therapy and find that it is not all you expected. Fine. Simply discontinue the treatment and inform your physician. You may also decide to seek the lowest possible dosage for the shortest possible amount of time and just wean off to get rid of your hot flushes. You may only want vaginal creams to aid this area. Or you may want to take long term treatment to insure the health of your bones. Whatever you choose, consider all of the facts. You know your mind and body better than anyone else. If you try hormone replacement therapy and it is good, continue. If it is not, stop. This decision, like any other, can be changed at any time. But remember, you will be spending a large part of your life as a postmenopausal woman. It is important that you make an informed, well-considered choice about what is best for your body and the quality of your life.

3

Osteoporosis: Preventing This Silent Killer

The most important reason to consider HRT is to prevent osteoporosis. Osteoporosis is a decrease in bone mineral mass that leads to an increased risk of fracture from minimal trauma. Now that women are living longer, osteoporosis has become a major health problem in the United States. It is more common than heart attacks or breast cancer. In fact, it is the twelfth leading cause of death in the United States!

Unlike hot flushes, which may be obvious and annoying, osteoporosis occurs silently. For the most part, there are no telltale symptoms until fracture occurs. Unfortunately, this major public health problem has gotten very little attention from physicians or from the press. Perhaps the *four billion dollars* spent last year alone repairing broken hips and verte-brae will thrust the problem into the spotlight—as it deserves.

Osteoporosis is a killer. Women sustain 85 percent of the 200,000 hip fractures that occur annually. And because of the complications that may happen during or after surgery, 60,000 women die every year within six months of their fractures. Furthermore, the incidence of osteoporosis is increasing, becoming almost epidemic. Hip fractures increased 40 per-cent between 1970 and 1980, and if this trend continues, there will be a half million hip fractures annually by the year 2000. This will result in 150,000 people being confined to nursing home care annually as a direct result of their fractures.

It is well known that in youth and middle age, women and men suffer approximately the same number of fractures.

49

Although both men and women progressively lose bone mass with aging, it is rare for men to develop symptoms of osteoporosis before age seventy. That is because the male skeleton contains more mineral and is denser than that of a female of the same size, and bone mineral content is directly related to bone strength. Men also have better statistics because their diets tend to contain more calcium and because they continue to have male hormones to protect their bones well into their seventies. After seventy, their hormone levels begin to decrease slowly. Therefore, male bone loss starts fifteen to twenty years later and occurs at a slower rate than in females. Consequently, men have lower fracture rates.

A study in Vienna by Kohn found that 84 percent of all patients requiring surgical procedures for fractures were women. The rapid loss of estrogen and progesterone after menopause makes women especially subject to bone loss. The seventy-year-old woman, for example, has a hip fracture rate fifty times higher than that of a forty-year-old woman.

Also, osteoporosis is most common in Caucasians and least common in blacks. In fact, bone mass seems to be directly related to the amount of pigment in one's skin. Approximately 25 percent of white women over age sixty will have compression fractures of their vertebrae due to osteoporosis, and this number increases to 50 percent by age seventy-five. Simpler fractures also take their toll. After age forty-five, there is a marked increase in forearm fractures in women. Fractures of the wrist usually result from a fall or other accident, while fractures of the bones of the spine usually occur as the result of normal daily activity.

Today a woman who is already fifty has a life expectancy of 85 years. Because of the increasing number of women living longer, we can expect that complications and death rates resulting from postmenopausal osteoporosis will become even greater.

Before painting too frightening a picture, however, the good news is that osteoporosis in most women is a preventable disease. Let us try to understand the factors that contribute to it, and then prevention will become easier to understand.

What Is Osteoporosis?

To understand osteoporosis, it is necessary to realize that bone is constantly being remodeled. An ongoing process of breaking down or resorption of the bone is accompanied by continuous bone formation. These processes of formation and destruction must be in equilibrium so that bone mass remains stable.

The skeleton attains a maximum bone density at approximately 35 years of age. The absolute amount of bone formed depends upon many factors including genetics, diet and, possibly, exercise. It is vitally important to build strong bones because this gives you the best odds against bone loss and developing fractures as you age (something akin to having money in the bank).

As a woman ages and her hormones become depleted she will lose bone at an accelerated rate of 1 to 3 percent a year unless preventive measures are taken. This loss begins at menopause or with the surgical removal of her ovaries. For example, if a woman has both of her ovaries removed at forty-one, her rapid bone loss begins immediately rather than years later, when she would have had her natural menopause. Therefore, she is at high risk for developing osteoporosis. On the other hand, if a woman continues to menstruate past fifty, she has less bone loss than women of the same age who have ceased having menses. Stated simply, the longer the post-menopausal period, i.e., the longer a woman lives without estrogen support (from her own ovaries or from HRT), the greater the loss of bone. The white woman who reaches the age of eighty will lose somewhere between 30 to 59 percent of her bone mass.

In addition to the effect of hormone depletion on women's bones, much current information suggests that osteoporosis may be a nutritional disease involving a prolonged calcium deficit in the diet. Insufficient calcium intake over several decades, plus the added factor of aging with its decreased intestinal absorption and increasingly poor food habits, creates the background for osteoporosis.

Most older women gradually become less active physically. This sedentary life pattern creates a "disuse osteoporosis." This condition is further aggravated in those who are confined to bed because bed rest causes loss of bone mineral, even in young people. Stress and strain on muscle, which transmits the force to bone, prevents demineralization. This is why patients are encouraged to get up and out of bed at the earliest possible time. Even people with fractures now have them stabilized and are encouraged to get up and move about.

As osteoporosis progresses, the bones become less able to withstand stress. The disease affects the axial skeleton first—that is, the spinal column, the head of the femur, and the pelvis. The weight-bearing vertebrae of the back collapse and compress, accentuating the roundness of the upper back.

The first vertebrae to collapse are the ones that bear the most weight, usually from the eighth thoracic vertebra down. (This is approximately at the level of the bottom of your scapula or wing bone.) The earliest change of the vertebrae is biconcavity. This is caused as the tougher intervertebral discs dig into the fragile vertebrae. Next, compression fractures occur, which cause the vertebrae to look like a wedge from the side. The posterior vertebral height is usually maintained while the anterior portion is squashed. This accounts for the dowager's hump and rounded back of the "little old lady" with a shortened upper trunk, who loses an average of two and a half inches in height.

One way to keep track of loss of height is, of course, to have good height measurements during your twenties, thirties, and forties. This should actually be part of your yearly examination. The degree of spinal change can then be estimated. Another way to estimate accurately the amount of height loss is to measure the span of your arms. Raise your arms sideways to shoulder level and measure from your longest fingertip on one hand to your longest fingertip on the other hand. In women with a normal spine, the height equals the fingertip-to-fingertip measurement. When the fingertip measurement is more than the height, the amount of spinal compression can be estimated from the difference between the two.

The loss of height is only one of the results of vertebral collapse. When the vertebral column is altered, the position of the ribs that attach to the vertebrae is also changed. This decreases the size of the rib cage, which in turn impairs breathing. The woman also notes that her waist line shortens or becomes nonexistent and that her abdomen protrudes. Bending or any other exertion may become difficult, and there may be pain caused by pressure on the nerves that exist from the spinal cord. In addition, the deformity of her back often causes cosmetic changes that become emotionally troubling for her.

The woman experiencing a spinal vertebral fracture will usually feel sudden, severe pain in her back accompanied by severe muscle spasm along the spine. The pain may radiate in ring-like fashion around to her chest or abdomen and is increased by standing or sitting. Multiple vertebral fractures result in chronic back pain, as well as other medical problems.

Presently there is no easy method of predicting exactly which women have the highest risk for the development of bone fractures. However, 35 to 40 percent of all women will develop osteoporosis, and this figure could be higher. It seems that the woman most likely to suffer from osteoporosis is small, thin, inactive, and more likely to be of northern European origin, with light hair and light skin. She also has a sedentary life style, smokes, drinks too much coffee and alcohol, and has a long history of poor diet with low calcium and vitamin D intake. She also may have had cortisone therapy for some reason, or a family history of osteoporosis, that is, female relatives who have had fractures or who developed rounding of the upper back.

It would be safe to state that any woman who has had her ovaries removed while she was premenopausal is at increased risk. Part of the problem is the loss of estrogen; another is the loss of the male hormone that is normally secreted by her ovaries. Two studies have shown that women who have osteoporosis have lower levels of male hormone.

The following factors increase your risk of osteoporosis:
• White or oriental heredity
• Slender build

- Fair skin, light eyes and hair
- Early menopause or ovaries removed
- Family history of osteoporosis (bone fractures/height loss in female relatives)
- Poor diet—
    low calcium intake
    low vitamin D intake
    increased alcohol intake
    increased coffee intake
    high protein intake
    often on a diet
- Sedentary life style
- Cigarette smoking
- Never pregnant
- Never took birth control pills
- Periodontal disease
- History of taking steroids
- Excess use of aluminum-containing antacids

However, while this list is useful, you should realize that osteoporosis can and does occur in women of every size, shape and color, and from a wide variety of backgrounds.

Methods of Assessing Bone Loss

There are several ways to measure bone loss. One is to gauge calcium levels in the blood and urine. When the patient is fasting, blood calcium levels reflect calcium that the body extracts from bone, the major storing place for 99 percent of this mineral. Since the kidney filters the blood, higher blood calcium levels mean that more calcium will pass out into the urine and be lost. Higher calcium levels in the urine, then, often reflect breakdown of bone.

A protein meshwork holds the bone minerals in place. The breakdown of this protein framework is reflected by the appearance of protein (hydroxyproline) in the blood. As women become menopausal, they show marked increases in the blood levels of hydroxyproline, more laboratory proof of an increased rate of bone loss. Such evidence occurs after the ovaries are removed regardless of the women's age.

Newer Methods of Measuring Bone Density

Bone loss can be seen on X rays, but by the time it shows up on the film, the woman has already lost 30 percent of her bone mass. Obviously, X rays have little value for preventive screening. Dental X rays which may be more routinely done, often show changes consistant with loss of mineral. In fact, this may be the reason for loss of teeth which become loose in the weakened jaw bone. Dental evidence of bone loss may in some cases precede generalized osteoporosis and be especially helpful.

More recently, however, procedures such as single photon absorptiometry and dual photon absorptiometry are being used in centers with special interest in osteoporosis to measure bone mineral content.

The single photon technique compares the bone mineral content of the patient's forearm with the bone mineral content from a standard graph based on sex and age. The test takes only a few minutes and is painless. It uses a source of radiation which gives approximately the same amount of exposure as an X ray of your arm.

If the test shows that your bone mineral content is low in comparison to other women your age, it will indicate that you may be at risk of developing osteoporosis. However, the prime usefulness of the test is in following patients from year to year to assess the rate of bone loss. This is more important than any one single determination. However, one of the problems of the technique is that if osteoporosis is already present, there may be poor correlation between the results derived from the bone in your arm and what is actually occuring in your vertebrae.

Dual photon absorptiometry can be used to further test those women with suspiciously low mineral content as determined by the single photon method, or may be used as a screening test itself for women in high risk groups. This machinery is more costly, but it directly measures mineral content of the vertebrae and therefore results are more reliable.

CAT scanning can also be used for measuring the amount of bone within the vertebrae. This method, although very accurate, is costlier, and exposes the patient to increased amounts of radiation. New techniques are being developed, however, which take only one film through the midsection of each of several vertebrae and compare their density to known bone normals.

As the appreciation of the enormous size of the problem of osteoporosis increases, these and other techniques to assess and follow patients will be developed. Most of these techniques are still only in specialized centers. Hopefully, as biomedical research proceeds, women will have better, more accurate and less costly means of evaluation at their disposal.

Estrogen and Osteoporosis

Osteoporosis is the most important problem associated with menopause. One of the strongest arguments for hormone-replacement therapy in menopausal women stems from long-term studies proving that such therapy prevents osteoporosis in postmenopausal women and in those women whose ovaries have been removed.

Estrogen preserves bone by preventing loss of calcium through the kidneys. Estrogen also increases calcium levels by increasing intestinal reabsorption of the mineral, so that for any given amount of calcium in your diet, more is absorbed. Also, estrogen protects the bones against the withdrawal of too much calcium. Therefore, at menopause, when estrogen levels drop, dietary calcium is absorbed less efficiently. But blood calcium must be kept stable. This results in a raid on the calcium supplies in the bones, which are now a more vulnerable target.

To date, it is not known exactly how estrogen affects bone metabolism. It does not stimulate bone building; rather it appears to decrease bone breakdown. But this is extremely important. If you can stop bone breakdown by taking estrogen for ten years, at the end of that time your bones will be ten years better off—that is, ten years younger than they would have been without therapy. They will have been maintained as they were. When you go off estrogen, however, the breakdown process will begin and at an increased rate, similar to that which occurs at menopause. Therefore, therapy should continue for a long time to give long-term protection.

Studies affirming the importance of estrogen are numerous. In one study of 1000 women treated with estrogens for a total of 14,318 patient-years of observation, wrist fractures were reduced by 70 percent from the expected rate. No hip fractures occurred during fifteen years of estrogen therapy in these 1000 women.

Whether 1.25 milligrams or 0.625 milligrams of conjugated estrogen were used seemed to make no difference in risk of fracture. This shows that higher doses of estrogen are not necessary to preserve your bones. Researching the minimum dose required for maintaining bone structure, Lindsey found that 0.3 conjugated estrogen decreases bone loss, but 0.625 provides better protection by keeping bone mass nearly status. These are the lowest doses of conjugated estrogen available. These are also the most frequently prescribed doses for HRT.

Because estrogen prevents osteoporosis and decreases vertebral and other fractures, it thereby also prevents loss of life. With appropriate therapy—one that includes calcium and exercise—the image of the little old lady with the rounded, hunched back can be replaced by that of a tall, erect older woman.

Perhaps the most exciting news is that scientists from across the nation met on April 4, 1984 at the National Institutes of Health in Bethesda, Maryland, to work out a consensus on the cause, prevention and treatment of osteoporosis. The fourteen member advisory board concluded that "estrogen replacement therapy is the most effective single modality for the prevention of osteoporosis in women." The panel also said the strategies for prevention of fracture include "assuring estrogen replacement in postmenopausal women, adequate nutrition including an elemental calcium intake of 1000 to 1500 mg a day, and a program of modest weight-bearing exercise." The panel reported that "case-controlled studies have shown an approximately 60 percent reduction in hip and wrist fractures in women whose estrogen replacement was begun within a few years of menopause.'' Even when started as late as six years after menopause, ''estrogen prevents further loss of bone mass but does not restore it to premenopausal levels.''

Interestingly, there are a couple of studies that show that the addition of progesterone to the estrogen regimen may actually increase bone mass by promoting new bone formation.

It is important to understand that to prevent osteoporosis effectively, we are no longer talking about a few months of hormonal therapy intended to tide a woman over her hot flashes. We are no longer talking about adding estrogen in minimal amounts now and then to keep her vaginal area functional. Osteoporosis demands long-term therapy, for it is a long-term disease. And long-term therapy should not be considered unless adequate doses of progesterone are cycled with the estrogen.

We have taken a lot of time and effort to understand the effect of estrogen and progesterone on bone. Remember, however, that their role in osteoporosis is primarily one of prevention. Once the fractures have occurred and the woman is well into her sixties, the hormones will not benefit her as much. This is another case where an ounce of prevention is worth a pound of cure. After substantial bone loss, a cure is difficult—we cannot rebuild the skeleton. Treatment at that point only can prevent (hopefully) further bone deterioration.

For the woman who already has osteoporosis, certain precautions are necessary. Sudden bending or lifting and carrying heavy objects should be forbidden. Women with osteoporosis have been known to fracture while lifting a turkey from the oven. Safety measures, too, are necessary— nonskid rugs, low-heel shoes; anything to avoid a fall.

Calcium

The most important function of calcium in the body involves normal cell activity such as muscular contraction and nerve-impulse conduction; keeping bones strong and healthy comes second. In order for your body to function normally, a certain level of calcium must be maintained in the blood. Most of this calcium comes from foods we eat, especially dairy products. If the calcium blood level drops below a specific point, the body reacts by absorbing more calcium from foods or a calcium supplement. However, if there is not enough calcium in the diet, or if it cannot be absorbed adequately, the body steals calcium from the bones, which are the major storage place for this mineral. If this problem exists only for a short time, no harm is done. But if the situation persists and your body runs at a chronic calcium deficit, the constant transfer of calcium from the bones to the bloodstream eventually weakens the structural strength of the bones. The bones become less dense and more likely to fracture.

Because calcium absorption declines progressively, the aging woman has an increased need for dietary calcium. Estrogen helps the body absorb calcium from food and supplements as well as conserve calcium by preventing loss through kidneys. Therefore, women taking hormones need less calcium than women who are not on therapy.

One five-year study showed that women who are postmenopausal on hormonal therapy need 1 gram (1000 mg) of calcium daily, while postmenopausal women on no hormonal therapy need 1½ grams. The current recommended dietary calcium allowance (RDA) is 800 milligrams—much lower than this. However, the typical American woman gets only 400 to 500 mg per day. Therefore, older women have higher calcium requirements than men and younger women.

Menstruating women also need calcium, in fact, their requirements are 25 percent higher than the current RDAs. It is a fact that most college women are calcium deficient. Women, to their detriment, often limit their intake of calcium. They frequently avoid dairy products, a major source of calcium, because of weight worries or because of concern about cholesterol, and thus they are operating their bodies at a chronic deficit.

Few women would ever let a car engine run for months on

low levels of oil, knowing the toll this takes on the engine. So in order to preserve their investment, they take proper care of their cars. Unfortunately most women take better care of their cars than of their bodies. Somehow we tend to forget that this is the only body we will ever have—we can't trade it in for a new model if it doesn't function well. Think about it. Preserve your body as best you can by giving it what it needs—now. Years of dietary neglect leave most women with large deficits that must finally be cared for.

Osteoporosis must become an acute concern of all women, and not just to those women approaching menopause or who are already elderly. We know osteoporosis as a debilitating and disfiguring disorder of old age, but steps need to be taken early to prevent the disease from occurring.

Calcium is needed by young women who are building their bone mass. The best way to prevent osteoporosis is to build the greatest possible bone mass. One of the keys to that is calcium. Young women, if they cannot be coaxed into a quart of milk daily, or equivalent amount in cheese and other dairy products should take a calcium supplement. Many experts feel that increased amounts of calcium intake should begin by 15 years of age. Calcium is the primary mineral of bone, and it has been well documented that inadequate dietary calcium is a risk factor for fracture in all age groups!

Side effects of excess calcium may be an elevated blood calcium level, soft tissue calcification, kidney stones, or kidney damage. However, such problems would almost never arise in patients with normal kidney function on the doses of calcium recommended in this book.

The following chart shows foods that are rich in calcium. If you eat sufficient amounts of these foods on a daily basis, then you may forego calcium supplements. Unfortunately most women's diets do not include enough calcium, and supplements should be considered. Researchers have concluded that menopausal women should get 1000 mg of their calcium in a supplement and 500 mg in food sources.

CALCIUM EQUIVALENCY CHART*

Item	Serving	Calcium (mg)
Milk products		
Whole milk	1 cup	288
Evaporated whole milk	½ cup	302
Powdered whole milk	½ cup	252
Skim milk	1 cup	298
Half and half	2 T	32
Sour cream	2 T	31
Cheese		
Cheddar	1 oz	218
Cheese foods	1 oz	160
Cheese spread	1 oz	158
Cottage cheese	¼ cup	53
Fish		
Salmon (with bones)	1 oz	51
Sardines	1 oz	115
Clams	1 oz	29
Oysters	1 oz	31
Shrimp	1 oz	35
Bread		
Biscuit	2" diameter	42
Muffin	2" diameter	36
Cornbread	1½" cube	36
Pancake	4" diameter	45
Fruit		
Orange	1 medium	41
Blackberries	¾ cup	32
Raspberries	¾ cup	30
Tangerine	2 small	40
Rhubarb	1 cup	96
Vegetables		
Beans, green or wax	½ cup	50

*Printed by permission of W B Saunders Co from *Food, Nutrition, and Diet Therapy,* by M.V. Krause and L. K. Mahan. Copyright © 1979 by W B Saunders Co.

Item	Serving	Calcium (mg)
Broccoli	½ cup	88
Cabbage	½ cup	49
Celery	½ cup	39
Spinach	½ cup	93
Turnip greens	½ cup	184
Artichokes	½ cup	51
Okra	½ cup	92
Kale	½ cup	187
Dessert		
Custard, baked	⅓ cup	112
Ice Cream	½ cup	110
Ice milk	½ cup	118
Pie, cream	⅙ of 9″ pie	120
Pudding	½ cup	117
Other		
Eggs	1	27
Yogurt, plain	1 cup	272

It is interesting to note that women who are and have always been overweight will benefit less from hormone-replacement therapy and calcium, for their bones are normally more dense.

Recent evidence obtained by studying 20,000 people reveals that hypertensives as a group have a lower intake of calcium than the general population; in fact, their average daily intake is only 200 milligrams. It is possible that increasing calcium intake in hypertensive patients will lower blood pressure. The elderly and blacks are more likely to have hypertension, and these two groups have known low calcium intake levels. So increasing your calcium may be good for more than just your bones.

Vitamin and Mineral Supplements

Now that you are aware of the need for calcium thoughout your life, you should also realize that osteoporosis does not have to be an inevitable consequence of aging. With diet and good dietary supplements, it should be a preventable disease.

According to nationwide surveys by the U.S. Department of Agriculture 40 percent of all women ages 19 to 50 consume low-calorie diets. These women do not get the minimum daily requirements of many essential vitamins and nutrients, especially vitamins A, C, B_6 and calcium. Women who are dieting clearly need vitamin and mineral supplements. Women also need vitamin D in order to properly metabolize the calcium they take.

Women on birth control pills may require more B_6 and folic acid to make up for metabolic changes induced by the pill. Vitamin B_6 decrease is thought to be the reason that some women become depressed when taking oral contraceptives. Vitamin B_6 may also help reduce premenstrual tension and allergic problems in some women. Other researchers feel magnesium is also important in decreasing PMS. Smokers have reduced levels of vitamin C. Drinking lowers thiamine and folic acid levels. It is also possible that different medications, tranquilizers and stress have untoward effects on vitamin metabolism.

New research has found that animals with normal levels of vitamin A have less breast cancer than animals with low levels. There is also evidence that selenium in proper dosage may protect against human breast cancer. Vitamin E has been reported to be helpful in women with cystic breasts. I also use it to treat women with night leg cramps.

I believe that the entire subject of vitamin and mineral supplementation has never been dealt with properly by the medical community. There has been almost no teaching available in medical schools on diet and nutrition for medical students or residents, and certainly nothing on supplementation until a few hours were added to the curriculum several years ago in some of the medical schools.

I feel that there soon will be a serious swing in medical thinking. There is increasing awareness that physicians should not only be taught to treat disease, but—more importantly—also should be in the business of trying to prevent disease.

Much of disease prevention may lie directly within our grasp through better nutrition (better eating habits) and vitamin and mineral food supplementation (dietary supplements).

The idea of preventive medicine has suddenly attracted intense scientific interest. The National Cancer Institute (NCI) has spent over $13 million over the last eighteen months for seventeen separate clinical trials of a variety of vitamin supplementation regimens. A $3 million Harvard study (one of six on beta carotene and a dozen on vitamin A and related compounds) should bring answers over the next few years. Dr. Charles Hennekens, the director of the Harvard study, suggested years ago that carotene could cut United States cancer rates by 20 to 30 percent and save 60,000 lives in the process. The enthusiasm for these studies is based on many laboratory studies that link vitamin A deficiency to changes such as excessive multiplication and intracellular abnormalities in individual cells. Vitamin A may possibly work by preventing subcellular damage from highly reactive charged oxygen "free radicals." This theory is also proposed as the mechanism of action for the possible cellular protection of vitamin E.

Animal studies have indicated that vitamin A activity may offer protection against some cancers of the lung, prostate, cervix, breast and gastrointestinal tract. Additionally, dietary surveys in Norway, Japan and the U.S. that involved more than a quarter million people found a significant inverse relationship between vitamin A intake and lung, stomach and bladder cancers, even in smokers.

One of the problems is that we are not entirely sure of what vitamin doses are essential. Research will not have these answers for many years to come. I feel, however, that it is important to have levels of vitamin A, for example, that are at least not below normal. And as important as it is to get adequate dosages of vitamins, I believe it is equally important not to overdose. Overdoses of vitamin A, for example, can lead to headache and neuralgias.

As you can see, there are many considerations that should go into the formulation of a vitamin and mineral preparation for women. I have not been able to find a properly formulated supplement to prescribe for women.

Most of the vitamins heavily touted for women contain iron and little else besides a few vitamins in low amounts. If there is one element that older women don't need a lot of, it's iron. Ironically, although younger menstruating women need the iron, it is believed that the accumulation of iron in men and nonmenstruating women increases their risk of heart attack. Those preparations that contain high amounts of iron and are currently aimed at older individuals are dangerous.

In my opinion, the most serious problem is that these vitamin preparations do not contain sufficient calcium for a woman's needs. Women from their teens to forty should supplement their diets with about 650 mg of calcium per day to assure that strong bones are built. Women over forty should supplement the 500 mg in their daily diet with 1000 mg of calcium to preserve their bones.

I am frightened when my patients take dozens of vitamin tablets from as many different bottles. All too often they overdose on some of the vitamins and neglect others entirely. Very often they create imbalances in their bodies. Some minerals, for example, should be taken in specific ratios or their benefit is lost.

I therefore resolved to make a vitamin and mineral formulation for my patients that would give them all the essential ingredients that they needed. And so I formulated a complete dietary supplement that included everything I had learned to be important. My specifications were that the preparation would contain sufficient amounts of the finest ingredients that money could buy. I named them simply, "Vitamins for Women."

Vitamins for Women come in two formulas because women have different nutritional requirements at different times in their lives. One formula is for women from teens to 40, the other for women over 40. (The over-40 formula is also to be used for women of any age who have had a hysterectomy.)

The twenty-three ingredients in the two formulas are the same: only the amounts vary. For example, the teen to forty

Day AGES 14 TO 40		*Day* OVER AGE 40	
Two tablets contain:		*Two tablets contain:*	
Vitamin A	5000 IU	Vitamin A	5000 IU
Beta Carotene	1 mg	Beta Carotene	1 mg
Vitamin D$_3$	400 IU	Vitamin D$_3$	400 IU
Vitamin C	500 mg	Vitamin C	500 mg
Vitamin B$_1$	20 mg	Vitamin B$_1$	20 mg
Vitamin B$_2$	25 mg	Vitamin B$_2$	25 mg
Vitamin B$_6$	100 mg	Vitamin B$_6$	75 mg
Vitamin B$_{12}$	50 mcg	Vitamin B$_{12}$	50 mcg
Niacinimide	25 mg	Niacinimide	50 mg
Folic Acid	400 mcg	Folic Acid	400 mcg
Calcium	100 mg	Calcium	300 mg
Magnesium	50 mg	Magnesium	100 mg
Bioflavonoids	100 mg	Bioflavonoids	100 mg
Rutin	10 mg	Rutin	10 mg
Iodine	25 mcg	Iodine	50 mcg
Iron	27 mg	Iron	15 mg
Zinc	12 mg	Zinc	15 mg
Copper	1 mg	Copper	1 mg
Selenium	30 mcg	Selenium	50 mcg
Chromium	25 mcg	Chromium	50 mcg
Manganese	5 mg	Manganese	5 mg
Biotin	25 mcg	Biotin	25 mcg

Nite		*Nite*	
Two tablets contain:		*Two tablets contain:*	
Vitamin E	100 IU	Vitamin E	200 IU
Calcium	550 mg	Calcium	700 mg
Magnesium	200 mg	Magnesium	200 mg

Two day and two nite tablets provide 650 mg of Calcium

Two day and two nite tablets provide 1000 mg of Calcium

formula contains more iron to offset menstrual blood loss, 650 mg of calcium to build strong bones, plus B$_6$ to help alleviate premenstrual tension. In contrast, the over-40 formula contains 1000 mg calcium, more selenium and E and a small amount of iron so as not to increase the risk of heart attack.

Because there are so many vitamins and minerals, it is necessary to take four tablets daily. These are divided into a morning and nighttime formula. Therefore, vitamins for women are sold as a package that contains two bottles. One bottle contains the morning multivitamin "wake up" formula, and one contains the night formula consisting of only calcium, magnesium and E to calm and help you sleep. The E in the evening helps get rid of night leg cramps.

You should understand that your body benefits most by taking your calcium and vitamins over the course of the day because it will better utilize the ingredients. In fact, although it is vitally important to take all of your calcium, it is not a good idea to take 1000 milligrams at one time. Therefore, the directions on Vitamins for Women read: Take one tablet after breakfast, and one after lunch for the morning formula (always taken with a full glass of water). The night formula is to be taken after supper and at bedtime. Dividing the doses of vitamins A, B, C, D, and E and minerals will enhance their effect, and your body will appreciate your concern.

Of course, in the less-than-ideal world, many women—including my teenage daughter and myself—are very busy. On hectic days we take two tablets together after lunch and two night tablets together after supper, rather than missing a dose.

You cannot make an intelligent decision about your vitamin regimen without knowing the sources of the vitamins and minerals that you are putting into your body. For example, dolomite and bone meal, frequently used sources of calcium, may be contaminated with lead. More recently, arsenic contamination has been found in dolomite. These preparations therefore would not be good sources for long term use. Vitamins for Women contains pure oyster shell calcium. (Each batch is carefully assayed for any heavy-metal contamination.) The product also contains the B complex vitamins. These were purposely not made from yeast, as many people are allergic to yeast in large quantities and react badly to it. The vitamin E is a dry vitamin E. The zinc, copper and manganese are from amino acid chelates, and the iron is supplied in the gentle form of ferrous gluconate.

Vitamins for Women are free of sugar, starch, preservatives, and are vegetable-protein coated. I believe they are the finest vitamin/mineral plan available for women today. Originally available only to my patients, they are now available to the public by mail order.*

One more thing you should understand before we leave the subject of calcium: how to read a label. There are several different forms of calcium. There is calcium carbonate, which can be obtained from natural sources such as oyster shells, dolomite or bone meal. Other forms include calcium phosphate, calcium lactate, and calcium gluconate. There are also others, less popular calciums.

It is most important that you understand how to make certain your supplement provides the total amount of calcium you require. Since women over forty require at least 1000 milligrams of calcium daily, I shall use this figure as an example. This refers to 1000 milligrams of *elemental calcium*.

calcium carbonate contains 40 percent elemental calcium
calcium phosphate contains 31 percent elemental calcium
calcium lactate contains 13 percent elemental calcium
calcium gluconate contains 9 percent elemental calcium.

In other words, to get 1000 milligrams of elemental calcium, you must ingest:

2,500 milligrams of calcium carbonate
3,225 milligrams of calcium phosphate
7,692 milligrams of calcium lactate
11,111 milligrams of calcium gluconate.

A milligram is a set measure and refers to weight. So while it is possible to put 1000 milligrams of calcium from calcium carbonate in two tablets because it contains 40% calcium, it would take ten to eleven tablets of calcium gluconate to provide the same 1000 milligrams of elemental calcium be-

---

*For further information about these supplements call toll free 1-800-331-1750, or write to Vitamins for Women; P.O. Box 305; Woodbury, N.Y. 11797

cause calcium gluconate contains only 9% calcium. Learn to read labels. The label must read 1000 milligrams calcium or 1000 milligrams elemental calcium. If it reads 1000 milligrams calcium gluconate, you are only getting 90 milligrams of calcium.

Alternative Treatments

All women should exercise, take calcium, and do all the rest of those good things mother told you to do like quit smoking and drinking coffee and alcohol.* But when osteoporosis is already well established, other, more experimental treatments may have to be pursued.

Fluoride in high doses is currently being used experimentally. This therapy is tricky, because fluoride is a toxic element that has many side effects when it is taken in large doses. It also can create bone structure that looks great on X rays but fractures easily.

Winstrol (stanozolol) is an anabolic steroid and a synthetic derivative of testosterone that has recently been marketed for patients with osteoporosis. The 1982 *Physicians Desk Reference* list it as "probably effective; as adjunctive but not primary therapy in senile and post-menopausal osteoporosis. Equal or greater consideration should be given to diet, calcium balance, physiotherapy, and good general health-promoting measures."

Winstrol should be considered specifically by women who have contraindications for estrogen therapy and are at high risk for development of osteoporosis. Male-type side effects, such as increase in facial hair and male-pattern balding have been noted, along with more general side effects such as nausea, vomiting, diarrhea, acne, liver-function abnormalities, and fluid retention. Winstrol is given in a dose of 2 to 6 milligrams daily. Like estrogen, this drug is often given in a three-weeks-on, one-week-off regimen. This supposedly re-

---

*Studies have found that women who smoke have an earlier menopause. Coffee causes a loss of 5 milligrams of calcium per cup.

duces the incidence of side effects. Liver-function tests should be done at six-month intervals, and if abnormalities appear, dosages should be decreased accordingly or the drug discontinued. Decreasing drug dose may also relieve side effects. Other side effects include adverse changes in blood fats.

In a clinical trial of 38 patients—21 treated patients and 17 controls—the treated group showed an increase in total body calcium as well as a decrease in urinary calcium loss. Both groups were given 1000 milligrams of dietary calcium daily. Hip-bone biopsy showed an increase in the rate of bone formation in the treated group. Moreover, no new spinal compression fractures occurred in the treated group, whereas 3 occurred in the control group. This twenty-four month study was short compared to the entire history of an individual's osteoporosis, and longer studies are needed to elucidate the role of this drug, which has substantial side effects but is potentially beneficial.

Decadurabolin is another anabolic steroid that is sometimes used in the treatment of osteoporosis. It is given by injection and causes an increase in muscle mass. It also has male-type side effects. No recent well-controlled studies have been done with this drug, but it has been used for many years and may have some benefit in those cases where estrogen-progesterone therapy is contraindicated.

Calcitonin is another drug that may one day play a part in the therapy of osteoporosis. It increases the total body calcium, primarily by decreasing bone reabsorption. This drug must be given by injection, and there are sometimes slight problems at the injection site, including redness and allergic reactions. Calcitonin is protein in nature, and therefore skin testing should be done before it is used to rule out the possibility of sensitivity to the drug.

Calcitonin's method of action in the body is still incompletely understood. It may work along with other hormones such as parathyroid hormone to control calcium levels in the body by balancing the transfer of bone calcium to the blood and vice versa, or it may decrease bone resorption by a direct action on the cells that break bone down.

Vitamin D is necessary for the absorption of calcium from the intestine and its deposition in bone. All women should take 400 IUs of vitamin D daily. (A certain amount of exposure to sunlight is required for conversion of vitamin D precursors to the active form of vitamin D. That is why we all need at least short periods of sunshine daily. Realizing this, even nursing homes are now beginning to get their patients out of doors for twenty minutes or so every day.)

The most active from of vitamin D is available as Rocaltrol. It is currently being used experimentally in a trial on Long Island, where women with documented fractures are being treated. Although this drug is a vitamin product, it is very potent and can produce many side effects; overdose can even be fatal. However, taken in correct dosages, it may well benefit patients with osteoporosis. Much more should be learned as this study proceeds.

The best therapy results to date have been seen with combination therapy—that is, calcium, estrogen, vitamin D, and exercise. Experimental studies adding fluoride have also shown promise.

Exercise for Prevention

Some months ago, because of the constant typing involved in writing a book, I began to feel that my upper back needed some exercise. I was spending many hours hunched over the typewriter, and for most of the rest of the day, I talked to and examined patients while sitting on a stool that has no back support. My shoulders and upper back grew tired by the end of the day, because like most women, I have very little upper-body muscle development. I felt that exercise would be a good thing for me.

My eighteen-year-old son has a bench in his room on which he lies and lifts weights. For some time, I have watched him struggle to lift 275 pounds. His upper body is obviously well muscled, much of that due to his genes and to his male hormones. But I need some muscle, too, and because lifting weight while lying on your back develops upper-body strength and protects your vertebrae from damage, I decided that I would try it. My son took one look at my skinny arms and set up the bar with no weight on it. The bar alone weighs 25 pounds.

It has been several months now. Although I must admit that I have not done the lifting on any regular schedule, just a few weeks ago, I was finally able to do three full sets of ten lifts with the bar alone. My son kept saying in dismay, "Mom, aren't you embarrassed to be lifting a bar with no weight on it? It looks funny." I have finally added 5 pounds of weight, and I feel that it is an accomplishment for me. I will obviously never be a weight lifter, but lifting even the 25 or 30 pounds at the end of days when I ache makes me feel better and makes my upper back and neck pain free. I also learned that even if you are over forty, your muscles will respond to stimulation and exercise. Women should do more to strengthen their bodies and to preserve the strength in their muscles and bones. I plan to practice what I preach and join a gym as soon as this book is written. (Weight lifting is contraindicated in persons with hypertension, osteoporosis, or cardiac disease.)

One of the best things you can do for yourself is preserve your body and prevent osteoporosis while you are still in your twenties, thirties, and forties. Exercise should be done faithfully. As you age, especially after your bones become brittle, you will not be able to do anything strenuous, especially exercise that involves lifting weight, because you will run the risk of collapsing your vertebrae or fracturing a bone.

I am not a fan of jogging—unless you have been doing it most of your life, beginning in mid-life can be treacherous. Knees, ankles, and hip joints take an awful beating unless you have good supervision, begin slowly, and build up slowly. In my estimation, walking is a much better and healthier choice.

One of the interesting facts is that you must exercise everything. If you exercise your legs only, the bones in your upper back and arms will not benefit. If you only stress the upper part of your body, your legs and hips will not improve. Therefore, an all-around exercise program that involves as many joints of the body as possible is best.

Stress or mechanical strain which are the result of physical activity prevent bone loss and increase bone mineralization. Two of the factors that act on bone are the contraction of muscle and the pull of gravity. If either of these forces is changed, as they are in exercise, bone mineral content is affected.[5]

Inactivity produced by immobilization, weightlessness, or loss of muscular activity results in bone loss. Even athletic young men have been demonstrated to lose large amounts of their bone calcium during prolonged bed rest. Well-trained astronauts have also been studied after space flight and have shown a loss of bone mineral due to the lack of the pull of gravity in space.

On the other hand, tennis players have heavier bones in their playing arms, and long-distance runners have better bone mineral content in their legs than nonrunners. Therefore, bone can respond to local stress and individual bones can be built up and made stronger through exercise. Interestingly, age does not seem to be a major limiting factor in the ability of bone to respond to stress. But the amount of time needed or the amount of work or stress needed to maintain the bones in older people is not precisely known yet.[6]

Smith, et al. studied a group of thirty elderly women who had an average age of 84. Eighteen served as controls in the study, while twelve participated in an exercise program for three years. The twelve exercised for thirty minutes a day, three days a week for three years. The exercises used in the study were designed to be done sitting in a chair and included sideward leg spreads, walking and running in place, knee lifts, toe touches, arm lifts, sideward bends, and toe taps. "The control group had a bone mineral content loss of 3.28% during the 36 months, while the physical activity group demonstrated a 2.29% gain. . . . The physical activity resulted in an increased bone mineral content in the physically active participants."[7]

Even in older women with severe bone loss, improvement in bone mineralization is possible. Swimming in a warm pool is great for improving the range of motion of joints and for stretching muscles, but it probably does little to add mineral to bones because there is little stress on the bones because of the buoyancy of the water. However, for women who are already known to have osteoporosis and who have fractured bones, it is one of the best ways to begin to get back into shape.

If you are premenopausal, you will realize that now is the time to start taking care of your body. Most likely it has been good to you through the years; now it is time for you to be good to it. Join a gym where you can get supervision by a professional. Remember, however, if you decide on a serious exercise program, check with your personal physician first.

Most important, remember that osteoporosis is not an inevitable consequence of aging. With a proper medical regimen, exercise, good diet, and diet supplements where necessary, it can be prevented.

4

No More Mastectomies

After 20 years in practice, I am convinced that the most devastating diagnosis I can give a woman is that she has a lump in her breast. She will immediately be overwhelmed by the spectre of mutilation which is more than some women can deal with. Since the hardcover publication of *No More Hot Flashes and Other Good News,* I have seen a number of women who were aware that they had breast masses but never went to their doctors. These were not uneducated women. Indeed, some were very well educated, wealthy and had professional husbands. In discussions, they were quick to agree that on an intellectual level they were aware of the risks, but on an emotional level they were unable to cope with the loss of their breast.

Although these women may not be the norm, most women are aware of the breast cancer statistics and consider themselves at risk. Yet, only a small percentage do breast self-examination. This makes some sense, for there is no immediate tangible reward for finding a lump. Even if the mass is small, that woman knows she is fated to lose her breast when she sees her surgeon. So many women find little reason to do breast self-examination, or if they have found a lump they may wait and lose precious time that can be the difference between life and death.

But there should be a reward for finding a small lump, and that reward should be that the woman can choose to keep her breast. If more women were aware that finding a small tumor would give them this option, more women might see the benefit of monthly examination. They might also better appreciate the need for screening mammography. And that might make a significant contribution to decreasing the death rate from breast cancer.

Five years ago, I wrote in my first book, *No More Menstrual Cramps and Other Good News,* that if I discovered that I had breast cancer, I would treat it by lumpectomy (removal of the lump only) and radiation therapy, rather than surgical removal of my breast. One out of every eleven women will get breast cancer, and I, like everyone else, have no special immunity, and so I have given a lot of thought to that possibility. Furthermore, the medical literature that appeared since then has convinced me that my decision is on even firmer ground. In fact, most of my patients have found lumpectomy and radiation the most comfortable decision for them.

This chapter was written not to tell you what to do, but to explain an option that is rarely discussed by surgeons with women who have breast cancer. It will not change the fact that you must respond to you own personal needs, but you should realize that there is more than one treatment option for early breast cancer. This information is offered to provide a background so that you can assume some degree of control over your body and what happens to it.

The emphasis on surgery in this country has all but overshadowed the role of radiation therapy as a primary therapy for this disease. Much of the current thinking and emphasis on surgery goes back to Halsted at the turn of this century.

William Halsted was a superb surgeon who practiced just after the discovery of anesthesia. For the first time, patients could be put to sleep and undergo surgical procedures that had previously been impossible. Before anesthesia, if a woman had breast cancer, only the swiftest of breast amputations could be accomplished. It is little wonder that women did not readily come forward. They were also reticent because in those days breast cancer was thought to be a form of venereal disease. Most patients suffered in silence as if they were doing penance for their sins. They did not come forward until their lesions made life unbearable. Many women came to Halsted. His meticulous surgical skill saved the lives of some fortunate women who were still in the early stages of the disease, and he and his operation became famous.

Halsted believed that breast cancer spread in an orderly manner into the lymph vessels, then to the lymph nodes closest to the tumor, and then to the nodes further away. According to his theory, further spread could be stopped by removing all the nodes in the area of the cancer. This would prevent escape of cancer cells into the bloodstream, and that is why he removed the entire breast, the underlying chest muscles, and the underarm lymph nodes all in one operation. He felt that if all the tumor was confined to the breast, lymphatics, and lymph nodes, removal of these tissues should cure the patient.

Halsted spent hours on each operation. For a short period of time, he even extended his surgery to remove the lymph nodes at the base of the neck. When he noted that this extended procedure did not increase the life expectancy of the patient, he abandoned it. He also believed that the surgeon controlled the patient's survival by being thorough and meticulous and by removing every last bit of fat, breast tissue, and nodes from the operating field. He felt that proper surgery was the primary factor affecting the woman's survival.

Hundreds of thousands of Halsted radical breast procedures have been done over the past eighty years. If his theory were correct, all women who underwent the Halsted radical before the cancer had obviously spread would have been cured. On the contrary, the death rate for breast cancer is high and has not changed significantly since the turn of the century!

Patients who have a Halsted radical mastectomy are left with a thin, bony chest wall that looks skeletonlike as far up as the collarbone. The shoulder is stiff and the affected arm weak because of the large amount of muscle that has been removed. Due to removal of most of the armpit lumph nodes, the involved arm often swells because of poor fluid drainage, and the affected hand and arm are susceptible to infection. A tiny nick or scratch can lead to massive infection.

Women who have had radical surgery can try to prevent swelling of the arm by regular exercise, elevation of the arm whenever possible (resting it on a pillow higher than the heart level during sleep), wearing an elastic sleeve when necessary, or using a Jobst pump (a mechanical device designed specifically to reduce swelling) if all else fails. Some women complain about chest pain from the cold on a winter day. Without the protective padding of muscle and fat, the rib cage and the internal organs are constantly exposed to temperature variations.

In spite of all the problems associated with radical mastectomy, it is still performed in *one fourth* of all breast surgery cases in this country. As far as I am concerned—and not every American surgeon would agree with me—the radical mastectomy should have been abandoned years ago. In Europe, medical textbooks regard the Halsted radical mastectomy as an operation only of historical significance.

Contrary to Halsted's belief, breast cancer may not spread in an orderly manner and may invade the blood stream directly and early. In fact, there may be spread of the cancer cells even before the cancer is detectable in the breast. It is the metastases to the brain, liver, bone or lung that contributes to the demise of the patient, not the local disease in the breast. Local control, however, is the basic for disease control. Whether mastectomy or lumpectomy and radiation is selected, keep in mind that these are local therapies that may at best control the disease while it is still confined to the breast.

Current theory is that there is no orderly pattern of tumor-cell spread. Spread through the lymph does not necessarily precede spread through the bloodstream, because tumor cells may bypass the nodes. Indeed, the bloodstream is a very important pathway for spread of cancer. This was discovered when, prior to a colon-cancer surgery, blood was drawn from a draining vein and then filtered. In this experiment, many cancer cells were caught in the filter. This demonstrated that cells break off the primary tumor and move through the blood to distant sites. Local factors in the body's defense mechanism influence the survival of these cancer cells that break away from the main tumor and circulate. Such factors determine whether the malignant cells will form a growing seed of cancer or be destroyed.

It follows, then, that having positive lymph nodes (finding cancer cells in them) simply means that the woman's immune defense system does not stop the growth of the cancer cells, while negative nodes signal that her defense system is effective or that the number of cancer cells is low enough for the body to be able to destroy them. In reality, lymph nodes are probably ineffective barriers to tumor spread.

Interestingly, among women who have early cancer of the breast where there is spread to the lymph nodes, there is no difference in survival if the lymph nodes are left intact or removed. Although the physician may not find these nodes enlarged, 40 percent of them contain microscopic cancer cells. The presence of cancer cells, therefore, does not necessarily mean that a tumor will develop.

Removal of the breast, chest muscle, and all of the axillary lymph nodes, as is done in the radical mastectomy, does not increase survival over lesser surgery but adds much to pain and suffering. In 1979, the National Cancer Institute decided that the radical mastectomy should no longer be the surgical procedure of choice. Yet surgeons continued to argue about how much breast has to be removed, and, like Halsted, they fail to realize that they are only affecting the local factors in a larger problem. This obsession with removing the breast stifles new ideas and has led surgeons to mutilate women without improving survival rates of breast cancer over the past eighty years.

Other forms of breast surgery include the modified radical and the simple mastectomy. But modified radical mastectomy does not mean quite the same thing to every surgeon. Some remove so much tissue that I have trouble distinguishing it from a radical, except that the incision is horizontal. Other surgeons remove the breast, underarm lymph nodes, and either remove the pectoralis minor chest muscle or leave it intact. Each surgeon fashions his surgery after the way he was taught. It may be extensive in some women or appear more like a simple mastectomy in others. Simple mastectomy removes the breast and leaves the chest muscles and lymph nodes in the armpit intact. But even simple mastectomy removes the entire breast. The fact is that five- and ten-year studies show that all these surgical procedures have survival rates that are no better or worse than lumpectomy plus radiation therapy, which leaves the breast intact!

The number of years that a woman lives after mastectomy is not affected by whether she chooses lumpectomy with radiation or mastectomy. However, the quality of those years may be drastically affected in some women. One study showed significant emotional distress in postoperative mastectomy patients—they suffered from depression, anxiety, and sexual difficulties. Other investigators have reported that the "psychological well-being of those patients who have had less radical surgery is so far superior to those who have had mastectomy as to defy comparison. The difference in the quality of life and in the degree of fear following the two operations is enormous."[1]

A recent retrospective study undertaken at Long Island Jewish Hospital revealed a number of important differences between twenty-one lumpectomy patients and forty-six mastectomy patients. Patients were matched for time since surgery, stage of their disease, and age:

Both lumpectomy patients and mastectomy patients reported feeling less attractive and less feminine in the first six months after their surgery than before. However, the mastectomy patients experienced a greater decrease in both...at 14 months, the lumpectomy patients had returned, virtually completely, to their presurgical feelings of attractiveness and feminity, whereas the mastectomy patients showed continued feelings of loss. As a result, at 14 months mastectomy patients felt significantly less attractive and less feminine than lumpectomy patients. There were no differences in the retrospective rating by lumpectomy and mastectomy patients of the importance of their breast presurgically to their self-image.[2]

Moreover, the study went on to find that mastectomy patients changed their clothing styles and were in general more concerned about their appearance. They more often wore clothing to bed and were significantly less likely to undress in front of their husbands. They were also less comfortable about their surgery and less able to talk to their husbands about their feelings. On the other hand, lumpectomy patients felt freer to discuss their feelings and also felt that they had received more support from friends after surgery, in contrast to the mastectomy patients, who were unable to talk openly about their surgical experiences. Their greater inhibition, self-consciousness, and concern over their appearance may have resulted in their receiving less support.

Both groups were found to be similar in their sexual habits before surgery. Even breast stimulation during lovemaking was the same. "After surgery, the importance of breast stimulation did not change for the lumpectomy patient, but decreased markedly for the mastectomy patient. Lumpectomy patients were more comfortable talking about their sexual feelings after surgery with friends and doctors than were mastectomy patients."

The two groups also differed sharply in their perception of their husbands' sexuality after their surgery. "Lumpectomy patients rated their husbands' sexual behavior as enhanced after surgery, compared to mastectomy patients who felt that their husbands' sexual behavior showed a decline."

Basically, the lumpectomy group was less pessimistic about the future and functioned at a higher level after fourteen months. Interestingly, when lumpectomy patients were asked to rank six possible reasons for choosing lumpectomy in order of importance, the highest-ranked reasons were that the mastectomy was unnecessary surgery or too disabling, and the least important reasons were concern over attractiveness, sexual desirability, or femininity.

From this study, then, it is clear that mastectomy persistently remains emotionally troubling for some patients long after their surgery. It also follows that most women who choose to retain their breasts have a better long-term emotional outlook.

I am convinced, furthermore, that fear of losing a breast subconsciously keeps women from checking their breasts for lumps, although the need to do this is well known. More distressing are the women who delay reporting a lump when they find one from the sheer dread of losing their breast. They lose precious time that could actually mean the difference between survival and death.

There are two other serious clinical disadvantages of mastectomy that must be considered. First, a cancer that recurs in the chest wall of a patient who has already had a mastectomy is very difficult if not impossible to treat effectively. Often there just isn't sufficient tissue available for a nice, clean surgical excision. Also, once surgery has been done and the blood supply to the area altered, the site may not heal well. On the other hand, a cancer that recurs in the breast after lumpectomy and radiation can be easily treated by removing the breast, and the woman will be cured in most instances. Therefore, I think women who have undergone a mastectomy have the worst time with recurrences.

The second disadvantage is that mastectomy is major surgery that may sometimes require blood transfusions. Transfusions either before, during, or after an operation impair the body's immune capabilities. It has been known for some time that patients who receive transplants accept them better if they are given a blood transfusion prior to their surgery. Their immune system will not fight the tissue that is newly transplanted into the bodies, that is, a kidney or heart donated from another individual. Lessening the body's capabilities to fight foreign cells, though it may be helpful in special circumstances such as transplant surgery, compromises the patient's ability to fight cancer cells that are present in the body or have escaped during the surgical process. A mastectomy patient should, therefore, request that no blood be given unless it is really a matter of life and death. The patient electing lumpectomy and primary radiation does not have this concern, because the surgery is so limited.

What, then, can you do to avoid ever having a mastectomy? Let's begin with your risk.

Who Is at Risk?

One woman out of eleven in this country will get breast cancer at one time or another, and almost half of them will be between the ages of forty-five and sixty-five. I feel that because of the high incidence of breast cancer, all women over thirty-five should consider themselves at risk. Without any treatment, 93 to 97 percent of women diagnosed as having breast cancer will die within ten years of discovery of the disease. With early detection and treatment, as we shall see, this statistic can be nearly reversed. Prognosis is best in women aged forty-five to fifty-four, worse in women under thirty-five, and worst in women over seventy-five, perhaps because they often suffer from other diseases as well.

Any of the following factors would give you a statistically higher risk:

1. A previous breast cancer or other previous cancers, such as ovarian or uterine.
2. Cancer in several members of your family (stomach, colon, ovarian, or uterine). A mother or sister who had breast cancer, especially if it occurred in both breasts *before menopause,* greatly increases the risk factor.
3. Multiple chest fluoroscopies or radiation treatments for postpartum mastitis when you were in your teens or early twenties.
4. Early menstruation (at age 11 or before) and late menopause.
5. Childlessness, or having your first child after age 30. Previous miscarriages or abortions don't seem to add to your protection. Having your first child before age 20, on the other hand, seems to decrease risk.
6. Multiple large cysts in your breasts.
7. Overweight, especially from a high-fat diet.
8. History of previous breast surgery for benign disease.

The more risk factors you have, the greater the chance of breast cancer, but no individual prediction can be made—statistics cannot be applied directly to the individual person.

However, knowing what your risk is will help you make decisions in the crucial process of prevention and early detection.

Detection of Breast Cancer

Early detection is the single most important thing you or anyone else can do to ensure that you will survive breast cancer. If we assume that a tumor once started out as a single cancer cell, which doubled and redoubled and redoubled as the cells reproduced themselves, it would take somewhere between two and eight years for most breast cancers to reach the size you can feel with your fingertips—1 cubic centimeter.* This takes about thirty doublings, and each doubling may take from forty to a hundred days. This small tumor already contains 1 billion cells. Its logarithmic growth pattern will quickly take it to 2 cubic centimeters and then to 4 cubic centimeters in only one or two more doubling periods. This is why early detection and immediate management of the cancer in its earliest possible stages is so crucially important. The risk of spread to distant sites increases with greater numbers of cancer cells present.

Breast Self-Examination

There are methods of detecting malignant tumors even before they are large enough to be felt, and we will discuss them later in this chapter. But the fact remains that more than 90 percent of breast tumors were found first by the women themselves. You, more than your doctor or anyone else, have the best chance of finding a suspicious lump earliest if you examine your breasts regularly.

Women over forty should return to the doctor's office every six months for a breast and pelvic examination. If they are in

*Not all breast cancers grow to a size that can be felt with the fingers. The incidence of undiscovered breast cancers in women over 70 years of age who die of other causes is nineteen times greater than the incidence of palpable breast cancer, suggesting that some breast cancers may regress without ever being detected.

a high-risk group, the frequency of breast examinations may be increased to three or four times a year. I have some patients whose breasts are so lumpy that they find it nearly impossible to do self-examination. I sympathize with them and tell them that examination of their breasts is difficult for me as well. These women have severe fibrocystic disease and are intimidated by the thought of being responsible for their own examinations, so I simply tell them to return every three months. This way at least one of us can check her at appropriate time intervals.

On the other hand, these women are just the ones who have the most to gain by examining their breasts every month. By being familiar with the anatomy as well as the texture of their breasts during their monthly exams, these women may be much better able to detect change early than a physician.

Some women find it easier to examine their breasts in the bath or shower, where soapy lather decreases the friction between their fingers and their breasts. I advise them that lying down flattens the breast against the chest and allows the best access to all the tissue. I have taken the hint, however, and tried using baby oil sometimes when I do office breast examinations. Patients often prefer this technique because it is more comfortable. The oil seems to help me do a more detailed examination, and I can feel subtle features of the breast more readily. At the end of the examination, it is easily wiped off with tissues.

As thorough as I like to think my exam is, a patient practicing self-examination can do an even better job than any physician. Studies at the University of Vermont have shown that the average size of tumors found by patients by chance is 2.2 cubic centimeters, whereas the average size discovered on a routine physical examination is 2.0 cubic centimeters and that found by women who practice regular self-examination is 1.8 cubic centimeters. As I have said, it is possible to feel a tumor that is even smaller than these averages—when it is only about 1 cubic centimeter, giving you an 85-percent chance for ten-year survival. And yet, although most women know about breast self-examination, only 18 percent practice it regularly. Perhaps now that you know that if you find a lump early you will *not* have to lose your breast, you can confidently make breast self-examination a monthly routine. I described the steps of BSE at length in *No More Menstrual Cramps,* but to be sure you've got them, here they are:

1. Wait until after your period. Premenstrually, many of the normal lumps in your breast may swell and become hard. If you have had a hysterectomy or are postmenopausal and no longer have periods, do the examination on the first of each month.

2. Looking in the mirror and noting the shape of your breasts, raise your hands over your head and press them together, then lower them to your hips and press down. Look for:

   • nipples that seem to be pulled out of position or newly inverted
   • scaling of the nipples or thickening of the skin
   • unusual dimpling of the skin

3. Lie on your bed and rest your left arm over your head. (If you have very full breasts, place a folded towel under your left shoulder. This arches your chest and helps to flatten the breast.) With your right hand, beginning at the edge of the nipple, make small circular motions with the fleshy part of your fingertips (not the very tips), moving from the nipple to the edge of the breast. As if your breast were a clock face, feel out along the entire breast at 12 o'clock, 1 o'clock, 2 o'clock, and so on until you have systematically felt the entire breast. Feel all the way to where the armpit begins and then in the armpit itself. You may or may not have noticeable lymph nodes there. Normal nodes move freely, feel soft, and are not painful to the touch.

The normal breast is composed of fatty areas and glands that produce milk. As you age, the glandular elements are slowly replaced by fat. The gland tissue tends to be more lumpy, whereas fat is softer and smooth. Most of the glandular tissue is found in the lateral upper portion of the breast near the underarm area; and it is there that most breast cancers (60%) arise. Look for:

1. A lump that is harder than the normal breast tissue. Cancers feel hard because firm scar tissue is formed by the body in a defensive reaction to the cancer.
2. A lump that is not mobile. Cancers often are attached to the overlying skin or underlying muscle.
3. Firm lymph nodes in the armpit area that do not move freely.

Repeat the process on your right side (shifting the towel, if you use one, to under the other shoulder).

At the end of the procedure, squeeze your nipples gently to see if there is any blood or discharge. Look for watery, pink, clear yellow, or bloody discharge. This is especially significant if it occurs in only one breast.

If they are present, these discharges call for an immediate visit to your doctor, who can easily check while you are in his or her office for the presence of blood cells in the discharge. Even if there is blood, the cause is most likely to be a benign papilloma (overgrowth of the lining cells in the ducts). Sometimes, however, papillary carcinomas can be present. As with all other breast findings, the likelihood of cancer is increased with increasing age. No matter what your age is, a watery, clear yellow, or pink or bloody discharge of the breast should be thoroughly investigated.

Other nipple discharges, for the most part, are not associated with breast cancer, but they should be brought to the attention of your physician so that he can determine if treatment is necessary. A milky discharge from both breasts, apparent only after slight squeezing of the nipples, is associated with pregnancy and delivery and may persist for months or even years in some women. This is almost always a benign condition. Milky discharge from both breasts also may be due to medications, such as phenothiazine tranquilizers (Compazine, Stelazine, Thorazine), tricyclic antidepressants, oral contraceptives, and hypertension medications like rauwolfia compounds and methyldopa. It may also be part of some endocrine disorders, especially those associated with the absence of menses (amenorrhea-galactorrhea syndrome). Multicolor or yellow-green discharges that tend to be sticky are also most often caused by benign disease, usually an inflammation within the duct system of the breast.

Paget's disease is a somewhat unusual form of cancer, because it produces early symptoms and these *first* involve the nipple. Patients complain of burning, itching, and discharge from the nipple and note that the nipple appears irritated, red, and wet. It seems like chronic eczema, for the nipple area weeps with a clear or slightly colored discharge and may have a scab or crust, especially if bacteria begin to infect the area. Many women believe that they have dermatitis, a skin problem, that simply will not clear up. Often they do not notice that the nipple is slowly being destroyed. If the surrounding skin and other parts of your body are affected, you probably do have dermatitis and not cancer. Paget's disease usually affects one breast, while dermatitis tends to affect both breasts at once; but you must consult your physician to have a proper evaluation. Paget's disease is special because it gives many early signals and can be cured. Many women, however, wait and apply salves for months, unaware that a cancer is growing. Sadly, this tumor, for all its warning signs, is usually brought to the attention of a surgeon only after long delays.

It is vital, if you find any of the signs mentioned at any step in your self-examination, or any change in the way your breasts looked or felt since the last time, that you see your doctor *at once*. Although most conditions turn out to be benign, you can't afford to take a chance!

Benign Findings

Cysts are the most common benign breast problem, occurring in perhaps 30 percent of women. If there is a lump that always seems to swell and become tender before your menses and then to become smaller and less tender afterward, you probably have found a cyst. Fluctuations in size are rare in other benign or malignant tumors of the breast. Cystic breast disease, also known as fibrocystic disease or chronic cystic mastitis, is the source of much concern in the thirty-to-forty age group, for it is often confused with malignancy. Cysts are most usually found in women of this age, though they may occur at any time in a woman's reproductive life. However, after a woman is a year or two into menopause, breast cysts rarely occur.

A cyst feels like a movable marble within the tissue of the breast. If there are multiple small cysts, the entire area may not be as freely movable as when there are only single cysts. Cysts may be tender or painful, depending on their number, size, location, and rate of enlargement. They may be firm to hard, because they contain fluid that is tightly compressed within the fibrous capsule, somewhat like a balloon filled to capacity with water. Before your menses, because of the increased fluid, these cysts fill and become bigger and therefore harder. Not only will the lump appear hard and even painful, but it may suddenly appear where last week you could detect nothing. If you can survive the week (mentally) until after your flow has stopped, you will find that the cyst either has disappeared or has gotten much smaller and softer. The cyst is still there, of course, but, like a deflated balloon, it no longer has structure or volume.

Although cancer hardly ever develops within a cyst itself, women who have cystic disease are slightly more likely to develop a cancerous tumor, although there is some controversy regarding this point. Women whose breasts produce very large cysts are at greater risk. It is also more difficult to detect a tumor when there are many cysts present, so women who have them should see a doctor three to four times a year.

Fibroadenomas are less common in women over thirty-five than in younger women. There are often several in a breast, and they are firm, smooth, rubbery, and not painful. They don't adhere to the surrounding tissue and will move from side to side as you push them. These tumors, like cysts, are firm because they are composed of a fibrous capsule that compresses the soft tissue inside. They are often removed in women over thirty-five, using local anesthesia, because they can be confused with malignant growths.

Postmenopausal Benign Findings

In the postmenopausal breast, fibrous and cystic lumps tend to subside; a new lump that is found is more likely to be a cancer. Some women have the mistaken impression that after they are menopausal, they no longer need yearly examinations. Nothing could be further from the truth. The incidence of cancer increases with age, so the older you are, the more diligent you should be about your physical examinations.

Benign tumors do occur in postmenopausal women. Many of them simulate cancers in the way they feel and in other breast changes that they cause. If you are postmenopausal and you find a lump, you will be a much more likely candidate for biopsy than a younger woman would be, simply because the risks of watching and waiting are too great. But there are women who have all the stigmata of breast cancer—nipple discharge; nipple retraction; a stony, hard mass that may adhere to the skin—yet have a benign disease (for example, mammary-duct ectasia). Only a biopsy can determine which is which, and survival depends on early detection in older women as much as in younger women.

In the postmenopausal breast, there also are soft tumors that are benign. These are fatty tumors called lipomas. Lipomas also occur in other parts of the body; in the breast, they are soft and completely nonsymptomatic. Let your doctor decide after examination and mammography (if indicated) whether biopsy is called for.

How to Proceed if You Find a Lump

Let us begin in your doctor's office, where, of course, you will have taken yourself at the first opportunity after discovering the lump. The easiest way for the doctor to diagnose a lump that is suspected of being a cyst is through aspiration, in which the doctor simply injects a tiny bit of local anesthetic and inserts a needle into the mass. Nothing pleases me more than to see and feel the lump painlessly disappear from a woman's breast as I withdraw·fluid into the syringe. In two minutes, it is gone along with my patient's fears.

If fluid is not obtained, we know we are dealing with a solid mass and more information is needed. I next turn to mammography or sonography—or both—depending on the patient and her age.

Mammography

Mammography is a technique for X-raying breasts. This technology produces a sharp, detailed picture that not only aids diagnosis but can reveal small tumors with impressive accuracy as long as two years before they can be felt. This makes mammography a most valuable tool. In combination with physical examination of the breast, mammography is the only cancer-screening technique with documented proof of increasing survival in asymptomatic women over the age of fifty. It is also an extremely valuable tool for evaluating women of any age who have signs and symptoms that could be related to breast cancer. There is evidence that screening with mammography can detect very small localized breast cancers in women thirty-five to forty-nine years old, which in turn suggests the possibility of better survival rates in this age group as well.

The American Cancer Society's National Task Force on Breast Cancer Control believes that mammography in addition to clinical examination and breast self-examination offers the best promise of significantly increasing the cure rate of breast cancer. ·

From all the publicity X rays have received as a carcinogen, you might wonder at the wisdom of using them to detect cancer. You may recall that in 1976, a flurry of reports about the dangers of mammography appeared in the media. In my opinion, the radiation scare that stopped many women from having mammographies was never really put into clear perspective. I have the distinct feeling that women read the headlines stating that radiation causes an increase in breast cancer and immediately assumed that women who had had mammographies were dying like flies.

It is important to realize that the background data that brought the headlines to light were retrospective studies of women who were exposed to unusual dosages of radiation, *none* of which were associated with any mammography procedure.

For example, data from the Hiroshima atom bomb explosion indicated that there was an increase in breast cancer among exposed women. Even under such extraordinary circumstances, older women were much less affected than younger women. Other studies from Massachusetts, where women were repeatedly given multiple fluoroscopies during tuberculosis treatment,* showed an increased risk of breast cancer. However, in further defining those data, even with this heavy X-ray exposure, there was *no* increased risk for women who were thirty years or older at the time of their treatment, in contrast to women fifteen to nineteen years of age, who had a 3.8-fold increased risk.

The third category of exposure was among women who underwent X-ray therapy to their breasts for breast inflammation after childbirth. Here, too, age played a significant factor.

I sincerely hope we will never again drop an atomic bomb, radiate young women's breasts after childbirth, or expose them to unnecessary fluoroscopy month after month. These sources of large, chronic radiation dosages have essentially disappeared.

While there is no way of determining the precise risk of inducing breast cancer by mammography, it is possible to estimate that risk. The most commonly accepted estimate is that if one million women were to receive a 1-rad dose of radiation to their breasts—which is more radiation than is used by many modern mammography machines—six or seven additional cases of breast cancer would occur per year after a minimum latent period of five to ten years. Since any woman already has a 9 percent chance of getting breast cancer (one

---

*Fluoroscopy is a special X-ray technique that uses high doses of X ray.

woman out of eleven), a single mammogram raises the risk by 0.07 percent to a 9.07 percent chance. If a woman has one mammogram a year for fifteen years, the risk factor will increase to 10 percent.

New mammography techniques involve tiny amounts of radiation. However, the more important factor may be that recommendations for mammography begin for patients past the age of thirty-five. By age fifty or over, there seems to be no concern among knowledgeable people that mammography is harmful. Therefore, the risk-benefit ratio is firmly weighted on the benefit side.

With the introduction of new, high-quality mammography examination, the radiation exposure has been cut to approximately 0.04 rad or less for two views of each breast. (This would be the typical exposure at the mid-breast level.)*

Most radiologists feel that women should have a baseline mammography at age fifty, and many feel that one is also justifiable between thirty-five and forty-nine. Although there may be disagreement as to just when the baseline mammography should be done, all agree that there is need for it. Having a normal picture of your breast anatomy can be extremely helpful in interpreting subtle changes that might occur in the future. There is also some evidence that the radiologic appearance of breast patterns can indicate whether you are in a higher or lower risk category, although this subject is still being debated.

In addition, although the purpose of baseline studies is to give a picture of normal breasts, these studies invariably detect a small but significant number of early cancers. In the Breast Cancer Detection Demonstration Project (BCDDP), mammography alone was responsible for positive findings in 41.6 percent of the cancers detected between 1970 and 1980 (1,481 of 3,557 cancers). It was also responsible for the biopsy recommendation in 35.4 percent.

---

*Another X-ray technique called xerography yields a clear, blue and white positive image, but since it uses nearly ten times the radiation dose of mammography—0.37 rad in new equipment—I don't recommend it for routine use. In special cases where calcifications are suspected on mammography, xerography may be used for better definition.

Finding an early cancer that is small and has not yet spread has a direct relationship to survival. Not only does early diagnosis give greater hope for cure but it also allows for less extensive surgical procedures and/or radiation.

There has been considerable improvement in mammography techniques over the past few years. Images are sharper and show more breast detail, thereby increasing the chances of finding small tumors. However, it is important to stress that your mammography should be performed and interpreted by physicians who are experienced and well trained and who have modern equipment that uses the lowest possible radiation dosage.

As impressive as the record is, mammography is not a hundred percent accurate; some 10 to 15 percent of breast cancers do not show up. I have had the experience of having negative mammograms on my last six patients who were subsequently proven to have breast cancer. Therefore, if you already have a mass that is clinically palpable, it should not matter much what your mammography reads. The physician must be guided by clinical judgment and order a biopsy if he or she is at all suspicious. However, mammography is important to the woman with a suspicious mass for the information it provides about the mass *and for ruling out additional tumors in the same or opposite breast.*

Because mammograms are especially difficult to read on younger women who have dense glandular, fibrocystic type of breast tissue, they may be of little value for those women. The accuracy of mammography increases as the woman ages, because her breast tissue gradually becomes replaced with less dense fatty tissue. This allows for better definition of the more dense tumor from its surrounding area.

Mammography is suggested:

1. At any age, if your doctor's findings indicate a significant suspicion of cancer when a mass is present or there has been a noticeable change in your breast whether or not a mass is palpable. For example: recent onset of nipple retraction, thickening or skin changes in a portion of the breast; nipple discharge that is clear or bloody; a firm

lymph node in the armpit. (Mammography should not be performed in women under the age of 35 when there are no specific, strong clinical indications. The incidence of cancer in this age group is very low. There are, however, occasional circumstances in which mammography in women under the age of 35 is justified.)

2. For women from age 35 to 39, when there is a personal history of breast cancer or high risk because of strong family history.

3. For women age 40 to 49, if there is a personal history of breast cancer in first-degree relatives, that is, mother or sister, or if a baseline is desired. How often to have such examinations should be determined by analyzing the relative risk factors present.

4. For women age fifty and over, annual or biannual preventive screening is statistically justifiable. For the occasional woman with low risk factors and with breast mammograms showing fatty replacement of the breast tissue (the normal sequence in the older woman), longer intervals might be justified. For the women at high risk, more frequent examinations might be considered (this group would also include those women with large breasts and confusing physical findings).

When you go for a mammography, make sure that the radiation dose is 1 rad or less for two views of your breast. Not all hospitals and private physicians' offices have new equipment. You should ask the radiologist about the dosage of the machine. If no one is available to tell you the dosages, don't hesitate to make further inquiries or to look elsewhere. In some localities, however, you may not have much of a choice.

Also make sure that the radiologist won't throw your films away. All of this talk about baseline examinations is nice, but five years after your examination, you may find that the radiologist has thrown out your films because so many have accumulated that finally he or she is unable to store them all. This should not happen. I suggest that you insist that your X-ray doctor put a large sign on your chart saying, "These X rays are not to be disposed of." If the radiologist cannot guarantee the safety of your films, then you should request that you be allowed to keep them. Assure the doctor that you will bring them back with you for your next examination as a basis for comparison. This is somewhat unorthodox, but it makes a lot of sense to me, especially after I learned that my own films had been discarded!

Ultrasound or Sonography

In this nonradiation technique of breast examination, high-frequency sound waves are projected into the breast, and the pattern of echoes they produce is converted by a computer into an image that shows the different densities of the interior of the breast. It is a painless, even pleasant procedure in which you lie prone on a table that has an opening at the chest area to allow your breasts to fall into a bath of warm water through which the ultrasound is projected. The room is usually semi-dark and quiet. If the technician is not too talkative, you may be able to catch a quick catnap. Or you might prefer to watch the television screen that projects the image of your breast tissue.

Breast ultrasound with the water-bath technique is not completely perfected yet, but it provides valuable information because it readily shows up cysts and differentiates them with fair accuracy from solid, more ominous lesions. Furthermore, because ultrasound has no known contraindications or potential danger to the patient, the examination can be repeated as often as necessary for optimum follow-up. And last but not least, it may give better information about breasts that are dense and fibrocystic than does mammography. This makes it an ideal method for young women who should not be exposed unnecessarily to radiation.

Experienced physicians using the water bath or hand-held sonography technique can sometimes even distinguish between solid malignant and solid benign tumors. This is especially good news for the young woman with a fibroadenoma in her breast. It appears as a smooth-walled mass with uniform echoes, while a cancer appears to have jagged walls and nonhomogeneous echoes. If a typical fibroadenoma image is obtained, the patient may be able to postpone her biopsy and to return for another look in six months, especially if she is under thirty years of age. Without sonography, such women are often subjected to repeat biopsies, perhaps needlessly. There is a strong need today for more physicians with enough expertise in ultrasound breast diagnosis to give an educated opinion about the status of such a solid tumor.

Ultrasound will never replace mammography. Also, it is less useful in the older patient. At present, there are too few machines and too few physicians trained to interpret their results available in the United States. In addition, ultrasound is not well accepted yet by all physicians.

Thermography

Thermography is a simple procedure that a doctor can perform in the office or the woman can even use at home. Liquid crystals of cholesterol are held in a plastic support, which is applied to the woman's breast. The device may be either rigid or flexible enough to be wrapped around the patient's chest. The crystals pick up the body heat and change color according to the variations in temperature of the breast. The color changes are reproducible and allow for quantitative as well as qualitative measurement. Cooler areas on the breast show up in one color, warmer spots in another.

Most cancers have a higher metabolic rate than the surrounding tissue, which causes an increase in temperature at the site. There is also an increase in blood vessels around tumors. The resulting heat at the surface of the breast is picked up by the crystals, and a picture is then recorded on special heat-sensitive film and kept for future comparison.

The most important evidence of a possible increased breast cancer risk seen on the thermogram is lack of symmetry in the temperature patterns between breasts. If the vascular patterns and the temperature differentials of one breast are the same as those of the opposite breast, it is considered normal. The abnormal thermal patterns to look for are diffuse heat and focal heat, or a "hot spot." The method allows comparison

of one breast to the other and also allows comparison of the
state of the breast at one point in time with a subsequent one.

Combined with a thorough physical examination, this new
method may alert the physician that the patient needs further
workup, such as a mammography. Thermography is still not
well accepted, because many problems in technique and
interpretation must be worked out. However, because it is
easy to do and involves no risk to the patient, we may see it
being used more often as time goes on.

Thermography misses a substantial number of cancers which
are clearly defined by mammography. It also has about a 20
percent incidence of false positives and does not locate a
tumor accurately enough for specific biopsy. Therefore, the
technique must be used in conjunction with others, never
instead of physical examination or mammography.

Dianphanography

This is another method of cancer screening that is currently
undergoing trial. It involves the use of light and special film
to examine the breasts. The white light shines through the
breast and gives an image. Some units are computerized and
the computer generates an image for analysis.

One of the problems with thermography and light methods
of breast diagnosis is that women who are examined by these
methods feel that they have been screened for breast cancer.
When these women are told that their results are negative,
they believe that cancer has been ruled out and are given a
false sense of security. But the methods are not meant to be
used in this way. Rather, they must be used along with
physical examination and mammography, which are proven
methods.

Nuclear Magnetic Resonance

Nuclear magnetic resonance, or NMR, is a new diagnostic
medical tool. NMR emits no radiation and is completely
noninvasive. It is based on harmless magnetic and radio
waves. Although the technique is still in its infancy, there is

hope that in the near future NMR may be able to identify tiny cancers in the breast. It also may be useful in following early chemical changes in the tumor as it responds to chemotherapy.

No matter what is found on mammography, ultrasound, or thermography, I follow my clinical instincts. If I am not sure that the lump is benign, and if I feel that it is not safe just to observe the mass for another few weeks to see if it will disappear during another part of the patient's menstrual cycle, I would order a biopsy.

The Biopsy

A biopsy is the removal and examination of tissue from the body for diagnostic purposes. I feel that most breast biopsies should be done with only a local injection of anesthesia, unless the patient is very apprehensive and does not feel that she could tolerate being awake. I explain to my patients that the biopsy is not very different from the breast aspiration procedure. Whether it is done in the office, the emergency room, or an out-patient or regular hospital operating room, the same local dental-type anesthesia is used. The surgeon makes a small incision and excises the tumor. Of course, if the tumor is deep in the breast or is very large, then admission to a hospital and general anesthesia may be required. If the tumor is large, sometimes only a piece of it may be excised. Tissue from the tumor can also be sampled with a needle, but if the finding is benign, there is always the question of whether the needle missed the tumor or sampled a portion that did not contain the cancer cells. The excised tissue is then sent to a pathologist for analysis.

Remember that most biopsied breast lumps are benign. A biopsy done in this fashion is much less threatening than one performed when you enter the hospital as an in-patient. Furthermore, it prevents you from being hassled by a surgeon who wants you to sign a consent form that allows him to go ahead and immediately remove your breast if the lump is malignant.

I recommend that my patients consent only to a diagnostic

biopsy and deny written permission for the combined biopsy/mastectomy that is so popular with so many surgeons. During that combined procedure, the surgeon sends the biopsy specimen to the pathologist, who quick-freezes it, takes a slice, and reads it—all while the patient is asleep on the operating table. If the pathologist finds cancer, the surgeon completes the mastectomy. If not, no further surgery is performed.

I have always felt that this combined procedure, while it is very convenient for the surgeon, leaves room for irreversible error, especially in cases where the pathologist is not greatly experienced or where the pathology is particularly confusing. It also needlessly subjects patients—most of whom will prove *not* to have cancer—to anxiety and fear. Along with an increasing number of medical professionals, I have been protesting this procedure for a decade, yet a great many one-step biopsy/mastectomies are still performed in this country today. The reasons to resist this pressure from the surgical community are vital:

1. The majority of biopsied lumps are benign, and consenting to a one-step biopsy/mastectomy needlessly subjects you to the apprehension of possible mutilation. I am convinced that once women are freed of the terror of mutilation, they would welcome a simple biopsy if only to rid their minds of the fear and anxiety of not knowing. We should resist also because we are all aware of cases where surgeons have believed and have convinced the woman that her lump is benign. He finds out differently in the operating room and performs a mastectomy. These women must endure the shock of waking up to discover they not only have cancer but have also lost a breast. To make matters even worse, because a malignant diagnosis was not anticipated, the patient was never given a full preoperative workup to rule out metastases, or spread of the cancer to other parts of the body. Should unexpected metastases exist, the patient has been unnecessarily mutilated when there was no hope of cure by mastectomy.

2. If the lump is malignant, you need time to absorb the fact,

get more information, talk over your future treatment and possible alternatives, and generally prepare to fight the disease. In this way, you remain in control of your body and your treatment.

Surgery does not have to be performed on an emergency basis. It has been clearly demonstrated that there is no danger in waiting one or two weeks after the biopsy to embark on further surgery, radiation, or whatever therapy is decided upon by you and your doctor.

3. If the lump is malignant, the medical staff needs time to give you an orderly, complete "workup," or series of tests, that assess the extent of your disease. It is simply wrong to subject all biopsy patients, the majority of whom will have benign findings, to the cost, mental anguish, and radiation exposure of liver and bone scans and further X-ray testing. On the other hand, if a malignancy is found, these tests are essential to determine if the cancer has spread.

4. In my judgment, this fact is crucial: removing your breast does not improve your chances for survival over primary radiation therapy. Ninety-five percent of malignant lesions up to 2½ inches in diameter can be treated by a lumpectomy, sampling of axillary lymph nodes, and radiation as an appropriate alternative to mastectomy. But if the cancer has already metastasized, removing the breast won't cure you; neither will lumpectomy and radiation, for they are both only local therapies.

In most cases, lumpectomy and biopsy are synonymous. Both remove the tumor. In some cases, where the woman knows that she wants a lumpectomy and cancer is most likely present, general anesthesia could be used and additional permission granted for sampling the underarm nodes. These nodes are examined to determine whether the patient will need chemotherapy, so checking them after a frozen section of her biopsy/lumpectomy reveals a malignancy may save a later surgical procedure.

Breast surgery is neither complicated nor difficult for the surgeon, since he is working on a surface area with tissue that is soft and completely separated from any vital organs. It is quite a different matter from opening up the chest and cutting ribs to look inside at the heart or lungs. It is also a lot easier than opening a belly to get at a diseased gall bladder or appendix. Most breast surgery, especially biopsy, is not a big deal for the woman physically. Afterward, a Band-Aid and aspirin are usually sufficient. But apprehension about the results makes it mentally traumatic.

The Pathologist's Report

The pathologist analyzes the tumor in the laboratory, and if it's benign, which is most likely, you're home free. If it is malignant, the pathologist may be able to confirm whether the tumor appears to be aggressive or if it has invaded the lymphatics or the blood vessels. Tumor type has much to do with prognosis, for some tumors are more malignant than others. For example, there are noninvasive breast cancers which tend not to metastasize and therefore have an excellent prognosis. They account for about 5 percent of breast cancer, of which about half are a type called lobular carcinomas in situ (see page 104).

The pathologist's observations are often more important than the original size of the tumor or its local spread and may help to explain why some women with small tumors do poorly, while other women with large tumors outlive them by many years. Blood-vessel invasion should alert us to the fact that early spread of the tumor may occur.

At the time of your biopsy, your doctor must also request that if the tumor is malignant it be checked for estrogen and progesterone receptor sites. If your tumor has these, you may be a candidate for hormonal therapy later on. Although you may not need such therapy right away, the biopsy is the first and possibly only chance you will have to get the information. Your surgeon and the laboratory must cooperate to see that this test is done. (See the section on Hormonal Therapy later in this chatper.)

Ruling Out Metastasis

If the lump is malignant, the most important task before anything more is decided is to determine that you do not have metastatic disease. If metastasis already exists, there is no reason for further breast surgery. No surgeon should attempt a *local cure* (radical, modified radical, or simple mastectomy) if there is already metastatic spread of the cancer. In such a case, surgery should be minimal and done only for biopsy or palliative purposes. If the cancer has not spread, the way is clear for you to proceed with radiation treatment or mastectomy, whichever you have decided upon.

All that is normally done before a biopsy (two-step procedure) are standard blood tests, urinalysis, and a chest X ray. So if your biopsy proves malignant, before any further surgery, you should have *normal* results in all the following tests and they should be entered in your medical record:

1. blood test for liver and bone function: CBC (complete blood count), alkaline phosphotase, SGOT, SGPT, bilirubin (liver function tests), calcium and phosphorus, all of which are included in the comprehensive SMA 24 blood test. This helps to rule out metastases to the liver or bones.
2. urinalysis
3. chest X ray, to rule out metastases to the lungs
4. bone scan, to rule out metastases to the bones
5. gynecological examination, to rule out spread to the ovaries
6. liver scan, to rule out metastases to the liver
7. mammography (if not already done), to rule out other unknown cancers in both breasts

Many surgeons feel that a liver scan is unnecessary if the bone and blood tests are normal, since breast tumors usually spread to the bone first and then to the liver. I almost always order one, however, because I've caught one or two cases in which metastases did occur in the liver first and another case in which the discovery of abnormal but noncancerous findings at this stage served as a baseline for comparison in later years and prevented the patient from undergoing unnecessary treatment then.

Cancers with Favorable Prognosis

If the results of these tests are normal, you are ready to proceed with further treatment. But before we continue, you should know that there are several cancers and stages of cancer that have an extremely *favorable* prognosis. Here they are:

1. Lobular carcinoma in situ (also called lobular neoplasia). Invasion into adjoining breast tissue occurs in only about 30% of cases over a 30-year period.
2. Intraductal carcinoma. The survival rate is one hundred percent if one can be certain that no invasion is present.
3. Paget's disease of the nipple. If found early and if no palpable mass and no invasive cancer is found, the prognosis is excellent. However, because the cancer is usually confused with an eczemalike problem, diagnosis is usually late, resulting in a poor prognosis with nearly 50% of cases having positive nodes.
4. Mucinous (colloid) carcinoma, in women over 60. A soft, jellylike tumor with mucinlike material occurring within the normal adjacent breast tissue. A slow-growing tumor.
5. Medullary carcinoma with lymphoid stroma. About twice the survival rate of ordinary breast carcinoma.
6. Adenocystic carcinoma. A rarity.
7. Tubular adenocarcinoma.

The following are favorable prognostic factors in ordinary breast cancer (infiltrating duct carcinoma):

- Small tumor: 0.5–1.0 cm in diameter.

- No lymp nodes involved.

- No blood vessel invasion.

- Mostly intraductal cancer, i.e., the tumor cells are confined to the physical areas within the milk ducts rather than haphazardly invading through all the different structures of the breast tissue.

• The individual cells within the tumor are only mildly abnormal in appearance.

• Stromal lymphocytes. When they are present in the tumor, these white blood cells give clues that the body is attempting to defend itself against the spread of the tumor.

• Favorable microscopic picture, in that the tumor tissue closely resembles the tissue that it represents. Normal structures, even if not perfectly formed, are recognizable. In tumors that carry the poorest prognosis, all resemblances to normal microscopic anatomy are lost.

The Lumpectomy-plus-Radiation Treatment

Retrospective studies in this country as well as reports of European randomized trials show that definitive radiation therapy and radical and modified radical mastectomy give comparable results in the local control of breast cancer.

The use of radiation therapy as the primary or curative treatment for breast cancer evolved from the pioneering studies of François Baclesse at the Foundation Curie in Paris. With well over five hundred patients treated with primary radiation therapy, survival rates were found to be no different from those of radical mastectomy patients at Memorial Hospital in New York.

As for local recurrence, all the details of the Halsted radical, from the removal of the internal mammary lymph nodes (the nodes alongside the sternum) to the removal of every noted lymph vessel, and leaving only the thinnest of skin flaps, have done very little to alter the rate of tumor recurrence in the chest wall. Surgical control of the disease for early cancers ranges from 92 to 97 percent, and for somewhat more advanced disease, between 73 and 81 percent. In contrast, control for patients with early cancer receiving radiation therapy is 95 percent, and for more advanced is 86 percent. (A small percentage of mastectomy patients are at high risk for local recurrence of tumor. Local radiation to the chest wall and draining lymphatics following mastectomy have reduced the overall local recurrence rate in these women to 5% or less.)

Researchers discovered early that radiation alone without lumpectomy is inadequate. Included in the old Foundation Curie study was a group of women with large tumors (greater than 3 cu. cm). Their tumors were not excised, and 50 percent of them eventually had a recurrence and had to undergo a mastectomy. Obviously, such data prove that lumpectomy is needed prior to initiating radiation therapy.

Likewise, lumpectomy without radiation does not yield satisfactory rates of cure. A recent report on an *unselected* group of women who underwent local surgical removal of the cancer alone showed a 31 percent local recurrence rate over a very short period of time. In a *very select* group of patients with early breast cancer, partial mastectomy without radiation has proven to be effective therapy. Crile has shown that when it is appropriately applied, this treatment achieves a low local recurrence rate as well as acceptable long-term survival. However, because of the variations that he used in selecting patients, it would not seem prudent to recommend partial mastectomy alone as therapy in unselected patients. Therefore, adequate local therapy (i.e., surgical removal of the tumor plus radiation) is essential.

A study at the Princess Margaret Hospital in Toronto ranged over a period of twenty-two years and included over eight hundred patients who were treated by both lumpectomy and radiation. This group of women had a survival rate comparable to another group of women treated with radical mastectomy, but 85 percent of the Princess Margaret women were able to retain their breasts. As you can see, the results of this study are most impressive, even though the treatment did not include the techniques of "boosting" or giving extra radiation to the site of the tumor that are in common use now.

Since then, several other studies have been conducted using both lumpectomy and boosted radiation. Dr. Bernard Pierquin has treated a large number of women in France. He has followed 408 women for at least five years and 268 women for up to seven years. He has found no difference in survival between his subjects and comparable patients treated with radical mastectomy. He used interstitial implants of iridium-192 in the area of the excision to boost the external radiation. With tumors smaller than 5 centimeters (2½ in.) in diameter, the local recurrence rate was less than 8 percent, and even with tumors greater than 5 centimeters in diameter, he had a very acceptable local recurrence rate compared to the surgical rate of 15 percent.

The largest primary radiation therapy study was conducted by Dr. Spitilier from Marseilles, France. His study followed 2,200 women for five years, 700 women for ten years, and 130 women for fifteen years. Again, the overall survival rates were comparable to any of the reported results from radical mastectomy. Although he did not use interstitial implants, he did boost the area of tumor excision with either cesium radiation or electron beam. After ten years, 88 percent of the women retained their breasts. Women who had local recurrence of their cancer then had a mastectomy. Of these, approximately half did well and are cured.

American studies, although smaller, have shown even greater success. The Harvard Joint Center for Radiation Therapy in Boston treated more than 260 women and used an interstitial implant to boost radiation—a technique that delivers a much higher local dose than that used in the Marseilles study. Excluding 27 women who didn't have a lumpectomy, the recurrence rate was only 5 percent, which means that 95 percent of the women were able to retain their breasts. The M.D. Anderson Hospital in Houston, Texas, treated 122 women with Stage II breast cancer and had the same local recurrence rate (4.9%), which was better than the recurrence rate (8.4%) among the hospital's radical mastectomy patients during the same period. Disease-free survival rates at five and ten years were also similar.

The surgical community continues to advocate mastectomy as the treatment of choice, claiming that statistics on the effectiveness of radiation are not yet in. I think they are. Certainly the trend is well established, and I think it is not only favorable but in fact better in some cases than that shown by surgical data.

Surgical Procedure for Lumpectomy

Here the value of having time after the biopsy to think through the treatments that lie ahead becomes apparent, for the surgical procedure must take into account the therapies that may follow. These may include chemotherapy or hormonal therapy in addition to radiation, and all require some advance preparation, as we shall see in the following sections.

The surgeon must be aware that the purpose is to remove only the lump, leaving the breast as much as possible as it was before. Teamwork among the surgeon, radiotherapist, and personal physician are of the utmost importance for the best results.

If possible, an incision should be made that follows the border of the nipple. This can be done if the tumor is located near the center of the breast. Such an incision heals with the scar concealed in the pigmented border of the nipple and gives an excellent cosmetic result. The gross tumor should be removed with only a minimum of surrounding normal tissue. This is because a wider excision, with removal of excessive amounts of surrounding breast tissue, compromises the cosmetic results. Many surgeons still feel uncomfortable unless they remove a large amount of breast tissue surrounding the cancer. But radiation will eradicate the microscopic tumors or cells that may persist in the area.

Because of the high incidence of metastasis in women who have positive axillary nodes—and because such women do significantly better when placed on chemotherapy—it is essential to sample the axillary nodes if the tumor turns out to be malignant in order to determine whether or not she should have chemotherapy. The nodes are not removed to cure the patient, but to assess her prognosis and need for chemotherapy. It follows then that *the two major factors determining whether a woman will survive are the size of her tumor and whether her lymph nodes are positive or negative*.

The only way to assess these nodes is to remove them

surgically and examine them under a microscope. With the patient under general anesthesia, the surgeon makes a low incision near the axilla, separate from the breast incision. Surgeons have advocated several ways of obtaining the nodes, ranging from removal of all nodes to removing only the lower ones.

The Harvard radiation therapy group in Boston feels that the *lower* axillary removal (or dissection) is sufficient for accurate assessment. In this surgery, the nodes below and underneath the pectoralis muscle are removed. *No attempt* to remove the lymphoid tissue surrounding the axillary vein is made. This lesser procedure avoids the risk of arm and breast swelling that occurs when the patient has extensive axillary surgery. It also avoids swelling that may happen when complete axillary dissection (axillary vein tissue removed) is combined with radiation therapy. From reports given at the International Breast Conference in Cambridge, Massachusetts, in 1982, it was clear that either procedure could accurately assess the status of these lymph nodes, although the more complete axillary dissection would be somewhat more accurate in predicting the total number of nodes involved in tumor. Chances for survival are better with three or less nodes involved than when four or more nodes are involved.

The seriousness of positive nodes is reflected in the fact that only 25 percent of all patients with positive nodes at the time of surgery are free of disease at ten years, whereas 75 percent of patients with no evidence of spread to the lymph nodes are free of disease at ten years. Women with positive nodes are advised to undergo chemotherapy, for studies have shown that this increases their survival rate.

Radiation Implants

A radioactive implant is placed in the area where the tumor was excised under general anesthesia, often at the time of the patient's lower axillary sampling. It gives an extra radiation boost to this area where microscopic cancer cells might persist. In this procedure, hollow polyethylene tubes are placed into the breast with a needle and then filled with radioactive seeds of iridium-192. These are left in the breast for two days. At the end of this time, the tiny tubes with their contained seeds are easily removed from the breast, without anesthesia, in the patient's room. The patient is discharged from the hospital that same day.

In other patients, the implants are placed after completion of the external radiation therapy. The implants deliver a dose of 2200 to 2500 rads directly to the site of the tumor. In other centers, no implant is used, but an extra boost of external radiation is given to the area from where the tumor was removed.

Radiation Therapy

External radiation treatments are begun as soon as possible after the lumpectomy if your axillary nodes are negative. If they are positive, thus indicating the need for chemotherapy also, the schedule of radiation treatments will be carefully worked out in conjunction with the chemotherapy. Radiation consists of five 10- to 15-minute treatments per week for five weeks. A 4- to 6-million-volt linear accelerator delivers a dose of 180 to 200 rads at each treatment for a total of 4,600 to 5,000 rads. Treatment times can be arranged around the patient's work schedule. Many women get their treatments before work, others at the end of the day or during a lunch break. Most patients tolerate their therapy very well, though they often complain of fatigue. Other side effects of radiation include some increase in skin pigment which may resemble a sunburn and some dry skin which tends to flake. In moist body folds, some skin irritation may also occur. Skin problems resolve spontaneously within two to three weeks of completion of the treatment. The radiation treats the breast, of course, but it also treats the chest wall, covering of the lung, lymph nodes in the axillae, those that are located alongside the sternum (the internal mammary nodes), and the nodes above the collarbone, too. Some 4 percent of women develop rib fractures. Others may have a temporary dry cough. But both cosmetically and functionally, from 75 to 98 percent of women treated have good to excellent results.

Primary breast radiation is an art. Radiation therapists must have special training to get the best results. Without it, they can still radiate breast tissue, but the fine points, such as cosmetic results, or even survival itself, may be compromised. The breast tissue must receive a sufficient radiation dosage to prevent recurrence of the tumor and decrease the chance that the tumor will spread. It must also remain cosmetically acceptable.

Many surgeons still believe that radiation therapy leaves a scarred, shriveled breast. That simply is not true. If radiation is done properly and slowly in small doses, the breast is well preserved. Good technique will cause minimal cosmetic deformity. Although the irradiated breast often cannot produce milk, it should retain its normal sensation and appearance.

I've come to believe that the radiotherapist must be especially interested in treating breast cases, for the treatment is exacting and time consuming. It takes special effort. Unfortunately, such trained and caring radiation therapists are hard to find. Some time ago, I had a patient who had a small tumor in her breast and was ready for lumpectomy and radiation. I called a local teaching hospital where I knew the proper equipment was available. I asked the radiotherapist if he could provide the therapy.

"Sure we can," he replied.

"How many cases like this have you done in the past year?" I asked.

He said, "One or two."

I hesitated. "She's a dear friend of mine," I said. "Please give me your honest evaluation. Should you do her therapy?"

"Well, perhaps you should send her elsewhere."

Another problem in breast radiation therapy is that the correct radiation therapy machinery is not always available. Or there may be a properly trained radiotherapist and the right equipment, but no patients to use them. In New York City, for example, mastectomy is the norm, and lumpectomy is hardly ever done. A radiation therapist who is an acquaintance of mine was well trained in breast technique but became frustrated about wasting her skills for lack of patients. She left New York City and moved to another state.

It must be apparent by now that in order to make lumpectomy and radiation therapy generally available, cooperation is needed from the surgical community. This is perhaps the biggest stumbling block in this country to the more widespread use of this therapy. Surgeons are convinced that their way is best. They have been trained to do surgery and find it difficult to consider another means of treatment. Furthermore, surgeons are convinced that only surgery can save lives. Fortunately, the statistics no longer back them up.

Is Radiation for You?

With your biopsy and tests to rule out metastases in order, the following criteria will help you determine whether you'll get the best possible results—both cosmetic and curative—from radiation therapy. Radiation is likely to be successful if:

1. The tumor is no bigger than 4–5 cm in diameter. If the tumor is larger than that, you may run an increased risk of tumor recurrence if you are treated primarily by radiation therapy.
2. The tumor is small in comparison to breast size. In a woman with small breasts and a large tumor or multiple tumors, excision may distort the breast so much that mastectomy may be preferable. If the patient wishes, radiation might still be done, but the cosmetic result will be compromised.
3. The tumor is not located directly under the nipple. This, too, poses the purely mechanical problem of preserving the shape of the breast.
4. The breasts are not large and pendulous. With radiation, such breasts become firmer and somewhat retracted. This can pose a cosmetic problem but is not an absolute contraindication. In fact, radiation therapy usually produces a somewhat more uplifted and firmer breast. Some women prefer this and have kidded their radiotherapists that they like their new shape so much they want the normal breast irradiated, too.

Pointers for Finding Good Radiation Therapy

Women who meet the criteria as candidates for radiation therapy may still face the problem of finding a good treatment center and staff. As you now realize, the techniques of radiation therapy are extremely important. Here are the things you should look for:

1. Are the surgeons at the hospital experienced in excisional biopsies or lumpectomies? If these procedures are not properly done, tumors can be left behind or the breast may be so distorted that its appearance is destroyed. Find a surgeon with experience in lumpectomies and discuss the type of incision he or she plans to make. You should be satisfied that the doctor will remove only a small area of surrounding tissue with the tumor. If a doctor says that he or she will remove more than you think is necessary, consult first with the radiotherapist, then with another surgeon.

   Finding an experienced surgeon may sound elementary, but the facts are that 80% of patients with breast cancer are operated on in hospitals of 250 or fewer beds by surgeons who do only one to three mastectomies per year. I can't help believing that such little experience reduces the surgeon's ability to perform the procedure optimally. I was recently shocked to find out that one of my new patients had had her breast removed by a rectal-colon surgeon, and I was frankly disturbed that he had not declined to do her surgery. When my patients ask me to help select a surgeon, one of my criteria is that he perform a fair number of the selected procedures yearly—the more the better. In large metropolitan areas, there are surgeons who specialize in breast surgery, and these may be the ones to seek. On the other hand, these surgeons may only consider doing a mastectomy, so be sure yours would be willing to do a lumpectomy before you make your appointment.

2. Is there a 4- or 6-million-volt linear accelerator available

for therapy? The keen focus obtained with the high-energy beams of these machines assures that the area they strike is sharply delineated, with no beams scattering beyond the boundaries of the desired field. Such overlapping, common in less advanced machines, results in excessive dosage and scarring of the skin and other tissue. A cobalt-60 machine may be used, but its more scattered beams may cause scarring. Higher energy machines such as those providing greater than 8 million volts probably don't deposit a sufficient dose of radiation in the skin and are not recommended. However, this problem can be overcome with extra care in treatment planning.

3. Is there a treatment-planning facility in the hospital? In such a planning area, a radiation physicist, radiotherapists, and a computer expert rehearse the treatment to determine the exact area of your body to be irradiated and the precise dose you will need. Accurately positioning the fields of radiation to maximize the dosage to the tumor area and minimize the exposure of normal tissue depends on the size and shape of your breast. At the best-equipped facilities, the treatment team places you in front of an X-ray machine that has been designed to resemble the linear accelerator. If your breast tends to fall too far to the side, a halter made of netting may be fitted on you to hold it in place. A test X ray shows whether the positioning is correct. At the Sidney Farber Cancer Institute in Boston, a styrofoam outline is made of your head and shoulders, with an area for your arm to rest upon. This simple measure assures that your position will be the same for every treatment and that you will be comfortable. In short, you're treated completely individually and with painstaking precision.

4. Does the radiation therapy team include both a physicist and a technologist? Without proper physics, a homogeneous distribution of the beam cannot be expected. For example, the radiation dose at the broad base of the breast should be greater in order to penetrate the flesh than at the tapered nipple area. This is easily accomplished by putting a piece of copper or other heavy metal in the shape of a

wedge in front of the beam as it exits from the accelerator. Understanding these factors is part of the training of specialized therapists and is vitally important to guarantee the accuracy of the daily treatment setup.

Where to Find Radiation Treatment in the United States

The following list of radiation therapists and radiation centers was not meant to include *every* therapist or center, but to provide you with a starting point. If none of these listed are near enough to be practical, contact the nearest ones anyway—they may be able to give you the name of a center nearer your home.

In alphabetical order by state

E. Rogoff, M.D.
S.W. Radiation Oncology
Tucson, AZ 85712

L. Botnick, M.D.
Valley Radiotherapy Assoc.
St. Joseph Medical Center
Burbank, CA 91505

P. Mowry, M.D.
Fresno Community Hospital
Fresno, CA

R. Grobstein, M.D.
Scripps Clinic
La Salla, CA 92037

R. Thompson, M.D.
Cedars Sinai Hospital
Los Angeles, CA

Robert Shapiro, M.D.
Dept. of Radiation Therapy
Hoag Memorial Hospital
Newport Beach, CA

R. Deffebach, M.D.
Sequoia Hospital
Redwood City, CA 94062

G. Hanks, M.D.
Radiation Oncology Center
Sacramento, CA 95819

K. Fu, M.D.
University of California, S.F.
San Francisco, CA 94143

D. Guffinet, M.D.
Stanford University
Stanford, CA

R. Goebel, M.D.
Whilter Oncology Medical Clinic
Whilter, CA 90602

A. Salner, M.D.
Hartford Hospital
Hartford, CT 06115

J. Fischer, M.D.
Dept. of Therapeutic Radiology
Yale University School of
  Medicine
New Haven, CT 06510

A. Dritschilo, M.D.
Georgetown Medical Center
Washington, D.C. 20007

S. Carabell, M.D.
G. Washington University
  Medical Center
Washington, D.C. 20037

D. Dosoretz, M.D.
Radiation Therapy Association
Ft. Meyers, FL 33901

R. Million, M.D.
J. Hillis Miller Health Center
Gainsville, FL 32610

J. Schwade, M.D.
Cancer Treatment Ctr.
Baptist Hospital
Miami, FL

A. Fiveash, M.D.
Medical College of Georgia
Augusta, GA 30907

F. Hendrickson, M.D.
Rush-Presby. St. Lukes Med.
  Center
Chicago, IL 60612

J. Harris, M.D.
Joint Center Radiation Therapy
Boston, MA 02115

E. Weber, M.D.
Salem Hospital
Salem, MA 01970

W. Park, M.D.
Baystate Medical Center
Springfield, MA 01107

S. Kadish, M.D.
St. Vincent Hospital
Worcester, MA 01610

P. Lambert, M.D.
Eastern Maine Medical Center
Bangor, ME 04401

A. Blumberg, M.D.
Greater Baltimore Medical Center
Baltimore, MD 21204

S. Order, M.D.
John Hopkins Hospital
Baltimore, MD 21205

E. Flatstein, M.D.
National Cancer Institute
Bethesda, MD 20205

S. Levitt, M.D.
University of MN Hospital
Minneapolis, MN 55455

L. Gunderson, M.D.
Mayo Clinic
Rochester, MN 55901

J. Bedwinck, M.D.
Barnes Hospital
St. Louis, MO

L. Davis, M.D.
Montifior Hospital
Bronx, NY

N. Ghossein, M.D.
Albert Einstein Hospital
Bronx, NY 10461

J. Bosworth, M.D.
North Shore University Hospital
Manhasset, NY

P. Rubin, M.D.
University of Rochester
Rochester, NY 14642

J. Fazekas, M.D.
Booth Memorial Hospital
Queens, NY

W. Bloomer, M.D.
Mt. Sinai Hospital
NYC

M. Nobler, M.D.
Dept of Radiation Therapy
Beth Israel Medical Center
NYC

S. Hellman, M.D.
Memorial Sloan Kettering
Hospital
NYC

J. Bruckman, M.D.
Bishop Clarkson Memorial
Hospital
Omaha, NE 68154

D. Weiss, M.D.
Elliot Hospital
Manchester, NH 03103

L. Proznitz, M.D.
Duke University Medical Center
Durham, NC 27710

D. Gorshein, M.D.
Cooper Medical Center
Camden, NJ 08103

G. Jelden, M.D.
Cleveland Clinic Foundation
Cleveland, OH 44106

R. Dobelbower, M.D.
Medical College of Ohio
Toledo, OH 43699

W. Moss, M.D.
Oregon Health Sciences
University
Portland, OR 97201

R. Goodman, M.D.
Hospital of the University of
Penn.
Philadelphia, PA 19104

M. Mohivddin
Thomas Jefferson
Philadelphia, PA

L. Brady
Hanneman Medical College
Philadelphia, PA 19102

J. Concannon, M.D.
Allegheny General Hospital
Pittsburgh, PA 15212

B. Webber, M.D.
Radiation Oncology Association
790 N. Main St.
Providence, RI 02904

J. Gefter, M.D.
Erlanger Medical Center
Chattanooga, TN 37403

A. Malcolm, M.D.
Vanderbilt University
Nashville, TN 37215

John Bedwinick, M.D.
E. Tennessee Baptist Hospital
Knoxville, TN 37901

J. Hussey, M.D.
Radiation Medical Association of
Dallas
Dallas, TX 75235

J. Belli, M.D.
University of Texas Med. Branch
Galveston, TX 77550

E. Montague, M.D.
M.D. Anderson Hospital
Houston, TX 77030

G. West, M.D.
Radiation Therapy
USAS Medical Center
San Antonio, TX 78240

J. Stewart, M.D.
University of Utah Medical Center
Salt Lake City, Utah 84132

G. Tonneson, M.D.
The Fairfax Hospital
Falls Church, VA 22046

T. Griffin, M.D.
University of Washington Hospital
Seattle, WA 98195

R. Steeves
Div. of Radiation Oncology
University of Wisconsin
Madison, WI 53706

J. Cox, M.D.
Medical College
Milwaukee, WI 53226

****

R. Bush, M.D.
Princess Margaret Hospital
Toronto, Canada

R. Calle
Institute Curie
Paris, France

All these institutions are academically oriented and are affiliated with major medical schools. If you don't live near one of them, call any one on this list for advice on locating qualified radiotherapists with modern equipment and good radiation physics in your area. (It may also be a way to locate a surgeon who has had experience doing lumpectomies.)

Chemotherapy

The most promising development in the treatment of breast cancer has been the use of chemotherapy in addition to surgery or radiation. There are three basic ways to combat cancer: remove it, destroy it, or stop the cancer cells from dividing. Cancer can be removed by surgery or destroyed by radiation. Surgery and radiation are similar in that they treat the breast and surrounding area only. They do not affect areas where metastases may have been carried away from the primary tumor by the blood or lymph. Chemotherapy, however, can reach these cells.

Patients with positive axillary nodes who have no distant metastases have shown longer survival when chemotherapy is given. Almost all patients who have distant metastases are helped by chemotherapy as well. Studies have proven the advantage of using chemotherapy as soon as possible after surgery to reduce the number of viable tumor cells that may remain.

In the past, women with negative nodes did not receive chemotherapy. However, the natural history of breast-tumor recurrence can cover a long period of time, with relapses occurring as many as twenty years after the initial tumor is diagnosed. Even if the axillary nodes are negative, there is still an overall probability of tumor recurrence in 25 percent of women over a ten-year period. Because of positive results reported from several different clinical trials, some investigators are now considering the use of chemotherapy for these women. However, this approach is still experimental, since there is a potential for long-term toxicity and all the facts are not fully established.

The drugs are given by mouth or injected into the muscles or veins, from which they spread throughout the body, attacking the main tumor as well as any metastases. Some drugs may cure certain cancers. Others keep the cancer under control. They often prolong the length and improve the quality of life.

Most of the drugs work by preventing cell division and are therefore most active in rapidly dividing cells. Since cancer cells usually divide more often than normal cells, they tend to be more susceptible to chemotherapy.

There are many potent drugs available today. Each acts differently and can be used alone or in combination with other drugs. When they are used in combination, they can be given at the same time or one after the other. Since the drugs work in different ways, each may produce different side effects, which may also vary according to the individual. These can be severe, but the important thing to remember is that most of the side effects are temporary and disappear after treatment stops.

I have a large number of patients on chemotherapy who breeze through, continue working and shopping, and have few if any side effects. I remember one patient in particular. When she was first diagnosed as having breast cancer, she stated that she would rather die than have surgery. But then she decided to have the operation anyway. Three years later, she developed a lung metastasis. Again she balked at therapy.

I finally convinced her, and she began therapy. We spoke at a follow-up visit. She was amazed. She had been convinced that chemotherapy would cause her unbearable agonies, sweats, fevers, pain, and such. But she admitted that she had been mistaken, for in two months, she hadn't missed a bridge game or a day at charity work. She had lost some of the hair on her head, but she was less chagrined than I expected because her local beauty parlor provided her with several wigs in different styles and she was "enjoying the change" from one to another.

Another patient whose chemotherapy failed twice was put on a third regimen. The drug is very toxic. She has now had therapy with it for a number of months. Her energy level is good, though she "feels tired after running around all day." Hopefully the drug will take care of her persistent cancer cells. It has obviously not much affected her busy life.

Although it is impossible to generalize about chemotherapy for any individual, many breast cancer patients have had dramatic results over the past few years with two multidrug regimens: CMF therapy, using the three drugs cyclophosphamide, methotrexate, and 5-fluorouracil; and CMF-VP, which adds vincristine and prednisone.

Both these multiagent chemotherapy programs have shown a benefit in both pre- and postmenopausal women when taken in near full doses (greater than 85% of the prescribed dose). Although there are no longterm studies on patients using them in conjunction with primary radiation, recent studies report that chemotherapy can be taken in full doses with primary radiation therapy, either simultaneously or sequentially. In fact, chemotherapy should be started within two weeks of the axillary lymph node biopsy, and even as soon as two days following this procedure. Depending on the kinds of drugs being used, the physician can carefully intertwine the radiation with the chemotherapy or do chemotherapy first and begin radiation when it is completed or nearly completed. Many physicians are unaware that it is possible to attack the cancer cells on a local level with radiation while simultaneously mopping up distant cancer cells with chemotherapy. Harvard's Beth Israel Hospital is currently using this aggressive and sensible regimen. If you need specific information, your physician might call for their protocol.

Hormonal Therapy

Some years ago, Beatson discovered that some breast cancers are dependent on estrogen for their continued growth. Further experience demonstrated that about a third of all patients with advanced breast cancer would respond to some type of hormonal manipulation. The next problem was identifying such patients.

Then researchers discovered that some breast-cancer cells contained certain protein receptors specific for estrogen and later discovered receptors for progesterone. The more receptors the tumor has, the more dependent on hormones it is likely to be and the more easily it responds to hormonal therapy. Also, if progesterone receptors are present, the prognosis is even better.

To find out whether a tumor has such receptors, estrogen- and progesterone-receptor assays are routinely done on patients who have a malignant breast mass. Remember, arrangements must be made before your biopsy for the estrogen-progesterone receptor test. The knowledge gained from the test may not influence your immediate therapy, especially if your nodes are negative and no tumor spread has occurred. On the other hand, if your nodes are positive, or should your tumor spread years later to another part of your body, this information will be invaluable. If your breast tumor contains hormone receptors, new tumors that develop elsewhere in the body will probably also have them. If further therapy is necessary, then hormonal manipulation alone or with chemotherapy will give you the best prognosis. The test will thus ensure that you receive the most effective treatment. Furthermore, if you have positive hormone receptors, your overall prognosis is better than if you do not.

Until recently, the treatment for hormone-dependent tumors was to deprive the body of hormones by surgically removing the ovaries, adrenals, or pituitary. (The pituitary does not produce estrogen or progesterone itself but controls the function of the ovary and adrenals. Its removal suppresses these hormonal sources.) Parodoxically, if a tumor develops in a postmenopausal woman who has long been deprived of estrogen, giving her large does of estrogen sometimes slows its growth. Other women have been treated with male hormone to shrink their tumors.

Today the most exciting news in hormonal therapy for metastasized breast cancer is a drug called Nolvadex (tamoxifen citrate), an antiestrogen medication that vies with estrogen for the receptor sites. Once the drug uses up these sites, estrogen can no longer attach to the cell. The cell then loses the ability to grow and reproduce itself. When this happens, the cancer cells die and the tumor shrinks.

For several years, Nolvadex has been considered the preferred means of producing hormonal change for postmenopausal patients with advanced breast cancer. It saves women major surgery to remove their ovaries. Because Nolvadex is an antiestrogen and not a hormone or cytotoxic (cell-killing) agent such as those used in chemotherapy, it doesn't produce the adverse reactions commonly associated with those drugs. Most patients have few or no side effects, whereas some experience slight hot flushes, nausea, or vomiting. Unpredictable increases in blood calcium levels may occur in patients with bony metastases—a rare side effect, but severe if it occurs. On the positive side, few patients are unable to tolerate the drug, which is given in pill form twice a day. All in all, it is a benign drug with no contraindications that improves survival rates in postmenopausal women with metastatic, hormonally dependent breast cancer. Megace (megestrol acetate) is another hormonal therapy used in the treatment of metastatic breast cancer. Megace is a long-acting oral progesterone derivative. It is used in patients where Nolvadex has stopped working or as primary therapy in cases where oophorectomy has failed. Side effects of the drug tend to be minor. Another drug, aminogluthethimide, suppresses adrenal production of sex steroid. With its use, major surgery for removal of the adrenal glands is no longer necessary in patients with far advanced metastastic disease. These new drugs not only give women new avenues of therapy, but they avoid the need for further surgery and thus improve the quality of life. They may also be combined with chemotherapy.

Interferon and Thymosin

Aside from chemotherapy drugs which act directly against the cancer cell, other new anticancer agents are currently under development. These are called biologic response modifiers, and they work by modifying the body's response to the cancer—that is, they improve the body's own immune system.

Normally manufactured by the body's cells, *interferon* originally was known for its ability to stop the growth of viruses by preventing their replication. Now it has been found to directly affect the body's natural "T killer cells," which destroy cancer cells, thus inhibiting tumor growth. Although there are three types of interferon known, until recently, the interferon in clinical use was less than 1 percent pure. Now, by using recombinant DNA techniques and cloning genes in bacteria, 100-percent pure interferon can be produced.

Thymosin is a little understood substance secreted by the thymus gland, located at the base of the neck. It is thought to play a role in the maintenance of the immune system. The loss of thymic function with aging may be one of the reasons why people develop cancers as they age. It also may lead to the development of autoimmune diseases such as arthritis. With the loss of thymic hormones, the ability of the body to destroy cancer cells or fight viruses is impaired. In patients who have a normal immune system, however, thymosin is not helpful and therefore should be avoided.

These substances are given by injection and are often used on an out-patient basis. Interferon may cause fever and malaise, while thymosin has few side effects other than local redness at the site of injection. Both interferon and thymosin increase the body's ability to fight viral infection. This is especially important in the cancer patient who often has had chemotherapy and poor nutrition.

To date, most of the studies have been done in patients with advanced cancer and with impure interferon or thymosin. They have shown responses similar to those with chemotherapy.

However, new studies using the newly available pure biological products are in progress, and more will be learned as research continues.

Photoradiation Therapy (PRT)

For breast cancer patients whose cancer has spread to the skin or chest wall after mastectomy and has resisted all other therapies, PRT is a spectacular new treatment now under development. A light-sensitive material called Photofrin (hematoporphyrin derivative) is injected intravenously and is absorbed selectively by many cancerous tissues. Normal tissue absorbs very little. When it is activated by visible light, usually red, the Photofrin undergoes a reaction that indirectly causes the activation of oxygen within the tumor. This activated oxygen exists for only one millionth of a second, but during that moment, it oxidizes and destroys parts of the cell, thereby killing it. Normal tissue may be damaged slightly if some Photofrin is present in it, but it usually heals readily.

Following extensive animal testing and approval from the Food and Drug Administration, the first clinical test began in 1976 at Roswell Park Memorial Institute, conducted by Thomas Dougherty, Ph.D., and Arnold Mittelman, M.D. For the patients at this beginning stage, conventional therapy such as surgery, chemotherapy, and radiation therapy had failed. Most had breast cancer that had spread to the skin or skin tumors such as basal cell carcinoma. Following injection of Photofrin, the researchers exposed the lesions on or under the skin to red light from filtered lamps or a special type of laser which emitted red light. Most tumors responded to the treatment, the response being stronger with more light or more drug. However, the researchers also found that if too much light was applied, normal skin also could be destroyed, since the level of Photofrin in the skin was sufficiently high to be activated by large amounts of light, including sunlight. In most cases, the amount of light could be controlled to partially or completely destroy the tumor without excessive damage to normal skin. For the twenty to thirty days it takes the drug to clear the skin, patients must stay out of bright sunlight.

Since 1976, many other institutions have used PRT to treat tumors of the skin and breast cancer that has spread to the skin. It is fair to say that in patients with a limited amount of disease (either confined to a relatively small area or fairly superficial), good palliation could be obtained even if other therapy had failed. Several patients have been free of disease in treated areas for up to four years. PRT has also been applied with considerable success to treat advanced cervical and vaginal cancer, especially in Australia and Japan. Studies to treat gynecological cancers in an earlier stage are now underway in the United States. Investigators are also considering PRT for treatment of tumors of the head and neck, eye, brain, colon, and rectum. In addition, Roswell Park is combining PRT with surgery for tumors that cannot be removed surgically completely or which have a high probability of recurring.

It is clear that PRT offers potential advantages over existing treatments for certain types of cancers. In the next few years, researchers will more closely define its uses.

In summary then: the total number of women who have undergone lumpectomy and radiation cannot begin to match the number of women who have had radical mastectomy. Any surgeon will be eager to tell you that. Because of the thousands of mastectomies that have been done, they feel that surgery should continue to go on ad infinitum. But the time to stand back and take a look at the forest instead of the trees is long past. The track record of decades shows no improvement. If their mightiest efforts have not proved more effective, why should there be so much resistance to change? Why plod along in the same destructive fashion? The surgeon's knife, in my opinion, is no match for the carefully targeted beams of radiation which affect individual cells and prevent their multiplication. Can the surgeon's knife search out these microscopic cells? No! It must destroy and remove all of the breast in order to get results equal to radiation and lumpectomy. The important thing to know is that the survival rates after lumpectomy and primary radiation of the breast at five, ten, fifteen, and even twenty years are as good if not better than those for treatment with surgery. The number of cases may not be as great, but the trend has definitely been established and is being reaffirmed with every year that passes.

I hope this chapter has given you enough evidence to see that today the optimum therapy for early breast cancer need not include losing your breast to surgery. A lumpectomy followed by radiation offers results that are similar to mastectomy. You finally have the opportunity to choose a treatment plan that preserves your breast and thereby spares you as much psychological and surgical trauma as possible.

I am looking forward to an era of breast cancer management in which preservation of both the body and the mind is the physician's aim. It already is in other cancer therapies. In early vocal cord cancer, for example, radiation rather than surgical removal of the larynx is now the treatment of choice. It stops the spread of cancer, it assures survival rates equal to those of surgery, and it preserves the voice in more than 90 percent of the patients. Who would choose to live without being able to speak when this alternative exists? And who would choose to live without a breast under the same circumstances?

For the woman who chooses to treat her breast cancer with less than a mastectomy, it is vital that her physician respect her choice and not desert her. Each woman has a right to choose her way of dealing with her malignancy. Whether the physician agrees with her or not, he has the responsibility to remain supportive of her decision and to guide her to the best possible therapy of the type she desires. The doctor must not make her feel guilty about her decision just because her choice is not his choice.

However, you should realize that life will not be simple for the woman with breast cancer who wants a lumpectomy unless she is lucky enough to live in an area where good radiation therapy is available and acceptable to her treating physician. Women who live in the average small town will often have to leave their community to get proper therapy. If you want to preserve your breasts, you must persevere and not become discouraged by surgeons who feel that mastectomy is the only adequate treatment for breast cancer.

In addition to finding a surgeon who will do a lumpectomy you also have to find a well-trained radiation therapist who has the proper radiation machinery to work with. Unfortunately, there are too few such centers in this country, and your local hospital is more than likely not one of them. If radiation therapy is not performed correctly, you risk cosmetic problems as well as recurrence of the disease and even death.

One of the real tragedies is that surgeons go to surgeons' meetings and radiotherapists go to meetings with other radiotherapists. It might be nice if one day surgeons combined their meetings with those of radiotherapists. They might then begin to understand what radiotherapy can do and become less prejudiced. Ignorance has all too often been the basis for decisions that involve the lives and future of someone else's body. It is finally time for surgeons to become more open-minded and aware of the latest radiation studies and statistics. The time is coming when surgeons and radiotherapists should see each other not as adversaries but as colleagues who are after the same goal—the best results for the patient with the least possible physical and mental trauma. When the patient's total welfare becomes the important criterion, then perhaps change will come. Until then, we must move forward and insist on our choice.

On a recent visit to Beth Israel Hospital in Boston, Massachusetts, I was encouraged to see women of all ages who had elected lumpectomy and radiation therapy. Their comments gladdened me.

"I didn't want to lose my breast."

"I decided it was better to have radiation than to live with a mutilation as a daily reminder that I had cancer."

"I wanted to have a good mental outlook. I think that's as important as any therapy they can offer me."

These women were almost smug about their choice. They were proud that they had voiced their opinions and had had the good luck either to have a physician who mentioned radiation or to have known themselves that radiation was available. Not that these women were not scared, for they were, but they felt they were coping with their cancer on their own terms and did not feel helpless and at the mercy of the disease and of their doctors.

Nor should you.

In November 1982, I was invited to give a keynote address to a group of 750 cancer nurses and physicians by the Michigan chapter of the American Cancer Society. I spoke about breast cancer and its treatment by lumpectomy and radiation. At the end of my hour talk, the head of the Michigan Cancer Society took the microphone and said, ''Dr. Budoff's views are not necessarily those of the Michigan Cancer Society.'' The audience was nonplussed and reapplauded as I approached the microphone again for questions.

Only seven months later, at the National Annual Breast Cancer Teaching Symposium, held by the American Cancer Society in Boston (June 1983), the president of the organization announced that lumpectomy and radiation therapy was a viable alternative choice for women with early breast cancer.

Having read this long chapter, you now know that there are choices for women. Some will only feel safe and comfortable with mastectomy and should request that type of surgery. Others who want to retain their breasts should have that option. Whatever the choice, I desperately want women at least to know there now exists a choice, for that alone will give comfort to many.

5

No More Unnecessary
Hysterectomies

When I wrote my first book in 1979, I was convinced that there were too many hysterectomies being done in this country. Too many women were undergoing surgery when less aggressive approaches would have sufficed. Too many women were dying unnecessarily or were suffering from surgical complications.

Women who read my book began to question their doctor's decision that they needed a hysterectomy (removal of the uterus, sometimes including removal of the ovaries), and many of them called me or came to my office seeking advice or a second opinion. Although a few of the hysterectomies proposed by gynecologists were justified, to my dismay, nearly all of them did *not* have to be done. The problem is much worse than I had ever suspected.

Many of these women had small fibroid uteri without other symptoms. Some had bleeding problems that needed progesterone, not major surgery. Most women came to my office having been told that they needed surgery without having had even an adequate workup. In some cases, this should include a pelvic sonogram to document the size of the uterus and, more important, the size of the ovaries. The sonographer can also, in another minute or two, explore the liver, spleen, and kidneys. This will show whether urine is backing up in the kidneys because of uterine pressure on the tubes to the bladder that empty them. The sonogram may also give the physician information about the ovaries that he or she was not able to determine on pelvic examination because of the enlarged uterus.

Other women came with pathology reports from a recent D and C in hand. They had been diagnosed as having one or another of the hyperplasias and were told that a hysterectomy would be the safest course to take. But many of them felt safer taking progesterone pills than undergoing surgery. I placed them on this medication and followed up four to six months later with an office intrauterine aspiration biopsy, to ensure that their medical therapy had reversed the hyperplasia and returned the uterine lining to normal.

I firmly believe that women are safer if it is possible to avoid hysterectomy surgery. But hysterectomy surgery is certainly popular in this country—800,000 are performed each year. At a cost of approximately $1,000 each, hysterectomies account for nearly $800 million in surgical fees alone. Hospitals collect many times that figure in yearly revenues for room rates, operating-room time, anesthesia, drugs, and the like. *According to statistics, more than half of American women will undergo this surgery by the time they are sixty-five years old.* Thirty percent (240,000 women) will have nonfatal complications ranging from fever and wound infections to bladder and bowel perforations. Another 15 percent (120,000) will require transfusions and run a significant risk of contracting hepatitis.[1]

It is easy to "sell" a hysterectomy to a woman who does not need one. The suggestion that it will solve your problems, provide lifelong birth control, guarantee that you won't ever get cancer of the uterus or cervix, and rid you of the bother of menstruation can be very appealing. Just the other day when I had my monthly period, I thought to myself how easy it would be not to have to put up with all this bother. Who needs it—I'm over forty and never plan to have any more children. I understand how it might be easy to go along with the suggestion of surgery.

On the other hand, major surgery is major surgery. I have no desire to have my belly opened. Somehow, after surgery, your insides may never be quite the same. While most women do not have life-threatening complications, substantial numbers do. Others suffer from late complications such as adhesions that cause pain, intestinal obstruction, or other problems. Unoperated-on abdomens are generally less annoying to their owners than abdomens after surgery.

There are also a number of other late complications that can occur after hysterectomy. Some cases of urinary incontinence due to appearance of an opening between the bladder and vagina occur within a week or two after surgery. While the situation is not life-threatening, subsequent surgery may be necessary to repair the problem. Otherwise the woman will be plagued by constant dripping of urine from her vagina.

There are some indications that do call for hysterectomy, as nearly all doctors would agree. These are:

1. Cancer of the uterus, ovaries, or vagina.
2. Obstetrical hemorrhage, making hysterectomy necessary to save the woman's life.
3. Uterine prolapse, the medical term for a uterus that has dropped sometimes to the point where the cervix is protruding outside the vagina. (This results from childbirth and is caused by loss of muscular support for the uterus due to stretching or tearing. The uterus itself in this case may be quite normal.)
4. Large fibroids, causing symptoms of pressure or bleeding *that cannot be medically controlled*.
5. Cancers or infections of nearby tissues which have spread to involve the uterus.

Beyond these criteria, there is much less agreement on exactly what conditions require hysterectomy. The Center for Disease Control (CDC) was quoted in *Medical World News* as stating that 15 percent of all hysterectomies were questionable. "Of the 3.5 million elective hysterectomies done on women of childbearing age in this country between 1970 and 1979 one of every seven had a questionable indication.... Researchers concluded that some 503,000 procedures in the surveyed period were done for such reasons as benign ovarian or tubal conditions, cervicitis, or gynecological problems treatable by less drastic means." The article went on to show that the problem was probably much greater than just 15 percent of cases. "There were another 1.3 million hysterectomies done for functional or anatomical diagnoses, and it is impossible to determine which are justified." This grouping includes uterine prolapse or malposition, menstrual problems, and pelvic congestion. The first two accounted for 70 percent of all vaginal hysterectomies over the nine years, and menstrual disorder was topped only by uterine fibroids as the most common indication for abdominal operations. Cancer, fibroids, endometriosis, and pelvic inflammatory disease were the indications for 38 percent of all hysterectomies; cancer accounted for only 2 percent.

Noninvasive cancer of the cervix, endometrial hyperplasia, and cervical changes resulting in abnormal Pap smears accounted for another 8.5 percent of the operations. The CDC started that these diagnoses "were considered separately because there are other acceptable treatments for all three." Dr. Irvin Cushner added to the dilemma by wondering "how many procedures may actually have been done for sterilization—a reason most insurers exclude from hysterectomy coverage and thus might be fudged."

The CDC found that by 1978, 20 percent of American women had had a hysterectomy by age forty-four. Other findings included the facts that the frequency of hysterectomy in the South was 11.5 per 1,000 women of reproductive age, more than double the Northeast's 4.5 per 1,000. Rates in the Midwest and Far West fell inbetween. Rates by age group were slightly higher among blacks than whites.

More than a quarter of all hysterectomy patients also had both ovaries removed. This rose to half when the oldest group (age 35–44) was studied.

In a survey of nine teaching hospitals, nearly half of 959 women who underwent hysterectomy through an abdominal approach developed at least one complication. One quarter of the 431 women who had their hysterectomies by a vaginal approach had complications. As Dr. Joel Greenspan of the CDC observed, "Hysterectomy cannot be considered benign surgery. We have to give more attention to its risks."

Second Opinion

If you are not positive that you need a hysterectomy, if you do not really want to undergo major surgery, if you are unsure of your doctor's decision that you need surgery, by all means, get another opinion. And remember, do not select your gynecologist's partner for that second opinion. Try to pick a physician associated with a teaching medical center or at least with a different hospital from your gynecologist's. Or try getting an opinion from a nonsurgeon, such as your family doctor. Patients who come to me, a family physician, know that I have no ax to grind—no financial interest in whether or not they ever have surgery—so my advice is based only on what I feel their needs are (and you know my surgical decisions for my patients are very conservative). If a woman really wants to keep her uterus, I will do my utmost to help her do just that unless, in my professional opinion, she truly has no other option than surgery.

Second opinions help. At Cornell Medical Center in New York City, a large teaching hospital with a top staff, second opinions did not confirm the original doctor's recommendation of hysterectomy in nearly one-third of cases. I would bet that if a second opinion from a well-qualified expert was obtained in small hospitals in areas of the country away from teaching centers, 50 percent or more of recommended hysterectomies would be avoided. In my practice, my patients receive greater than 70 percent negative second opinions. This may be partly because of the questioning nature of the patients who elect to see me, but I suspect that my findings are not all that uncommon.

I still hear stories every day from patients who say, "He wanted to clean me all out, so I wouldn't have to worry anymore." "Clean me out" is a most disturbing expression. Does the doctor consider the uterus and ovaries dirty? Is the patient really cleaner without them?

I recently spent an hour at a teaching conference at Harvard Medical School. Problem patients were being presented, for physicians' recommendations as to how they should best be treated. One patient was a seventy-three-year-old man with prostate cancer. The urologist was extremely concerned with his therapy as was the radiation therapist. The conversation went something like this:

> *Urologist:* I think that a surgical approach might work, but I am really afraid that it would make him impotent.
> *Radiotherapist:* Yes, but I'm not sure if the tumor can be well radiated because of its position. Radiation may not be a good choice for him.
> *Urologist:* I am concerned. I wouldn't want him to lose his potency. Surgery in that area may ruin his sex life.

I almost had to pinch myself to make sure I wasn't dreaming. Here we had a patient with a spreading cancer who was seventy-three years old. His surgeon was carrying on and on about his sexuality. I'm not against sex, but where are the surgeons who defend women's sexuality when they are presented for castration (removal of the ovaries) in the hundreds of thousands? I have never heard so much as a peep from my surgical colleagues on their behalf. The decision was finally made for the patient: radiation therapy would be the answer, and the urologist was off the hook. He did not have to be accountable for a fellow male's sexual demise.

I remember an occasion when I was still a medical student and naively suggested that a patient have a testicular biopsy. I was snubbed for at least a week after that, but I learned fast and never mentioned such an unacceptable idea again. Women, however, were not considered to have "precious jewels." Their cervices were—and still are—routinely biopsied every hour of the day, sometimes under the gaze of six to eight medical students. Their uteri and ovaries are removed during the morning surgical hours with a shrug of the shoulders and the saying, If there's doubt, take them out. No one ever seems to consider what the consequences might be for the woman and what it might do to her body image. I suppose if you are a man, it might seem that the loss of a uterus and ovaries is not important to the woman's sexuality. She can still have a sex life. And if her scar is well hidden, how could she even know the difference? What they fail to realize is that women have feelings about their sexual organs, too. They may not be visible, but I still think that they are precious to us.

Psychological studies prove that this is so. Women who have hysterectomies are five times as likely to have severe depression that requires psychiatric care as women who do not have any surgery, and they are twice as likely to need psychiatric care as women who have had other types of abdominal surgery. More than half of the women under forty who have hysterectomies will suffer severe postoperative depression.

To my mind, we hardly needed formal studies to tell us this. Society has conditioned us to invest a great deal of our feelings of self-worth in our sexuality, particularly as it relates to our childbearing ability. Even after menopause, the loss of the childbearing organ may make us feel incomplete, neutered, and unattractive. The woman who loses her uterus may feel castrated, and, in fact, if she loses her ovaries, too, she *has* been castrated. As I pointed out in my first book, the woman who has a clearcut, health-threatening reason for a hysterectomy, such as endometrial cancer, rarely suffers from postsurgical depression because she is not ambivalent, either before or after the surgery. Since her life was at stake, she has little reason to regret taking the step, whereas the woman who undergoes elective hysterectomy may feel guilt or rage at her loss if she was pushed into the decision without having been able to come to terms with it on an emotional level.

So if a hysterectomy has been suggested for you, satisfy yourself that it is absolutely necessary for your health by getting a detailed second opinion. In the following sections, I will describe how the diagnosis of endometrial cancer is arrived at and what the so-called precancerous states of the uterine lining are. But before continuing, here are a few pointers for thinking about the inevitable question, Shall we take out the ovaries, too?

A Word About the Ovaries

This question almost always arises when a hysterectomy is performed. If you are postmenopausal, the ovaries should be removed because they are no longer functional and the risk of ovarian cancer increases with age. If you are premenopausal, however, there are several things to consider.

First, as you know from Chapter 1, removing the ovaries will immediately bring on menopause. Although hormone-replacement therapy can substitue for the lost estrogen and progesterone, the ovaries play other roles in metabolism and in other body systems that are not yet fully understood and thus not replaceable. Removing both ovaries before menopause also increases the risk of heart attack, up to a sevenfold risk if the woman is thirty-five years old or younger. (Hormone-replacement therapy can decrease this risk.)

Second, the reason most often given for removing the ovaries is to avoid ovarian cancer, but it is important to note that the ovaries are at no greater risk of cancer than normal if they are left in after hysterectomy. *The most important thing a posthysterectomy patient must do if her ovaries are left intact is to have her ovaries checked by pelvic exam twice a year to make sure they are not enlarging.* Actually, all of my patients over forty are instructed to return every six months for a pelvic exam so that I can follow any changes that may occur in the uterus or ovaries. Paps, however, are done routinely only once a year. Possible future cancer, then, is not by itself sufficient reason to remove the ovaries but must be considered in the context of the woman's age and overall health picture. So if your doctor cites some "automatic" reason for removing them, be it a cutoff age (40? 45?) or that you "might as well" to avoid future problems, get specific answers and a second opinion.

"Precancerous" Conditions

I have often said in my lectures that uterine cancer does not just sneak up one day and bite you. The warning stages are there for a long time, and the endometrial tissue is easily sampled. In fact, between a normal uterine lining and a cancerous one, pathologists have identified and labeled six major progressive stages that the endometrium can undergo. If one of these is found and noted on your medical record after an endometrial biopsy or D and C, it may constitute the basis on which your surgeon recommends a hysterectomy. I described the stages in my first book because I wanted women to know exactly what each one means so that they could assess for themselves the need for a hysterectomy. I feel that as women approach and pass menopause, knowledge of these changes is particularly valuable to them. Not only does endometrial cancer strike most frequently in this age group, but also a postmenopausal woman who undergoes hormone-replacement therapy may want to understand these various diagnoses. Here, then, is a review:

1. *Normal endometrium.* As we saw in Chapter 1, the normal endometrium undergoes two major phases in the menstrual cycle: the follicular or *proliferative* phase and the luteal or *secretory* phase. The first phase is governed by estrogen, which causes the cells of the uterine lining to proliferate and the glands in it to grow. When ovulation occurs, progesterone joins the estrogen in its influence on the endometrium, causing the cells and glands to become better defined and secrete glycogen to nourish a possible fertilized egg. The loss of estrogen and progesterone eventually causes the built-up layers of the lining to break down and slough off in the menstrual flow.

2. *Hyperplasia.* If, for some reason, estrogen is present alone and no progesterone appears to oppose it, the endometrium continues its first phase of growth—the proliferative phase—unchecked. Cells and glands accumulate and are not sloughed off normally. Under the microscope, the cells look a little crowded. This can happen as a woman approaches menopause and, perhaps three to four times a year, does not produce an egg, thus failing to trigger the release of progesterone. Also, as we've seen, it can happen if a postmenopausal woman takes only estrogen-replacement therapy without progesterone.

Ninety-eight to 99 percent of women with this type of endometrial hyperplasia will never get uterine cancer. One to 2 percent get cancer eight to twelve years after having hyperplasia. That is a long time to detect, think about, and treat the condition. It is hardly a reason to rush into a hysterectomy. Simple hyerplasia can easily be treated with an oral progesterone-type preparation.

3. *Cystic hyperplasia.* The same buildup process continuing for perhaps six straight months creates this more crowded condition, in which the endometrial secretory glands appear under the microscope to be fat, rounded, and lined by more crowded cells. Two thirds of the cases of cystic hyperplasia that are treated with a D and C will not recur. (If it does recur, it can be treated again by another D and C.) Only 0.4 percent of women with cystic hyperplasia get endometrial cancer eight to ten years later. Again, there is no need to lose your uterus just because you have this condition. Again, the oral progesterone-type preparations easily cause the lining to revert to normal.

4. *Adenomatous hyperplasia.* Here the endometrial cells, though still normal individually, are very densely crowded, and the rounded walls of the glands have begun to fold in and out on themselves. The number of women with this condition who subsequently develop cancer increases sharply to 15 percent, with the cancer usually appearing only three to five years after the diagnosis of adenomatous hyperplasia by D and C.

Most women who come to me after a hysterectomy have had it for this reason. But I still consider this condition to be on the normal end of the scale. First, 85 percent of adenomatous hyperplasia cases will *not* go on to become cancer. Second, as you know from Chapter 1, *all* the cases of both adenomatous hyperplasia and atypical adenomatous hyperplasia (the next stage) that I have ever treated have been reversed by progesterone, and I certainly believe that a trial of this therapy is worthwhile. All my patients who received progesterone treatment followed by an office aspiration four to six months later regained a normal endometrium. Finally, fully two thirds of these cases can be cured by one hospital-type D and C and another 20 percent by a second. Having two D and Cs is still less traumatic than one hysterectomy. If a woman is approaching menopause, these procedures may tide her over this period without a hysterectomy. The postmenopausal uterine lining is rarely able to regrow after a D and C.

5. *Atypical adenomatous hyperplasia.* This is the first stage in which the endometrial cells begin to look unnatural. They may be too dark or jumbled out of their normal pattern. The presence of white blood cells indicates the body's attempt to straighten things out. Atypical adenomatous hyperplasia has been diagnosed about one to three years before cancer appeared, but 85 percent of women with this condition were still able to be treated successfully by D and C, neither regrowing the abnormal lining nor developing cancer. Hysterectomy might be a reasonable treatment for this stage of abnormality, but a carefully monitored trial of progesterone therapy also stands a good chance of reversing the condition without surgery.

However, the diagnosis of atypical adenomatous hyperplasia can be tricky for the pathologist. If he is not very experienced in reviewing such slides, he may overread and call the condition adenocarcinoma, which is cancer, or underread and not cause the gynecologist enough concern. Any patient who comes in for a consultation with a D and C diagnosis of atypical adenomatous hyperplasia has her slides reviewed by my favorite expert endometrial pathologist, Dr. Sheldon Sommers of Lenox Hill Hosiptal in New York.

I saw just such a patient not too long ago. She was only thirty-two and single. Her D and C diagnosis was atypical adenomatous hyperplasia. Two gynecologists were adamant about doing a hysterectomy, both cautioning about the danger she would incur without one. Dr. Sommers agreed with the diagnosis but further told me that the atypicality was only moderate. I treated her for four months with progesterone on a cyclic basis. In the fifth month, she had a second hospital D and C. The findings—secretory endometrium. Absolutely perfect!

She will, of course, continue to be monitored. However, she avoided a hysterectomy and now can look forward to having the children that she so desperately wants one day.

6. *Carcinoma-in-situ*. An uncommon and debatable condition, this is actual cancer of the uterine lining that has not invaded the muscular wall of the uterus. It occurs at the average age of fifty. Although it is believed to eventually and inevitably spread to the surrounding tissue unless destroyed, removed, or altered by hormonal therapy, it may take from one to ten years to do so. You have time, therefore, to double-check the diagnosis. Some cases have been reversed by progesterone therapy, but the usual treatment is hysterectomy.

As you see, there are a great many opportunities to detect, analyze, and treat "precancerous" conditions. Hyperplasias can be dealt with early and the more sinister changes easily avoided. Now the reasons to have a hysterectomy can be viewed from a much clearer perspective.

Besides the definite indications for hysterectomy that I listed earlier in this chapter, there are certain relative indications, upon which most doctors agree, that take into account the degree of abnormality and other risk factors of a particular case. These are:

1. cystic hyperplasia or polyps recurring two to three times after D and C (especially in an obese or diabetic patient)
2. recurrent adenomatous hyperplasia
3. atypical hyperplasia (dysplasia) or carcinoma-in-situ in a woman who will not come back for a followup examination
4. any hyperplasia of the endometrium in a woman with a family history of endometrial or gastrointestinal cancer
5. certain cases of bleeding from an endometrium that cannot regenerate (atrophic endometrium)
6. certain cases of bleeding from blood-clotting abnormalities or leukemias

Diagnosing Endometrial Cancer

Endometrial cancer is now the second most common type of cancer in women, usually striking them at age fifty to sixty. The incidence is 25 per 100,000 per year in women of all age groups but rises from age thirty-five on, reaching 75 per 100,000 by age fifty. Because the proportion of women over forty-five is increasing in the United States—they made up one third of the total female population in 1979—we are seeing an increased number of cases.

Since a major cause of hyperplasias is prolonged continuous estrogen stimulation of the endometrium without the modifying effect of progesterone, conditions associated with continuous estrogen states such as polycystic ovary syndrome, estrogen-secreting ovarian tumors, chronic lack of ovulation, and infertility are risk factors. Estrogen-replacement therapy without progesterone is the major physician-caused problem. However, age is still the prime risk factor. Obesity can also be added to this list, for women who are 30 percent overweight double their chances of getting endometrial cancer. Diabetic women, hypertensive women, and women with a family history of breast or ovarian cancer may also be at increased risk.

Although endometrial cancer is seen in a greater number of women than either ovarian or cervical cancer, it has a lower death rate. This is primarily because it has early warning signals.

The most usual early sign of endometrial cancer is unexplained bleeding. Approximately 80 percent of patients with endometrial cancer have this experience. Premenopausal women with endometrial cancer often have unusually heavy flow during their menses or have abnormal bleeding patterns with breakthrough bleeds occurring anytime in their menstrual cycle. In postmenopausal women, bleeding may occur in the guise of light spotting, a pink discharge, or a return of "menses." As a general rule, the further past menopause the patient is, the more likely it is that her bleeding spells endometrial cancer. The woman who still has regular menses and is older than fifty-two is also at higher risk. Of course, other diagnostic possibilities include endometrial hyperplasias, polyps, ovarian or vaginal tumors, atrophic vaginitis, and even an unexpected pregnancy.

Routine Pap smears sometimes provide clues, but because they are accurate in only 50 percent or so of endometrial cancer cases, this method is not reliable enough. A positive smear, however, will alert the physician that trouble is brewing and that the patient needs a full diagnostic workup.

Diagnosis by Intrauterine Aspiration

One of the nice office procedures (it's not really super, but it's effective and quick) is the suction endometrial biopsy, a two- to three-minute procedure that can diagnose endometrial hyperplasias or cancers with up to 95 percent accuracy (compared with a theoretical 100 percent in a hospital D and C). Unfortunately, the procedure is not good at detecting and removing endometrial polyps as a cause of bleeding. For these, you need the cutting edge of a curette as is used in the hospital D and C. But the suction method is usually all that is necessary to make a diagnosis and establish a basis from which to treat the patient knowledgeably.

With a perimenopausal patient who has a bleeding problem, there is not a lot of room for guesswork. An accurate pathological diagnosis must be established and cancer ruled out so that specific treatment can be undertaken with peace of mind for both the patient and her doctor. Aspiration can be used again some months later to follow up on her therapy and to make sure that her endometrium reverts to normal.

There are a variety of suction methods on the market. Most consist of a hollow steel or plastic tube connected to a tissue-collecting receptacle. I insert the strawlike narrow tube into the uterine cavity, and then turn the suction on. The tissue is sucked from the endometrial lining, down the tube, and into the collecting trap. By moving the device back and forth over the entire inside of the uterus, I obtain a complete sampling of the tissue. At the end of the procedure, the trap is sealed off and sent with its chemically preserved contents to the pathology laboratory. In the lab, the tissue is sectioned thinly, stained, and examined microscopically. The entire device is disposable. Some doctors who object to paying for disposable niceties use a long, hollow cutting instrument which they simply attach to a syringe. By pulling on the barrel of the syringe, they get suction which provides for a smaller sampling.

Some doctors do only hospital D and Cs, but I like the convenience of the office procedure, the lack of mental anguish of hospitalization and anesthesia risk, and the relative low cost compared to a hospital bill plus a surgical expense. A few patients who have had the office procedure informed me that they would rather have total anesthesia in the future, but they have been in the distinct minority. One woman, a psychologist, came for her second aspiration carrying a big black stick consisting of a piece of rubber hose covering a wood dowel. ''What's that for?'' I asked. I wondered whether the article in question was meant for her own use or to hit me with if she was displeased during the procedure.

''It's a squeeze stick,'' she proclaimed. ''I'm going to hang onto it and squeeze it when and if the going gets rough.''

And she did. She decided that an aspiration with a squeeze stick was better than an aspiration without a squeeze stick, so she offered to leave it for other patients to try. They have and they like it, too. My nurse also appreciates it, because before the squeeze stick, she always offered her hand and sometimes got squeezed too hard!

Actually, the discomfort of the three-minute office aspiration is very fleeting. Within two to three minutes afterward, all cramping pain is gone, and all my patients have left my office on their own and smiling. Honestly. I pointed out to my last patient after her follow-up aspiration that she indeed was smiling and she laughed. I think women are great patients. I know what they are going through, because I have been on the other side of the table.

As a matter of fact, before I ever did an aspiration on a patient, I went to my doctor and asked him to do one on me. I think that he thought I was a little strange making such a request. But I said that I had had some irregular bleeding and just wanted to check it out. He complied, and I felt that the whole thing was tolerable as an office procedure. If it had not been tolerable for me, I never would have been able to subject my patients to it. (I have also been a subject in three of my menstrual cramp studies. I feel that no patient should be subjected to any study that I could not freely participate in myself.)

Sometimes it is not possible to perform an office aspiration. For example, in an older woman whose regular menses ended several months or years ago, the cervical opening may be too tight to permit the introduction of even the slender aspirator tip. Because dilating or stretching the cervical opening is painful, it is not usually attempted in the office. Therefore these women must often undergo anesthesia and a hospital D and C.

In a hospital D and C, the cervical canal is usually dilated in order to pass a large, sharp-edged, spoon-shape curette into the uterus. This cuts the endometrial tissue away along with any endometrial polyps that are present. Again, the tissue is collected, chemically preserved, and examined under the mircoscope.

Because a D and C removes more tissue than do the suction methods, it is therapeutic in itself in cases where the woman has a hyperplasia. It may prevent the regrowth of the abnormal tissue as well as decrease bleeding caused by it. On the other hand, if the basic hormonal problem persists and is not corrected, the bleeding will resume within a month or two as the hyperplasia returns. I am continually frustrated by gynecologists who do repeated D and Cs on women, but never treat them medically with a progesterone-type medication to prevent the problem from recurring or becoming worse.

If invasive cancer or carcinoma-in-situ is found during an office aspiration, then a hospital D and C should follow. However, such a finding is rare, and so the office procedure is usually all that is ever necessary. The pathologist's report will state whether the abnormality is hyperplasia or cancer. If the diagnosis is cancer, then the report must include the type of tumor, the amount of abnormality of the cells (the tumor grade), and any evidence of invasion of the uterine muscle.

Removal of the uterus and ovaries is the usual procedure when a malignancy is found. If spread has occurred outside the uterus, or deep into the uterine muscle, then radiation will usually be done. It is frequently given after surgery.

The prognosis depends upon the extent of spread of the cancer, on the degree of cell differentiation (how normal or abnormal the cells appear under the microscope), and on the presence or absence of cancer in the endocervical canal (the mouth of the womb). The good prognosis that most cases have is due to the fact that 75 percent of these cancers are found when they are still confined to the uterus and the uterus is normal or only slightly enlarged.

It is fairly certain, then, that by knowing the signs of endometrial cancer, avoiding the use of unopposed estrogens, having appropriate testing done before beginning hormone-replacement therapy, and getting good gynecologic care early if you are in a high-risk category (menopause later than age 52, postmenopausal bleeding, premenopausal heavy menses, history of grossly irregular menses), you can greatly reduce the risk of ever getting endometrial cancer.

And if you never get endometrial cancer, there are very few circumstances indeed in which you would absolutely need a hysterectomy. Far fewer than the current 50 percent of all women should ever have one. Now that you know as much about uterine pathology as most non-specialist doctors, it's up to you to use this knowledge for the preservation of your own body and peace of mind.

Dysfunctional Uterine Bleeding (DUB): Another Reason for Hysterectomy

DUB is abnormal bleeding from the uterus that is not associated with a tumor, inflammation, or pregnancy. It refers to any abnormal bleeding for which no organic cause can be found. Eighty-five to 90 percent of such cases are due to lack of ovulation. In the remainder, ovulation has occurred but the life span of the corpus luteum may be either shortened or prolonged.

Doctors use several medical terms to describe the many different bleeding patterns that occur. You may see them written on your insurance forms and should know what they mean.

- *menorrhagia:* normal cycle but with flow that is excessive in amount or duration

- *menometrorrhagia:* prolonged uterine bleeding occurring at completely irregular intervals.

- *polymenorrhea:* normal flow with a cycle of less than 21 days

- *polymenorrhagia:* excessive flow with cycle of less than 21 days

- *metrorrhagia:* excessive flow which is acyclic, i.e., occurs at irregular but frequent intervals

Other problems include light bleeding or spotting prior to menses in a normal ovulatory cycle, or bleeding that occurs in mid-cycle with ovulation.

Women who have spotting with ovulation generally have had such a pattern for most of their lives. The spotting is caused by a slight fall in the estrogen level that occurs with ovulation. Some patients, however, may think that they are having a period every two weeks, especially if there is bleeding at mid-cycle rather than their usual spotting. Reassurance is the only required therapy. Sometimes such bleeding can provide a convenient way to determine the time of ovulation for conception and contraception. Some women also have pain associated with their ovulation. This is known as mittelschmerz. It is caused by the egg popping out of its follicle accompanied by tissue fluid or bleeding that spills and irritates the abdominal lining.

Similarly, women with light premenstrual spotting general-ly have always had this pattern to their menstrual flow. Some, however, may develop it when they reach a certain age, and then the pattern will persist for years. After ruling out other problems, I tell such patients that their menstrual pattern has simply changed, and not to worry.

The physician may often think that she or he is dealing with a case of DUB, but further investigation may prove that the cause is thyroid disease, blood abnormalities, submucous fibroids, endometrial polyps, or other pathology. Pregnancy must also be considered. But after pathology and pregnancy have been ruled out, then you can assume that the bleeding is caused by hormonal imbalance. As you can see, DUB is not a specific diagnosis. It is the term used to denote abnormal bleeding patterns after organic causes of disease have been ruled out. This is most important in the perimenopausal women, for one third of all adenocarcinomas of the uterus occur in this age group.

Symptoms

You should now understand the normal menstrual cycling of the endometrium or lining of the uterus. If not, look back at Chapter 1. The vast majority of DUB cases are due to lack of ovulation and the consequent lack of progesterone. Here the endometrium is constantly stimulated by estrogen (without the balance of progesterone), and the lining becomes too thick and finally outgrows its own blood supply. At that point, it begins to break down a little bit from one spot, a little bit from another. The woman notices that she is bleeding at odd intervals. Then, because the lining is thicker than normal, her flow is often heavy. And this is usually what finally brings her to the physician's office.

All normal women fail to ovulate once or twice a year, but as you head toward menopause, this may happen four or more months out of the year, predisposing you to the problem of irregular menses. Because this is the exact mechanism by which hyperplasia of the endometrium develops (as described previously), you must be certain to get an accurate diagnosis to determine whether such a process is taking place or whether cancer may already be present.

Diagnosis

The most important step in the diagnosis of DUB in women over thirty-five is the endometrial aspiration biopsy done in the doctor's office or a hospital D and C if your physician does not have an in-office setup. If it is at all possible, the procedure should be scheduled when you are premenstrual, during the secretory or postovulation phase of the cycle. In that way, it can be determined whether the bleeding is associated with lack of ovulation. If there is still proliferative endometrium or hyperplasia during the secretory phase of the cycle, then you are not ovulating and your bleeding is probably due to hormonal imbalance. In those rare cases when the woman is ovulating but still has DUB, the hormonal imbalance is due to the corpus luteum or luteal phase persisting too long or, the other extreme, not lasting long enough. Short luteal phases may result in frequent bleeding, whereas long luteal phases can delay the menstrual period by anywhere from a week or two to several months.

Other Factors in DUB

Obese women generally tend to have more menstrual disorders, including longer menstrual cycles, more irregular cycles, heavier flow, and hirsutism—an abnormal increase in body hair due to hormonal imbalance. Obesity is also associated with infertility, as the cycles of obese women tend to be anovulatory more often than those of their thinner sisters.

Smoking has an aging effect on the ovaries. Women who smoke have an earlier menopause by some two years than women who don't smoke. I wonder how many women would smoke if they realized it physically aged them by two years. Marijuana, too, has been tied to increased incidence of hormonal disorders, including more anovulatory cycles and shortened luteal phase, according to research from the Masters and Johnson Institute of St. Louis.

Treatment After the Diagnostic Endometrial Biopsy

Treatment of DUB is usually administration of a progesterone-type drug to stop the bleeding. Norethindrone acetate seems to work especially well. Other products such as medroxyprogesterone acetate can also be used. Then, in subsequent cycles, ten days of progesterone therapy may be taken from days 15 through 24 of each cycle for as long as necessary.

DUB may account for as much as 10 percent of hospital admissions and 25 percent of all gynecologic surgery. Because of this fact, it is important that you realize that it is almost always possible to treat DUB with hormonal therapy. Hysterectomy should not be considered unless the bleeding is unresponsive to hormonal therapy and/or D and Cs.

Fibroids: Still Another Reason for Hysterectomy

Fibroids may be the reason for the roundness of your lower abdomen. Usually, of course, it's overweight, but nearly one third of women approaching their menopause have uterine fibroids. Some of these are large enough to make a difference in your silhouette.

Actually, most women are surprised when the doctor says, "Hmmmmmmmm, you have fibroids," during a pelvic examination. "Really? I feel fine, I don't have any symptoms." "Well, don't worry, just come back in six months and I'll check again."

And that's all there is to it. You have joined the ranks of those who have a fibroid uterus.

However, you must be aware that fibroids are one of the most popular reasons for hysterectomy. It follows, then, that you should have a basic working knowledge of fibroids so you don't get trapped into having an unnecessary hysterectomy.

Fibroids are benign tumors—in fact, the most common benign tumor of the uterus. They make their appearance during the reproductive years of a woman's life and therefore are probably linked to hormonal stimulation. The highest incidence, almost 30 percent, is in the middle and latter half of the woman's menstrual life, and black women seem to be particularly susceptible.

Fibroids or leiomyomas are solid, benign growths within the muscular wall of the uterus, enclosed in a capsule that separates them from the surrounding tissue. There are usually several of them, though they may occur singly. From their site within the muscular wall, they may expand, pushing muscle aside either in the direction of the outer surface of the uterus or, more rarely, toward the inner surface just beneath the endometrium. Submucous fibroids lying just beneath the endometrium may be responsible for excessively heavy bleeding during your period, because they distort the lining of the uterus or decrease the ability of the uterus to contract during menstruation. Some women have gushes so heavy that they may become anemic and require surgical attention.

The uterus does not seem to tolerate submucous fibroids as well as it does fibroids in other positions. Severe menstrual pain can sometimes result, as these fibroids are the object of uterine contractions to expel them. Because of their location, they cannot be felt by the physician, but they can be spotted by pelvic ultrasound. Fortunately this placement of a fibroid is rare so that most women who have fibroids are asymptomatic.

Still other fibroids may start off near the outer surface of the uterus, and some may continue to project outward until their only connection to the uterus is by a slender stalk which contains the blood supply to the fibroid. These rare fibroids may "float" within the pelvis and be confusing to the physician, who must carefully differentiate them from an ovarian tumor. Sometimes such a fibroid may twist on its stalk and create severe pain due to loss of its blood supply and tissue death. In all my years of practice, I have only seen this occur once.

Other fibroids, even those within the uterine wall, may also degenerate—probably due to an alteration in blood supply. This often occurs in pregnancy, though I have seen a small number of women in their fifties who had such an episode. The patients complain of pain and uterine contractions. On physical examination, the fibroid is seen to have changed in texture and is soft and tender. Luckily, many of these simply get better on their own, but accurate diagnosis is necessary first.

Fibroids must be differentiated from pregnancy, the usual cause of increasing uterine size. Another cause of uterine enlargement is called adenomyosis. In this condition, islands of endometrial glands and their supporting tissue produce a uniform enlargement of the uterus, which on palpation feels much like a uterus with a symmetrical solitary fibroid within its walls. Adenomyosis is a pathological diagnosis, for it is primarily made after hysterectomy, when the uterus is opened. With adenomyosis, rather than seeing the fibroid with its capsule, there are endometrial glands mixed into the tissue of the uterine wall. Women with adenomyosis often have menstrual pain that begins with the onset of flow and only ends at the end of their period.

Fibroids are one of the most common reasons given for hysterectomy. I am convinced that many of these hysterectomies are unnecessary and that most fibroids should just be watched. Those that are causing symptoms such as obstructing your kidney outflow or interfering with bowel function or are increasing rapidly in size will probably require surgery. But my advice to most patients in their late forties who have fibroids—even those that have slowly enlarged to the size of a twelve- or fourteen-week pregnancy—is to continue having regular checkups and to watch and wait.

Most women with fibroids tend to be perimenopausal. With menopause, their fibroids and uterus will decrease in size. Therefore, if you can hold off, it is likely that menopause will make surgery unnecessary. If you decide to wait, you must have frequent checkups to monitor the size and consistency of your fibroids—that's part of the deal that I make with my patients. If they want to avoid surgery, then they must be willing to have me follow them at intervals that I think are appropriate.

It is important to know the size of your uterus and fibroids. Without such knowledge, it is impossible to participate intelligently in decisions about whether to have surgery. For example, suppose that during your examination in the doctor's office, you are told that your uterus contains fibroids and is enlarged to the size of a three-month pregnancy. If you know that your uterus has been that size for the past four years, you will not be alarmed. On the other hand, if your uterus was normal size just six months ago, this is a significant finding because fibroids that enlarge rapidly may be cancerous. Unless you keep track of the size and condition of your uterus, you won't be able to evaluate changes. Therefore, don't settle for a doctor's knowing "ummmm" as he or she examines you. Speak up and ask what is being found. (This information can also be very useful to a doctor who is seeing you for the first time. If you can say what previous findings have been, the doctor can more accurately evaluate your uterine potential for future problems.)

Listen carefully to what you are told, and if surgery is suggested, be smart and get a second opinion.

Leiomyosarcoma of the Uterus

One other subject must be discussed here—a malignant change called leiomyosarcoma that occurs in only 0.5 percent of fibroids. Uterine leiomyosarcomas are rare malignant tumors with an incidence of 0.67 per 100,000 women. It is possible for these tumors to arise out of an existing fibroid, or they may arise within the muscle of the uterine wall. Those that are confined to the fibroid have the best prognosis; those that arise de novo from the uterine wall have the poorest. However, if spread does not occur and the sarcoma is confined to the uterus, the survival rate is excellent.

Abdominal or lower pelvic discomfort or abnormal bleeding are the most usual complaints, but a fair portion of patients have no complaints. Preoperatively, the patient is usually assumed to have a fibroid. Suspicion may arise, however, if there has been a rapid increase in the size of the "fibroid." Interestingly, a large tumor does not necessarily carry a poor prognosis. Premenopausal women also have a better prognosis (a 5-year survival rate of 93% in a recent review of cases)[2] than postmenopausal women.

Vaginal Hysterectomy vs. Abdominal Hysterectomy

The Center for Disease Control (CDC) in Atlanta set up a two-year study to evaluate the complications of elective hysterectomy. The study found that vaginal hysterectomy was safer than the abdominal approach when the women who underwent the vaginal procedure were given antibiotics prior to surgery.[3]

It is important to realize that not all women are candidates for vaginal hysterectomy, but the CDC felt that some 10 percent of women who usually would undergo surgery by the abdominal approach might benefit from the vaginal procedure's shorter and less complicated postsurgical course. Surgeons traditionally use the vaginal approach for hysterectomies in which the ovaries will not be removed and for those women who have carcinoma-in-situ of the cervix, uterine bleeding, or small fibroid tumors of the uterus. The vaginal approach is also used when the surgeon is correcting a cystocele (dropped bladder) or rectocele and does a hysterectomy as an adjunct to these procedures to ensure their success.

The abdominal procedure is performed when there are large uterine fibroids, adhesions from previous surgery, pelvic inflammatory disease; when the ovaries are to be removed; or when there is need to look at the abdominal cavity for tumor, endometriosis, or other pathology, especially when the patient has complained of pelvic pain that has remained undiagnosed.

Another factor that determines which approach the surgeon will take is his training. Some medical centers prefer one procedure over the other, and the surgeon's training will therefore be better in that procedure. He will feel more comfortable using that technique and will elect it whenever possible.

Interestingly, before the use of prophylactic antibiotics in the vaginal procedure, the complication rates for both procedures were approximately 40 percent. Now the vaginal procedure done in conjunction with the administration of antibiotics has a much lower complication rate. Women who were given antibiotics for abdominal hysterectomy also showed a reduced complication rate, but there remained a significant difference between the two approaches even when antibiotics were given to both surgical groups.

Here are some questions you might consider asking a gynecologist who has suggested that you need a hysterectomy:

• Does this condition ever lead to cancer? How often?

• Is there a medical (as opposed to surgical) way of treating this condition? Would you be willing to try it?

• Is there minor surgery (such as a D and C) that might clear up my condition so I wouldn't have to have major surgery? Would you be willing to try it?

• Since I'm 44 (or whatever), do you think that menopause might soon relieve me of my symptoms without surgery?

If your doctor says that your condition is not life threatening and might respond to medication or a D and C, ask that it be so treated if you want to avoid hysterectomy.

Above all, be wary of going ahead with a hysterectomy if the physician emphasizes the "no more babies or fuss with birth control" reason for surgery. Be wary, too, if the doctor indicates that he or she believes in hysterectomy almost routinely for older women.

I certainly am not advising that you simply ignore your physician's recommendation for hysterectomy. But you should know the *exact* reason for this advice. Your doctor will probably be willing to explain fully—if not, look for one who *will*. And if you have a condition that is not life threatening and treatable with medication, find a physician who is willing to try such therapy if you wish to avoid surgery. After all, it's *your* uterus, and you—not the doctor—are going to be risking the possible serious complication of having it removed.

6

Ovarian Cancer: Be Aware

Ovarian cancer is the most frustrating problem that a physician faces, because although it is highly curable in its early stages, it is rarely detected until it is far advanced. Ovarian cancer is a ''hidden'' cancer and is not associated with significant symptoms in its early stages. The result is that ovarian cancer is the leading cause of death among women with cancer of the pelvis. It will occur sooner or later in 1.4 percent of all females born in the United States this year, and of these 18,000 cases, 11,500 will be fatal. Every decade more than 100,000 women at the height of their social and economic productivity die from this disease. Ovarian cancer is one of the greatest challenges of the 1980s, because its prognosis is no better now than it has been for the past two decades.

Cancer of the ovary is on the increase in the Western world, especially in the highly industrialized countries. It seems to occur mainly among middle- and upper-class women. Women who have never married or have never borne children have two or three times the risk of developing this malignancy that married women have. On the other hand, women with four or more children have a lesser risk. It is possible that pregnancy exerts a protective effect or, conversely, that an abnormality in ovarian function predisposes a woman to both infertility and ovarian cancer. Also, recent studies have shown that oral contraceptives offer some protection against ovarian cancer by shutting off ovarian function and allowing the tissue

155

to rest. Giving the ovary a break from the repeated stimulation of "incessant ovulation" seems in some small way to reduce the cancer risk.

The use of talcum powder for dusting sanitary napkins or the external genitalia doubles the risk of developing ovarian cancer, according to Dr. Daniel Cramer of Harvard Medical School. In his study, women who used talc for both dusting activities were in an even higher risk group. The researchers did not investigate the use of talc on diaphragms; neither did they inquire whether women washed the talc off their diaphragms before using them.

Like asbestos, talc is a hydrous magnesium silicate, but it has a somewhat different structure. Talc is not a pure product and may be contaminated with asbestos. During ovulation, when the surface of the ovary folds inward, the talc could be carried into the interior of the ovary and lead to the development of cancer. Dr. Cramer was quick to state, however, that he was not proposing talc as the only cause of ovarian cancer and that more studies would be done to clarify this new lead. I have always advised my own patients to dust their genitals or diaphragms with cornstarch. It's cheap, effective, and in the light of this new study, less likely to cause problems.

Anatomy of the Ovary

The ovaries are solid, slightly nodular, pink-gray bodies the approximate size of unshelled almonds. They have an inner core and an outer portion called the cortex, and a few thin covering layers of cells, the outermost of which is known as the germinal epithelium. The inner portion of the cortex consists mostly of follicles—microscopic clumps of cells each encasing an immature egg. (See Chapter 1 for their role in the menstrual cycle.) The ovaries are situated on either side of the uterus, behind or below the fallopian tubes. They are usually not symmetrical, the right ovary often being larger than the left.

The ovary changes markedly in size, shape, consistency, and position during its lifetime, and there are also microscopic changes brought about by the stimuli of various hormones.

When checking for abnormalities, it is therefore important to know the changes that occur in the ovary at different ages as well as within any given menstrual cycle.

The ovary undergoes a complicated development, for it arises from several different embryonic tissues. Each of the early tissues that composes the ovary retains its own potential to form a tumor. Many different cancer types can occur in this small organ, each type originating from its own cell line that dates back to the formation of the ovary itself. Consequently, there is no single "ovarian cancer." Instead, there is a long, complicated list of ovarian cancers, each with its own mode of spread and response to therapy.

Symptoms of Ovarian Cancer

There are no specific early symptoms associated with ovarian cancer. Rather, the list consists of vague, insidious abdominal complaints that a woman usually attributes to anything but her ovaries. This lack of significant symptomology is a major contributing factor to late diagnosis and, therefore, poor prognosis of the disease.

The earliest manifestations are vague abdominal discomfort, dyspepsia, indigestion, gas with constant distension, flatulence, belching, a feeling of fullness after light meals, slight loss of appetite, and other mild digestive disturbances.

Women rarely feel discomfort from the ovaries themselves—they are fairly insensitive to distension, since they do not have a restraining capsule. Therefore, a tumor or a cyst can become large without the patient ever being aware of it (unless the increase in size occurs very rapidly). If the ovary were a sensitive organ, the diagnosis of cancer could be made more easily at an earlier stage. (The ovary, though it is not sensitive to distension, is exquisitely sensitive to squeezing or compression—a fact that is well known to physicians because patients routinely complain about slight discomfort when their ovaries are lightly squeezed during a pelvic exam.) Pain is, therefore, not commonly present unless an unusual problem occurs. For example, if the expanding ovary becomes heavy and cuts off its blood supply as it twists and falls into the lower pelvis, the pain can be extreme and of sudden onset. But otherwise, unfortunately, a tumor may grow to huge proportions before a woman seeks medical attention. All too often, she finally goes to her doctor because her abdomen has swollen to an embarrassing extent. By this time, the tumor may be very large and its weight may also be causing swollen ankles and varicose veins, much as pregnancy does. She may also complain about frequent urination.

There are, of course, ovarian enlargements that are not cancer. In young women, ovaries that are functioning at peak performance routinely enlarge every month as part of their normal hormone secreting function. Most monthly fluctuations in ovarian size go unnoticed.

It is unfortunate that the symptoms of malignant ovarian tumors are the same as those produced by benign tumors. One of the problems in trying to diagnose ovarian tumors clinically is that, at least early on, the benign growths act very much like the malignant ones and vice versa.

If a woman complains of gastrointestinal symptoms that cannot definitely be diagnosed as originating from her stomach or intestines, she should have ovarian cancer ruled out by an appropriate examination and medical workup. Most doctors tend to ignore vague abdominal and pelvic symptoms, but these complaints should be taken very seriously. If you wait until the usual symptoms associated with ovarian cancer are present, for example, abdominal swelling, pain, weight loss, increased frequency of urination, or a mass that can be felt through the abdominal wall, the disease is usually far advanced. Even with extensive spread of the ovarian cancer within the woman's abdomen, the patient's only complaint may be abdominal enlargement or a sense of fullness low in the pelvic area.

Unlike the cervix, the ovaries are hidden within the abdomen and cannot be seen. So while the death rates from cervical cancer have fallen, ovarian death rates have shown a slow but persistent climb.

Types of Ovarian Tumors

Some tumors have their origins in tissue that has the capability to produce male or female hormones. These are known as functional tumors, and some of them are malignant. Tumors producing estrogen (female hormones) may cause bleeding problems. Only 10 percent of malignant ovarian tumors disturb the menstrual rhythm or alter menstrual flow. Recurrence of monthly bleeding should alert a postmenopausal woman and her physician that such a tumor might exist. On the other hand, tumors that produce male hormones may bring an abrupt end to a woman's monthly period, cause her breasts to shrink, change the hair growth pattern on her body to a male type, cause her clitoris to enlarge, and, later on, even cause her voice to deepen.

Masculinizing tumors arise in the ovary because in the course of its normal development, the ovary contains some testicular elements. These disappear with further differentiation of the ovary, but in many women, tiny remnants can remain. However, most ovarian tumors do not secrete hormones and so do not produce the symptoms that might alert a woman that a catastrophe may be brewing within her abdomen.

Other tumors contain bits and pieces of bone, teeth, or cartilage, also left over from the various embryonic tissues which get incorporated into ovarian tissue. These show up easily on X rays and give clues to their nature.

The ovary is unique in that it not only gives rise to a number of different cancers but is also the recipient of metastases from cancers in other parts of the body, particularly from breast, stomach, and colon. Colon cancer spreads to the ovary by direct extension of the tumor from the colon. Endometrial cancer (from the uterine lining) spreads through the open fallopian tube onto the ovary. The method of spread from the stomach or breast is thought to be through the lymphatic or blood vessels.

The second ovary becomes involved with metastatic cancer via the lymphatic flow that carries malignant cells from the first ovary to the uterus and then across to the opposite ovary.

Though the initial cancer may be only in one ovary, the spread to the opposite one occurs so frequently that the uterus and both ovaries should be removed as standard therapy in ovarian cancer. The uterus also often contains tumors that have come from other sites.

Because the ovarian enlargement may be due to metastatic disease, any patient with a suspected ovarian mass should undergo a thorough preoperative evaluation to rule out a primary cancer elsewhere in the body. Women forty years of age and older comprise the high-risk group here, for at this age, cancers of all kinds are more common.

Ovarian growths may be either cystic (round in shape and filled with fluid) or solid, and both types may be either benign or malignant. Benign cysts change in size with the menstrual cycle and may be associated with alterations in the menstrual pattern.

Often a benign cyst is a follicle that partly matured during the normal menstrual cycle but did not release its egg (see Chapter 1 for a description of the mechanism of ovulation). These "functional cysts" usually disappear in one or two menstrual cycles. Cancers, on the other hand, tend to persist or to become larger. The rate of growth can range from extremely slow to very rapid.

Benign tumors, either cystic or solid, are most prevalent in the years preceding the menopause. Solid tumors (fibromas being the exception) usually possess some degree of malignant potential.

Although fewer than 4 percent of all ovarian tumors are solid, the majority of these are malignant in the over 40 age group. Two thirds of these solid tumors are metastases from other sites, and, in fact, all tumors that metastasize to the ovaries are solid. A malignant solid tumor also tends to be bilateral, occurring in both ovaries.

Although cystic tumors may be either benign or malignant, the more solid portions that are mixed with the cystic elements, the greater the likelihood that the tumor will be malignant.

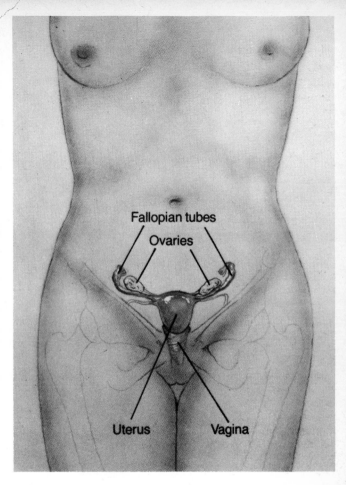

The normal female reproductive organs.

Diagram © Warner-Lambert Company 1981.

When your doctor performs your pelvic examination, one of the things he looks for is a pelvic mass in the uterus, fallopian tubes, or ovaries. Many pelvic masses cause no symptoms and are discovered only by pelvic examination.

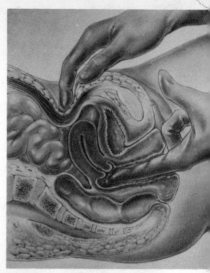

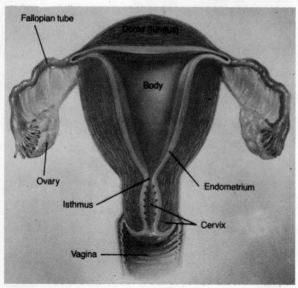

The normal uterus.

Diagrams © Warner-Lambert Company 1981.

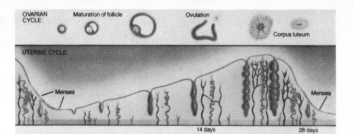

The menstrual cycle. Cyclic growth and destruction of the endometrium with comparable stages of the ovarian cycle.

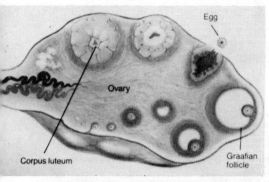

The ovary. A schematic representation of ovulation.

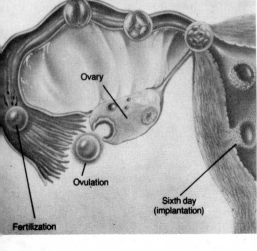

The fertilization process.

Diagrams © Warner-Lambert Company 1981.

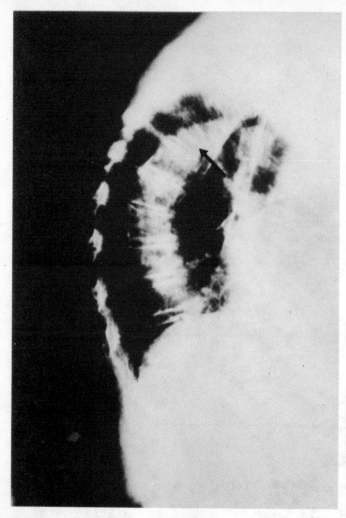

Osteoporosis. Note washed-out, pale bone structure. Arrow points to vertebra that has collapsed due to osteoporosis. Upper back is rounded, causing the "dowager's hump."

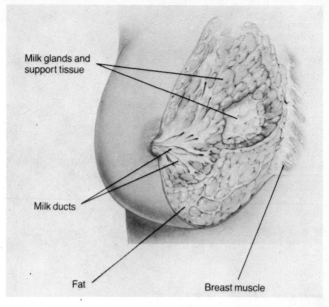

Milk glands and
support tissue

Milk ducts

Fat

Breast muscle

The breast is divided into several lobes in which are embedded milk glands arranged in clusters around tiny ducts. Fatty deposits lie around the glands, beneath the skin, and between the lobes.

Fibroadenomas are benign tumors which are firm and rubbery, nonpainful, and move about the breast freely.

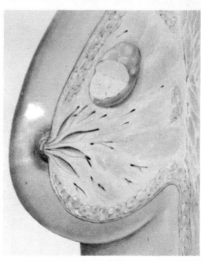

A single large cyst (blue dome cyst) is a common manifestation of fibrocystic disease of the breast.

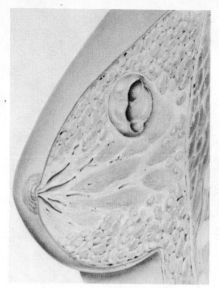

Another form of fibrocystic disease involves multiple small cysts with fibrosis. .

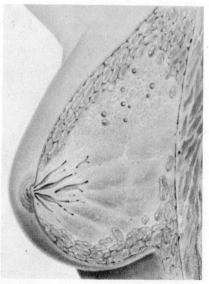

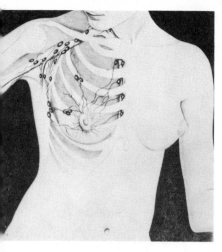

Each breast contains a network of lymphatic vessels that drains either into the lymph nodes of the armpit or the internal mammary nodes. Presence of cancer cells in the axillary lymph nodes is an indication that the disease may have spread to other parts of the body. *Courtesy of the National Cancer Institute.*

Radical mastectomy, six years previously.

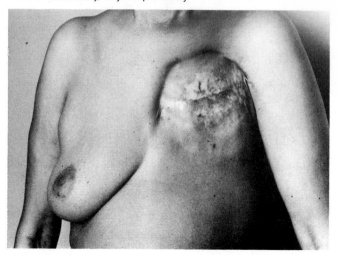

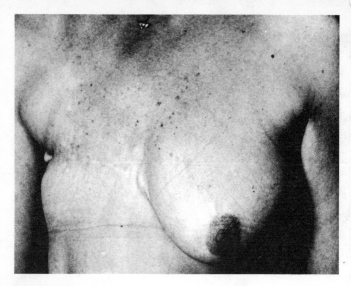

Modified radical mastectomy.

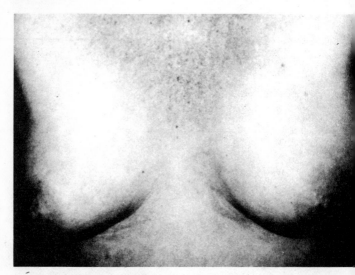

Breasts of a fifty-five-year-old woman treated for cancer of the left breast by irradiation six years previously.

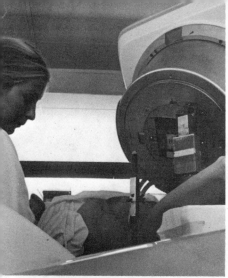

A radiation technician prepares breast-cancer patient for radiation therapy using the linear accelerator. *Courtesy of* Wellbeing, *Beth Israel Hospital, Boston, Mass.*

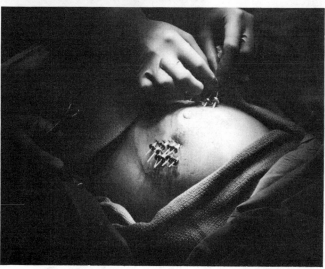

Insertion of fine plastic tubes into the breast under general anesthesia. Radioactive seeds of iridium-192 are then added. This booster dose of radioactivity remains for 48 hours and destroys any remaining cancer cells in the area of the breast from which the cancer was removed. *Courtesy of* Wellbeing, *Beth Israel Hospital, Boston, Mass.*

Endometrial hyperplasia means overgrowth of the lining of the uterus. It frequently causes heavy or irregular menstrual bleeding.

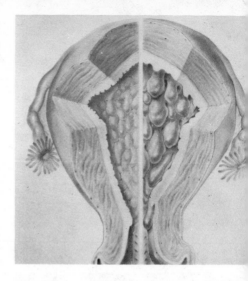

Endometrial cancer may cause vaginal bleeding between menses, after intercourse, after menopause. Usually no pain occurs.

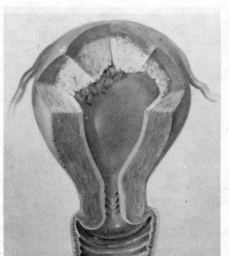

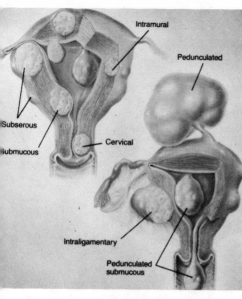

Benign uterine tumors called fibroids are extremely common. The symptoms vary with the size and location of the masses. Some huge growths cause no discomfort or abnormal bleeding. Others produce pressure and pain in the pelvic area. Submucous fibroids may alter menstrual bleeding.

Intramural

Pedunculated

Subserous

submucous

Cervical

Intraligamentary

Pedunculated submucous

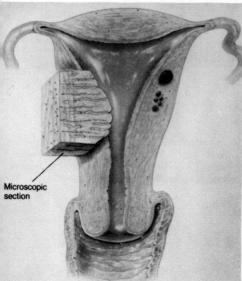

Adenomyosis. The cells of the uterine lining may invade the muscular portion of the uterus. This disorder is benign but may cause painful menstruation.

Microscopic section

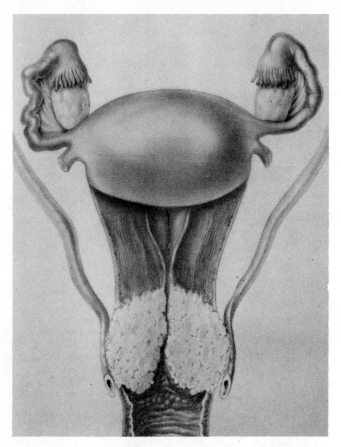

Cervical cancer. The most common pelvic malignancy, cervical cancer is a preventable disease. Usually it is detected with a Pap smear before it becomes a tumor or pelvic mass. Even when first discovered in the invasive stages, cervical cancer is curable in over 60% of women.

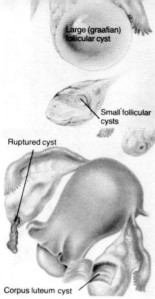

Follicular cysts and lutein cysts. Each time an egg is produced, a small cyst forms. Occasionally such cysts fail to rupture and continue to grow in size. Most regress or finally rupture. Some occasionally become so large that they require surgery. After releasing its egg, a follicular cyst normally changes into a small hormone-producing corpus luteum. Occasionally these develop cysts. They may become large enough to require removal or may rupture and hemorrhage.

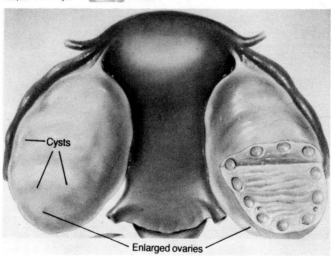

Some women develop large numbers of follicular cysts in both ovaries—a fairly common disorder called Stein-Leventhal syndrome. This may result in menstrual irregularity and sterility and may be associated with excess body hair and mild obesity.

Diagrams © Warner-Lambert Company 1981.

Ovarian cancer usually occurs in older women and frequently involves both ovaries.

Endometrial cysts are tiny implants of the type of cells that line the uterine cavity. These cysts (chocolate cysts) may enlarge, producing endometriosis of the ovary. If they rupture, they may spill over onto adjoining organs, which become bound to each other with scar tissue (adhesions).

Diagrams © Warner-Lambert Company 1981.

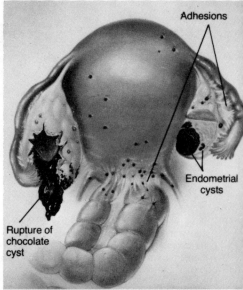

Adhesions

Endometrial cysts

Rupture of chocolate cyst

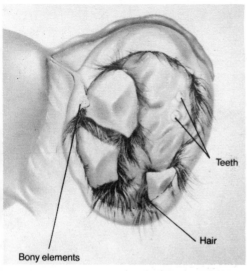

Benign cystic teratomas (dermoid tumors) arise from embryonic cells in the ovary. They may produce a strange tumor with a few fully formed teeth or a mass of hair, or, occasionally, portions of bones. Teratomas are usually benign.

Teeth

Hair

Bony elements

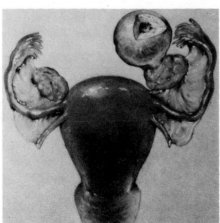

Benign solid ovarian tumors frequently produce no symptoms but may grow to large size and cause accumulation of fluid in the abdominal cavity or even in the chest cavity.

Diagrams © Warner-Lambert Company 1981.

Ovarian tumors, benign and malignant, can produce inappropriate amounts of hormones. These then affect the menstrual cycle as well as sexual characteristics. Granulose and/or theca cell tumors produce excessive amounts of estrogen.

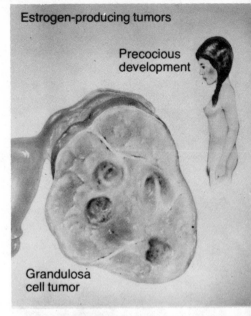

Estrogen-producing tumors

Precocious development

Grandulosa cell tumor

Arrhenoblastoma tumors produce male sex hormones in large amounts and cause masculinization. These abnormal sexual changes usually reverse themselves after the tumor has been removed.

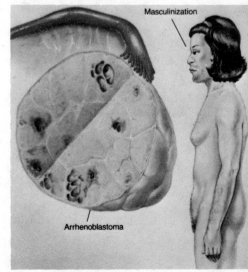

Masculinization

Arrhenoblastoma

Diagrams © Warner-Lambert Company 1981.

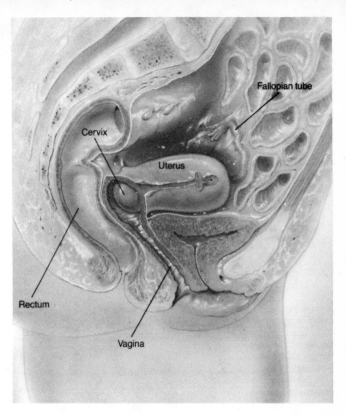

Normal pelvic anatomy.

Diagram © Warner-Lambert Company 1981.

Prolapse of the uterus is any descent of the uterus below its normal position in the pelvis. It is due primarily to relaxation or tearing of the supporting pelvic structures, usually during labor.

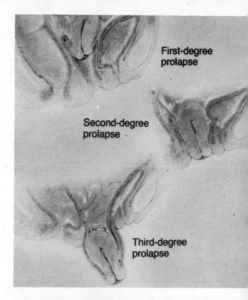

First-degree prolapse

Second-degree prolapse

Third-degree prolapse

Cystocele, the bulging of the urinary bladder into the vaginal wall, is caused by weakness and relaxation of the supporting structures. Rectocele, bulging of the rectum into the vagina, is also due to loss of support.

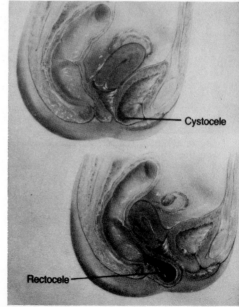

Cystocele

Rectocele

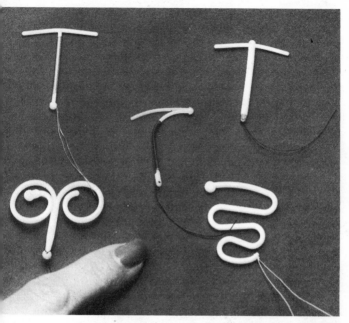

IUDs currently available in the United States: *Top left:* Tatum-T. Note copper wire wound about stem of T. *Top right:* Progestasert. Hollow stem contains natural progesterone. *Center:* Copper 7. Note copper wire wound about stem of 7. Wire appears dark, as copper has come off during three years' use of this device, just removed from a patient. *Bottom left:* Double spiral, inert device. (No longer being manufactured.) *Bottom right:* Lippes Loop, inert device.

To insert an arcing spring diaphragm (left), hold the diaphragm with the arc facing downward. Using the fingers of the other hand, spread the labia and insert the folded diaphragm.

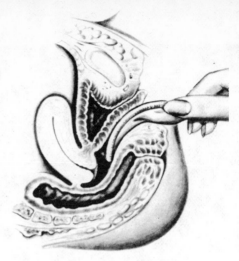

For a coil spring diaphragm (right), hold it between your thumb and fingers with the dome either up or down, and place your index finger on the back outer rim of the compressed diaphragm.

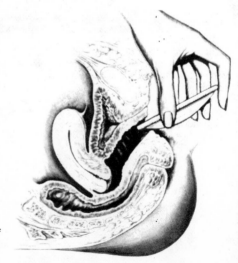

Diagrams courtesy of Young Drug Products Corp.

Tuck the front of the rim behind the pelvic bone so the rubber hugs the front wall of the vagina.

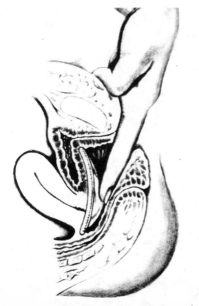

Feel for your cervix through the diaphragm to be certain it is securely covered by the rubber dome.

Diagrams courtesy of Young Drug Products Corp.

To insert a coil spring diaphragm with introducer device, direct the introducer downward and backward into the vagina as far as it will comfortably go past the cervix.

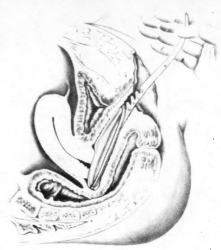

To release the diaphragm, rotate the handle of the introducer gently to the right or left.

Diagrams courtesy of Young Drug Products Corp.

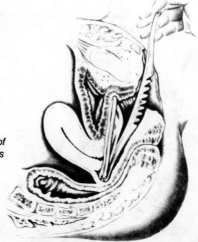

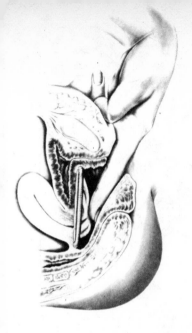

After the introducer is removed, tuck the front of the rim of the diaphragm behind the pelvic bone so that the rubber hugs the front wall of the vagina.

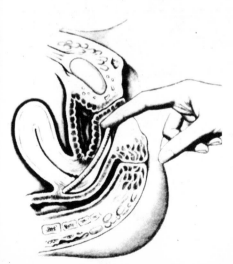

To remove, insert your forefinger up and over the top side of the diaphragm and slightly to the side. Turn the palm of your hand downward and backward, hooking the forefinger firmly on the top of the inside of the upper rim of the diaphragm, then pull it down and out.

Diagrams courtesy of Young Drug Products Corp.

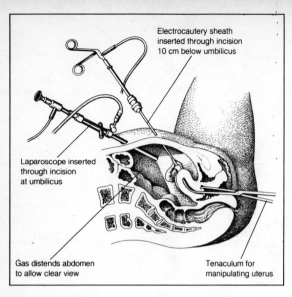

Electrocautery sheath inserted through incision 10 cm below umbilicus

Laparoscope inserted through incision at umbilicus

Gas distends abdomen to allow clear view

Tenaculum for manipulating uterus

Laparoscopy by the double puncture technique. *Ben R. Goode.*

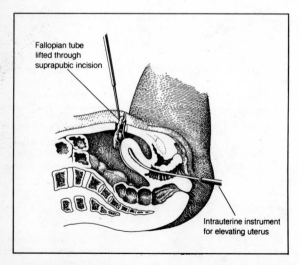

Fallopian tube lifted through suprapubic incision

Intrauterine instrument for elevating uterus

Minilaparotomy. *Ben R. Goode.*

The Pelvic Exam for Early Diagnosis

With better public and professional education, more diagnoses of ovarian cancer are being made at early stages. The best method we have at present is the pelvic exam. Unfortunately, although women know about the importance of going to a doctor to have their "Paps" done, a Pap smear itself very rarely picks up an ovarian cancer. Since the American Cancer Society has come out with its recommendation that women who have two consecutive normal Paps need subsequent Paps only every three years, many women have decided to see their doctors only once every three years. To their discredit, the American Cancer Society never educated women that they must still go to their doctors for an internal, or pelvic, examination at regular intervals. This is the only way that her ovaries can be evaluated before it is too late.

The pelvic examination to rule out ovarian cancer is most important for women over forty. The common epithelial ovarian cancers usually occur in women over forty, and although the greatest number cluster around ages forty-five to fifty-five, the incidence peaks at age eighty. The ovary gets too old to function, but never gets too old to form a cancer. (For unknown reasons, the common epithelial ovarian cancer has been increasing in frequency in young age groups and is even seen now in teenage girls.)

This is why I insist that my patients who are over forty come in every six months for a physical examination, so that I can check their ovaries and evaluate any change in the size or consistency of the uterus that might have occurred. The exam also includes a breast examination. I take their Paps on a yearly basis. (I ask my patients, especially those who tend to be constipated, to take an enema before coming in for the examination. Stool in the rectum is all too confusing when the doctor is trying to sort out odd lumps caused by stool from other lumps that might prove to be a tumor.)

In 1971, Barber and Graber pointed out a reliable sign for detecting early ovarian cancer called the postmenopausal palpable ovary syndrome. The ovary shrinks as menopause occurs, and three to five years after the woman's last menstrual period, it cannot be palpated by the examining physician. Consequently any ovary which *is* palpable in a woman three to five years after her menopause most probably contains a tumor. The high incidence of malignancy in ovarian tumors in women older than forty-five makes it incumbent upon the physician to prove that a malignancy does not exist.

In postmenopausal women, there are naturally no functional cysts, so time should not be wasted in observing a postmenopausal patient with a palpable ovary to see if the enlargement will resolve spontaneously. Such a delay will only allow local and metastatic spread to occur.

And so it follows that any pelvic mass that has appeared after the menopause and cannot definitely be identified as a uterine fibroid should be considered malignant until proven otherwise. The early diagnosis of ovarian cancer requires a high degree of suspicion. Because of the aggressive nature of ovarian malignancies, the only hope for successful treatment lies in the early diagnosis and complete surgical excision of the tumor.

Clinically, a benign solid tumor cannot be distinguished from one which is malignant. Because the incidence of malignancy in these tumors is high, it is best to assume that the tumor is malignant until proven otherwise. And the proof comes only after the tumor has been removed and examined under the microscope. Even in the operating room with the tumor in his hand, it is often impossible for the surgeon to tell whether it is benign or malignant just by looking at it.

The tumor should be opened in the operating room and a quick-frozen section of it examined under the microscope. Although such a biopsy is not the final word on the analysis of the tumor, it is an essential step. It is a shame that so often the diagnosis of ovarian cancer is made only after the patient's surgery has been completed and the final pathology report has come to the gynecologist's attention some days later. Then the woman must undergo further surgery and an additional anesthesia.

Sometimes, even with a benign cyst, surgery should be

performed. By removing the cyst, the surgeon can preserve an ovary which would otherwise be destroyed by the expansion of the cyst. Thus the ovary can be saved in a woman who is still premenopausal and wants to preserve her ovarian function. On the other hand, if the cyst has already destroyed all the functioning ovary, there is nothing that can be done other than to remove the entire mass.

The physician must be alert to and suspicious of:

1. A mass in the ovary.
2. Relative immobility of the ovary due to fixation and adhesions.
3. Irregularity of the tumor, often mixed with areas of increased hardness.
4. Relative insensitivity of the mass. Normal ovaries are tender when palpated during the pelvic exam; ovarian cancers usually are not.
5. Increasing size.
6. Bilaterality (70% of ovarian cancers are bilateral, versus 5% of benign lesions).

Knowing what to look for, however, will not suffice if the pelvic exam is not performed carefully. It is difficult to palpate the ovaries, but I am still alarmed at the number of masses that physicians miss. Not long ago, while I was doing a pelvic exam on a fifty-four-year-old woman, I felt a very soft mass in the area of her left ovary. As she lived far from my office, I sent her to an experienced surgeon near her home for an evaluation. He felt nothing. Am I crazy, I wondered. I asked the woman to return to my office; I had to be sure. Again I felt the soft mass. "Maybe it's a cyst that ruptured when he saw you and has refilled," I said. "Let's get a sonogram." The sonogram showed a large cystic mass. Back she went to the surgeon with the sonogram, for at her age, a large mass in the adnexal area meant she must have a complete workup to rule out cancer. Finally the surgeon did a laparoscopy (this procedure is explained later in this chapter). The woman turned out to have an old tubal abscess—fluid in her fallopian tube from a previous infection. It needed no therapy and was no cause for concern. At last, all the worry about an ovarian tumor was over.

I have also picked up another half-dozen ovarian tumors in women who had seen their gynecologists within the past few months. Doctors must pay more attention to their patients' complaints. They should also spend more time performing a thorough, careful, methodical pelvic examination.

Diagnosis of Ovarian Cancer

If your physician finds a mass on pelvic examination, then it is important to try to determine whether that mass is a uterine fibroid, an intestinal tumor, or an ovarian cancer. Each of these requires a somewhat different approach and therapy.

Ultrasound

One of the easiest and best methods of diagnosis is pelvic ultrasound or sonography. Ultrasound uses painless, high-frequency sound waves to "visualize" organs inside the body. The examination begins with a light application of oil to your abdomen. A small probe, called a transducer, is held against the skin and sends sound waves into the body. The transducer also listens for returning echoes that are reflected off the internal organs. These echoes are converted by computer into a visual image on a television screen. Permanent photographs, film, or videotape records are kept of the examination.

There is a no radiation involved. Furthermore, sonography is 80 to 90 percent accurate in diagnosing the size, location, and consistency of ovarian tumors and in separating ovarian tumors from uterine fibroids. Failures of ultrasound occur when the pelvic mass is 2 centimeters or less in diameter. It also cannot differentiate some other pelvic problems, such as endometriosis or pelvic inflammatory disease, from ovarian tumors. However, ultrasound is easy from the patient's point of view and has no contraindications. I tend to order pelvic sonograms freely. I use them to confirm my pelvic examination findings, to give me a better idea as to the exact consistency of a mass I am feeling, i.e., whether it is solid or fluid filled, and to provide a precise measurement that I can compare with another sonogram measurement in the next month or two to come.

CAT Scan

Computerized axial tomograph (CAT scan) is another method for diagnosing a suspect pelvic mass. This method does involve radiation as well as the risk of reaction to contrast dyes that are sometimes used during the procedure. It also has the disadvantage that there may not be good detail in very obese or very thin patients. It would be fair to say that there is room for much improvement in both ultrasound and CAT scan methods.

Laparoscopy

Laparoscopy provides an opportunity for a direct view of the patient's ovaries. Commonly called Band-Aid surgery, laparoscopy requires an incision about an inch long, made near the navel. The laparoscope is a tube slightly longer than a pencil, which is inserted into the abdomen. Fiberoptic light illuminates the inside of the abdomen. The laparoscope functions like a hollow flashlight, enabling the surgeon to see the ovaries and other internal organs. This is obviously an important alternative to full surgery in distinguishing benign uterine conditions and benign ovarian pathology from ovarian cancer. It can spare many patients with a pelvic mass the risk of actual abdominal surgery, for many of them have benign disease that does not require it.

Surgical Staging

Survival rates in most ovarian malignancies are determined purely by the tumor's stage, that is, whether it is limited or has spread to other areas. Consequently, the best prognosis occurs when lesions are strictly confined to the ovaries. When the tumor has broken through the surface of the ovary, the tumor cells may shed into the abdominal cavity and spread. Here the prognosis is somewhat worse.

The Cancer Committee of the International Federation of Gynecology and Obstetrics (FIGO) has recommended the following classification of the progressive stages of tumor growth:

Stage I.   Growth limited to the ovaries.
    Ia.   Growth limited to *one* ovary; no ascites.*
        1. No tumor present on the external surface of the ovary; the ovarian capsule remains intact; i.e., all the tumor is confined to the inner portions of the ovary and has not broken through the covering of the ovary.
        2. Tumor present on the external surface of the ovary and/or capsule ruptured by tumor breaking through its surface.
    Ib.   Growth limited to *both* ovaries; no ascites.
        1. No tumor on the external surface; capsule intact.
        2. Tumor present on the external surface and/or capsule(s) ruptured.
    Ic.   Tumor either stage Ia or stage Ib, but with ascites or positive peritoneal washings.†
Stage II.   Growth involving one or both ovaries with pelvic extension.
Stage IIa. Extension and/or metastases to the uterus and/or tubes.
    IIb.   Extension to other pelvic tissues.
    IIc.   Tumor either stage IIa or IIb, but with ascites or positive peritoneal washings.
Stage III. Growth involving one or both ovaries, with widespread metastases within the abdomen or with

*Ascites is an accumulation of fluid in the abdominal cavity which exceeds normal amounts.

†Positive peritoneal washings refer to the fact that fluid sampled from the abdominal cavity is seen to contain cancer cells under microscopic examination.

microscopically proven malignant extension to small bowel or omentum or lymph node chains that are located between the back and the abdominal cavity.

Stage IV.   Growth involving one or both ovaries with distant metastases.

Special Category: Unexplored cases which are thought to be ovarian cancer.

Remember, not all enlarged ovaries are dangerous. However, the following need to be *thoroughly* investigated:

1. Any ovary 10 centimeters or larger in any age group is dangerous. It is extremely rare to see functional (corpus luteum or follicle) cysts or even an endometriosis cyst of this size. Therefore, any cysts of this size would be highly suspect.

2. Any ovarian enlargement that occurs after menopause.

3. Any mass in the area of the ovaries in a woman of any age that progressively enlarges beyond 5 cm while under observation, particularly if it remains that size after her period. It is important to know that of cancers that are discovered in the ovaries, 95 percent are more than 5 cm in diamater. Therefore, the finding of a 5 cm or larger ovarian mass on pelvic examination, especially in a 40- to 60-year-old patient, requires further evaluation for malignancy. Exceptions would be a 5 cm cystic mass in a young mestruating woman which may be a benign functional cyst. This should be treated with observation and/or hormonal therapy. However, if after two months of treatment, no decrease in size occurs, it should also be suspected of being an ovarian malignancy.

4. Any persistence or new appearance of an ovarian mass while a woman is on an oral contraceptive.

5. A mass that cannot definitely be diagnosed as a fibroid. A pelvic mass must be considered an ovarian cancer until both ovaries are identified as being normal on palpation.

6. A normal-size ovary in the premenopausal woman represents an ovarian tumor in the postmenopausal woman.

Meigs' Syndrome

I must at least mention that sometimes all the classical signs of ovarian cancer are present, yet a benign tumor is found to be the culprit. This condition is known as Meigs' syndrome.

Usually the symptoms are ominous. The woman has increasing abdominal girth, often described as bloating, and her skirts and pants become tight. Her legs may ache and she may feel short of breath. Her physician finds a substantial amount of fluid accumulation within her abdominal cavity. Moreover, X rays may reveal that she also has fluid surrounding her lungs. The diagnosis must be made by a complete cancer workup and surgery. But here the good news is that the tumor that is removed is benign, and soon after it is removed, the fluid within the abdomen and lung cavity disappears.

Treatment

If the results of your workup point to a diagnosis of ovarian cancer, you must assume an all-out aggressive attitude to fight the tumor. The horizontal bikini-type incision (pfannensteil incision) at the top of the pubic hairline that women have grown accustomed to for routine hysterectomy is not for you. Your surgeon will have to make a long vertical incision. He must explore the entire inside of your abdomen, not just the pelvic portion. So plan on the old-fashioned up- and-down incision.

I would also personally advise a patient of mine whose workup was highly indicative of an ovarian tumor to seek the services of a gynecologic oncology surgeon at a fairly large medical center. The gynecologic oncologist will have better training in cancer surgery than the general gynecologist. He will know that it is important to look under the diaphragm for tiny metastases. He will also know how to remove the omentum (the loose membrane covering the small intestine) which improves survival in patients with early ovarian cancer and be trained in how to biopsy the pelvic and para-aortic nodes. He will head the team that integrates the woman's care. That team should include her family doctor or gynecologist, a medical oncologist, a surgical pathologist, and possibly a radiation therapist.

I sent a twenty-two-year-old patient to a local teaching hospital when, at her routine physical exam, I thought her right ovary felt irregular in shape and of not quite the right consistency. The residents there could find nothing unusual. Unwilling to let it go, I ordered a sonogram, which yielded suspect results. When she underwent laparoscopy, the gyn-oncologist found an early cancer of her ovaries, and her ovaries and uterus were removed. I felt strongly that for her best chance of survival, this very young woman needed chemotherapy in the hands of someone especially experienced in the treatment of ovarian tumors. So after surgery, I had her transferred to a major cancer center. Seven years later, she is alive and well and free of disease.

On the other hand, I saw a forty-one-year-old patient who was thought to have a right tubal abscess because of an old case of pelvic inflammatory disease (PID). I was suspicious of this ''abscess'' and ordered a sonogram. It showed a complex mass with multiple solid elements within which no normal ovary could be identified. I sent her to a fine gynecological oncologist in her own state. She turned out to have an ovarian cancer buried in scar tissue from her previous PID. She too is alive and well, for her tumor was caught early and was of a type that grows slowly.

Preoperative Evaluation

A thorough preoperative workup and a physician with extensive experience in tumor surgery are essential for good results in these cancers.

Aside from physician examination, ultrasound examination, and CAT scan or laparoscopy where indicated, before under-going abdominal surgery, women with a suspected ovarian cancer should have blood tests and X-ray examinations to rule out tumors elsewhere that may have spread to or from the ovary. The following tests should be performed:

1. A chest X ray should be done to check the lungs.
2. A barium enema should be performed because of the high frequency with which colon cancer metastasizes to the ovary.
3. An upper gastrointestinal (GI series) examination checks for stomach cancer.
4. An IVP, or intravenous pyelogram, can rule out the possibility that the doctor is feeling a kidney that is situated very low in the pelvis and not an ovarian cancer. Pelvic kidneys are fairly common. Sometimes this exam also reveals tumor involvement of the tubes that lead from the kidney into the bladder.
5. Blood tests, which are easily done, can reveal abnormal liver chemistries, indicating that liver metastases may have occurred.

Most patients will undergo chemotherapy or radiation therapy after surgery to destroy any microscopic cancer cells that might remain in the body. Even if there is a tumor so large that it can't be totally removed, surgery should remove or debulk as much of it as possible. This rids the patient of a large volume of cancer cells and gives chemotherapy the best of all possible chances to work. The anticancer drugs work by eliminating a certain percentage of cells during the various phases of their growth cycles. Therefore, results are best when fewer cells are physically present. This is also true with radiation therapy.

Reducing the volume of the tumor is important also because the tumor itself is an immunosuppressant agent; that is, it interferes with the patient's own immune system. Less tumor should mean less immune suppression, which should aid in restoring the patient's immune competence.

Tumor Markers

One of the most exciting areas of tumor study involves the effort now being made to diagnose ovarian cancer by means of a test for substances in the blood, called tumor markers, which indicate the presence of ovarian cancer. Because of the lack of symptoms in early ovarian cancer, early diagnosis rests upon the development of such a specific test. Unfortunately the tests that are currently available are not sensitive enough yet to be used for early diagnosis. But research is continuing, and there is a great deal of optimism in scientific circles that a method for early detection of ovarian cancer will be forthcoming in this decade.

A radioimmunoassay using a monoclonal antibody to monitor the course of the common epithelian ovarian cancer has been introduced by R. C. Bast and his colleagues from Boston. With this method, rising and falling levels of the tumor antigen can be correlated with progression or regression of disease in 93 percent of the cases studied. The Research Ovarian Carcinoma team at Lenox Hill Hospital in New York is working on a similar project using an enzyme-linked immunosorbent assay technique which should be a thousand times more sensitive than the radioimmunoassay method.

Vaccine

Currently Hollinshead and Barber are working on an ovarian cancer vaccine. It has been cleared by the Food and Drug Administration and the Bureau of Biologics for human use and is currently in experimental use with patients who have advanced epithelial ovarian cancer in stages IIb and III. These women have had surgery to remove as much of the cancer as possible. Half of the patients are randomly assigned to the vaccine, the other half to placebo. To date, it is apparent that the vaccine produces no major side effects. Its therapeutic effects will be determined as the investigators follow the course of the disease in these women.

As you are now aware, it was certainly not possible to title this chapter No More Ovarian Cancer. Ovarian cancer presents a real problem to women and a real challenge to physicians. This chapter was written to make you aware of the existence of the problem and to make you aware of the many small symptoms that you might have been ignoring, but which might be significant. It was also written to get you to your doctor once every six months for a pelvic examination if you are over forty. And if you are obese or if your pelvic examination is unsatisfactory for any other reason, get a pelvic sonogram. This simple test may give you and your physician the information that could set your mind at ease or begin a series of investigations. Ovarian cancer is not a pleasant subject, but it is one that should be part of your medical knowledge about your own body, for this information may truly save your life.

7

Urinary Tract Infections

The National Center for Health Statistics reports that lower urinary tract infection (UTI)—cystitis and urethritis—accounts for more than 5 million visits to doctors' offices per year in the United States. One fourth to one third of all women between the ages of twenty and forty have been diagnosed as having a UTI at one time or another. It is a much more common problem for women than men, and 80 percent of sufferers will have a recurrence of the problem.

A UTI is classified according to the site of the infection. Urethritis is an infection of the urethra (the tube through which urine flows out from the bladder), cystitis affects primarily the bladder, and pyelonephritis, the most serious of the three, affects and may damage the kidney. Urethritis and cystitis are relatively benign infections, but if they are ignored, they can sometimes lead to pyelonephritis, which often brings chills, fever, and back pain, sometimes accompanied by nausea and vomiting. Thus it is important to treat cystitis and urethritis early and prevent more serious problems. However, bacteria can reach the kidney directly through the bloodstream—from an abscessed tooth, for example. But the ascending route, with infection spreading from the urethra and bladder to the kidneys, is much more common.

Symptoms

Common symptoms of UTI are dysuria (pain with urination); increased frequency of urination, with the patient often feeling a need to void with only a tiny amount of urine present; and hematuria (bloody urine). All these symptoms may develop within just a few hours. Sometimes the patient will also note a bad odor to her urine or that it seems cloudy rather than clear. She will also often note a dull lower abdominal pain that intensifies as urination is completed. Approximately 50 percent of women with these symptoms have positive urine cultures containing such organisms as *Escherichia coli* (*E. coli* for short), *Proteus, Enterobacter, Enterococci, Klebsiella, Pseudomonas,* or *Staphylococci*. Most of these bacteria are normally found in the intestinal tract.

Approximately 20 percent of symptomatic women do not show enough bacteria to be considered significant, and 30 percent may have completely sterile cultures, in which no bacterial growth occurred. These sterile urine cultures usually mean that the patient has no bacterial infection, but she could have a viral or *Chlamydia trachomatis* infection. These organisms do not grow in the usual culture media used for bacteria, and outside of research labs and state health departments, few laboratories are yet able to culture them. However, new rapid ways of diagnosing *Chlamydia* by "fluorescent" antibody techniques are now being marketed and will soon be available for use in clinics or doctors' offices.

Causes of UTI

There are many possible explanations of why women are affected three times more than men. First, a woman's anatomy makes her more vulnerable. Her urethra is much shorter than a man's, which stretches from his bladder to its outlet on his penis. In women, bacteria have a much shorter distance to travel from the outside of her body to her bladder. A woman's urethra is also in very close proximity to the vagina and the rectum, making contamination easy. Fecal or vaginal contamination can occur if a woman wipes herself improperly after a bowel movement or urination. The correct hygienic technique is to wipe from front to back with one wipe. This prevents transporting fecal bacteria to the area of the urethral opening.

Sexual intercourse, with the thrusting and massaging action of the penis, can actually cause bacteria to be pushed up into the bladder. To counteract this, a woman should empty her bladder prior to intercourse, because an empty bladder is less susceptible to infection, and within ten minutes afterward to mechanically wash bacteria out of her urethra. Also, allowing sufficient time for foreplay will aid lubrication and help protect the urethra from irritation. If necessary, one of the new excellent lubricants that are now marketed specifically for this purpose—Transi-Lube, Personal Lubricant, K-Y jelly, Surgilube, to name a few—can be used.

Women who have the anatomical opening of their urethra within the vagina may be more susceptible to recurrent infection from sexual trauma or because the area is constantly bathed in vaginal secretions.

The presence of vaginitis may cause confusing symptoms for the patient and her physician. Because her tissues are irritated, this patient also complains about burning on urination. However, she usually does not have frequency of urination, and the burning is produced only as the urine touches the irritated genital area. In such circumstances, it is necessary that a pelvic examination also be performed. A vaginal culture might be in order, or examination of the vaginal discharge under the microscope might reveal the presence of *Trichomonas vaginalis,* a tiny motile organism which has the ability to create marked discomfort. *Chlamydia trachomatis* also may cause urethritis in women, much as it does in men. Certainly this organism must be thought of in sexually active women who have recently met new partners. It is probably the most common sexually transmitted urethritis in men in the United States, more common than gonorrheal urethritis.

And while we are on the subject of men, if you are frustrated because of recurrent or chronic infections, it might not be a bad idea to send your partner to the urologist to make sure that he is not the source of your problem. If he has an infection, it is possible that by clearing it up, your troubles will go away, too. Many men have infections and yet are asymptomatic.

Certain sexual practices may transport foreign bacteria to

the urethra. One patient who had recurrent vaginitis and cystitis told me that she had given up her usual sexual activity and was only having orogenital sex, but her problem was worse than ever. I reminded her that the human mouth carries many bacteria and yeasts (fungi) as well. I treated her and told her to go back to her regular sexual habits and discontinue orogenital sex. Six weeks later, she was "cured." Rectogenital sex can also spread bacteria to the urethra, and the use of a vaginal vibrator may lead to urethritis or cystitis because of its mechanical irritation of the area. •

Sometimes bacteria are introduced into the urethra by medical instruments when it is dilated in the urologist's office or when a catheter is inserted. *Contact with instruments in the doctor's office should be avoided during acute infection.* Cystoscopy and dilation of the infected and inflamed tissue only spread the disease.

Diagnosis

Male urinary tract infections are easy to diagnose. If pus is present in the urine, the man has a urinary tract infection. But pus in female urine may be coming from her vagina, because its opening is so close to the urethral opening. If the woman has vaginitis, a large quantity of pus (white blood cells) will be present, creating a vaginal discharge, or if the time is just before, during, or after her period, red blood cells from her vagina may drop into the specimen cup and confuse the diagnosis. So to decrease the chance of contamination of the urine specimen, patients are asked to provide a "mid-stream, clean-catch specimen." After first washing the genital area, they wipe themselves and void the first part of the urine directly into the toilet. Then they catch the rest of the specimen in a sterile container without touching the inside to their body or with their fingers. Then the container is carefully closed with a sterile cap. Inserting a tampon prior to giving the specimen assures that vaginal contamination of the specimen will not occur. This is necessary when the woman is menstruating or has a heavy vaginal discharge.

If the urine shows abnormal numbers of white blood cells

or of both red and white blood cells, infection is probably present, and it is important to identify the number and type of the bacteria that are causing it.* To do this, the bacteria from the urine specimen are grown in the laboratory, identified, and tested for their sensitivity to various antibiotics. If such testing isn't done, the patient may not get the correct antibiotic, the bacteria will not be destroyed, and the patient won't get well. The culture should be obtained before the patient begins antibiotic treatment. But since first cases of cystitis and certain uncomplicated cases are most often caused by *E. coli*, many physicians immediately treat such cases with sulfa drugs, ampicillin, tetracycline, nitrofurantoin, or nalidixic acid, all of which work against this bacteria.

If the patient does not improve, then a culture is taken and, once the results are known, the patient can be put on an appropriate antibiotic. For most first infections, any one of these antibiotics usually suffices, and therefore some physicians don't consider a bacterial culture cost effective.

Treatment

If possible, I initially culture all patients. Because symptoms are severe in so many cases, I begin treating the patient with antibiotics immediately and have the patient call forty-eight hours later, when the culture and sensitivity results are completed, to make sure that the antibiotic is the correct one. If all is well, I remind them to complete *all* their medication and not to stop taking it just because their symptoms have gone away. We must do more than just hinder the bacterial growth—we must kill them all! Some women take only some of their medication, feel better; and stop taking the drug. But a partial dose doesn't kill all the bacteria, and those that survive are the ones best able to resist the antibiotic. With the medication now prematurely gone, these remaining bacteria take over, multiplying and producing a super strain of son and daughter bacteria that have learned how to live and grow with the antibiotic. And now when the woman gets her symptoms

*For information as to how proper urinalysis should be done, see page 306.

back and takes the same antibiotic again, it doesn't work. In this way, patients create their own resistant organisms and must have a repeat culture and sensitivity test done to see what other antibiotic will work now. This is why it is important to follow instructions and complete any medication regimen that is prescribed. Often it is not the total number of days that are important but the total dose of drug. New antibiotic regimens are currently being investigated which give the drug in a large dose over a day or two. But until these are perfected, please take all your medication as the doctor has ordered.

I also instruct my patients to rest. For some reason, women with urinary tract infections never consider themselves sick and therefore do not consider rest important. If I tell a patient that she has bronchitis, she will put herself to bed so that her body can have a better chance at fighting the infection. But women with urinary tract infections often ignore them and go on working, traveling, or partying and almost never consider getting extra rest. They rely totally on the antibiotic to cure them of all their ills. That is wrong. Infection is infection, whether it is in your lungs or bladder or kidney. All locations demand the same respect and concern.

In addition, I instruct my UTI patients to increase their fluid intake enough to make the urine colorless. Increased urine output dilutes the bacteria, and frequent voiding removes infected urine. Increasing fluids also aids the action of the antibiotics. Sulfa drugs especially should be accompanied by eight glasses of fluid per day, preferably water.

Acidification of urine will increase the antibacterial activity of tetracycline and nitrofurantion (Furadantin). But it won't affect the activity of ampicillin or nalidixic acid (NegGram), and it decreases the effect of sulfonamides, penicillins, and aminoglycosides. Cranberry juice or vitamin C make the urine acid. If they are compatible with your antibiotic, you may wish to take your fluids in the form of cranberry juice. On the other hand, if you are being treated with antibiotics such as erythromycin or sulfa, dietary intake of fruits and milk will make your urine more alkaline and increase the activity of these drugs.

After your antibiotic treatment is completed, it is a good idea to try to keep your fluid intake high and drink cranberry juice in order to help keep your urine acid. This creates an environment in which bacteria are less able to multiply. Some physicians prescribe drugs such as Mandelamine, Hiprex, or Urex to keep their patients' urine acid.

Increasing fluid intake is a good idea generally. Women who void infrequently are more prone to UTI. Holding the bladder full for long periods makes it overdistended, which interfers with the blood flow within the bladder walls and thus impairs resistance to infection. Women who void only twice per day have more urinary infections than those who do so the optimum four to six times daily. Men who void infrequently, such as truck drivers and bus drivers, are also more prone to urinary tract infection, which is otherwise uncommon in men. Medications such as antispasmodics, antihistamines, anticholinergics, and sometimes tranquilizers may interfere with the normal voiding action of urinary tract muscles and make it difficult to urinate or cause patients to develop urinary retention.

Relapse, or bacterial persistence, is defined as a recurrence of infection with the same bacteria usually within two weeks after stopping therapy. An X-ray study called an IVP may be needed in some cases to rule out any abnormalities of the genitourinary tract, such as stone formation or obstruction that prevents complete clearing of the infection. Some patients have an abnormality in the urinary tract that causes improper flow of urine (stasis). A cystocele or a defect in the bladder muscle wall may keep the bladder from emptying completely. Such residual urine becomes a chronic source of infection and will predispose patients to the development of recurrent cystitis. An obstruction to the outflow of urine, such as stenosis (narrowing) or scarring in the urethra will also increase the chance for urinary tract infection. Women who have recurrent cystitis should take care to empty the bladder completely and maintain an acid pH and a free flow of urine. If no anatomic problems are found, they should have new sensitivity tests to guide the selection of an appropriate antibiotic. They then may be advised to undertake a longer course of therapy or to empty their bladder after intercourse and then take an antibiotic.

Reinfection refers to a new infection with a different organism. Women who become reinfected are candidates for long-term prophylaxis. For example, for the women whose reinfections seem to be directly related to her sexual activity, taking an antibiotic just before or after intercourse may be considered. Such women should carefully cleanse the vulvar area and make sure that they void as soon as possible after intercourse to push any bacteria out of the urethra mechanically. Reinfection should be treated for the usual ten to fourteen days, and some women may also need appropriate prophylactic therapy.

Urethral syndrome is one of the commonest complaints of women. Such women have perineal pain and discomfort, and a feeling of incomplete emptying of their bladder as well as frequency and urgency. They do not, however, usually complain about awakening at night to urinate. Cultures of the urine are invariably negative. If a flow study is done on these patients, the urinary stream often reflects some degree of intermittency with a poor flow. The poor flow is not based on a real obstruction, but is due to spasms of the external sphincter muscles. These patients may undergo urethral dilations which dilate the external sphincter, relax it for a short time, and then the symptoms return once the external sphincter regains its tone.

I believe that if these women are taught to relax while voiding and are aware that urethral syndrome is a manifestation of anxiety, then a lot of unnecessary urethral dilations and trauma to the urethra can be prevented. Once that patient understands the basic underlying problem and is aware that anxiety can provide the symptoms in much the same way as anxiety can produce a tension headache, they are able to stop taking antibiotics and avoid additional procedures to the urethra—which has already been sufficiently mutilated.

Interstitial cystitis is fairly rare when compared to the problems described above, but this chapter would not be complete without its mention. Interstitial cystitis causes pain and frequent urination with urgency. Such patients have around-the-clock frequent voiding and find such voiding relieves their abdominal pain. Such patients are often incapacitated by their symptoms even though culture after culture proves to be negative, and many are labeled as neurotic.

Most of these women have a bladder capacity of less than 200 cc. The bladder is seen to undergo ulceration and hemorrhage when the urologist gently distends it with water. Management of these patients includes passive bladder dilation—that patient is advised to delay voiding for as long as possible and to increase their fluid intake at the same time. In addition, they are given anticholinergic drugs to decrease their bladder sensations and reduce the urge to void, and occasionally they are given prophylactic antibiotics. Those that fail are brought into the hospital and have their bladder dilated mechanically with a balloon or just a regular catheter. This will increase the bladder capacity and also cause a decrease in tone of the muscle. Invariably, the patient benefits from the procedure for several weeks. Those patients who do not respond to repeated bladder dilations or any other form of conservative treatment can be dramatically helped by excision of the dome of the bladder and replacing this with a segment of cecum (part of the bowel).

Some women are simply more prone to UTIs than others. They probably have some unknown factors that predispose them to infection. There is also evidence that these women have large numbers of intestinal bacteria in the area of the vaginal and urethral openings. One study found that such bacteria are rarely found in this area in uninfected women. Perhaps the normal defense mechanisms break down in some women. A few experts blame this on deficiency of immunoglobulins; others on evidence that such women have a greater amount of bacterial adherence to the cells lining the bladder.

I feel that close follow-up of patients with UTIs will prevent many infections from becoming chronic. My patients have their urine checked for the second time when they are on their second to sixth day of therapy. Urines are rechecked on day 2 if patients are still symptomatic, because they should be feeling much better by then. The majority do well, however, and they bring in their second specimen on day 5 or 6 or in some cases when therapy is ending. I then ask to see them seven to fourteen days after discontinuing therapy, not for an office call but just to check their urine once more. If it is satisfactory and this was their first case of cystitis, this ends the follow-up. But if they have had two or more cases of infection, I like to recheck one more time, two weeks later. I want to make sure that the problem has not recurred, and if it has, I want to be the first to know about it. By closely monitoring a patient's progress, I have had few cases of problem-persistent infections. I think it is really important to stay on top of the situation—to control infections early and completely and then to check and recheck to make sure that you really have done all that is necessary. The cost is low; urinalyses are cheap. But the physical and financial cost to a patient who develops a chronic infection or one that ascends to infect and possibly destroy her kidneys is dear.

I also consider any woman with painful and frequent urination to be an emergency. She is always treated the day she calls if it is at all possible. The longer the infection has to get a foothold, the harder it may be to get rid of. Besides, no patient should have to suffer from the symptoms of a problem that in nearly all cases can be quickly alleviated.

Some patients, however, put off calling, thinking that the infection will go away by itself. Delays may lead to pain upon urination that is so severe they finally are unable to urinate. I immediately start antibiotic therapy and add a medication to soothe the irritation, but for a while, these women may find it possible to urinate only while sitting in a warm bath or in a sitz.

Other patients may panic when they discover that their urine is red. Hematuria, blood in the urine, may be microscopic and produce a smoky or red-brown color urine, or it may contain enough red blood cells to look exactly like one is urinating blood. In younger women, this is most often associated with acute urinary tract infection. Bleeding may come from inflammation caused by infection either in the bladder or, less often, in the kidneys. However, in women between fifty and sixty years old, the most common cause of such bleeding is a kidney tumor; between sixty and eighty years old, a bladder tumor. A stone anywhere in the urinary tract system may also be the culprit. A small stone that is being passed is ordinarily accompanied by severe colicky pain. Yet a large stone lodged securely in the kidney may create hematuria but no pain.

There are long lists of causes of hematuria, from anticoagulants, anticancer drugs, and even drugs like Pyridium, which color the urine orange and may be confused with bleeding; to many diseases which can affect the kidneys and cause bleeding into the urine. So if you have hematuria, your physician may want to order some standard laboratory blood tests as well as a routine urinalysis and culture. Make sure that the source of bleeding is documented if you are forty or over. This will often involve consultation with a urologist or a gynecologist who is well versed in and used to dealing with such problems. Be satisfied that your care is thorough and that you receive sufficient follow-up until the problem has completely cleared up. Or if the problem won't clear up, at least get a satisfactory explanation of the cause or seek a second opinion.

8

No More Urinary Incontinence

What could possibly be more devastating than to be dressed in your newest frock, standing at a cocktail party, when someone tells a joke and you suddenly realize that your own laughter has started a stream of urine running down your leg. Or it might happen with a cough or sneeze, or running to catch a bus. No matter when it occurs, it's awful and enough to make any sane woman panic. Yet many women suffer from this problem and live with it. Some are forced to wear sanitary napkins to avoid unexpected episodes; some never stray too far from a ladies' room.

The problem of urinary incontinence in women is often due to the trauma of giving birth, but it is also a result of the normal aging process and is accentuated by the loss of estrogen. When you realize that the pelvic organs (the uterus and bladder) are held in place against the forces of gravity only by muscles and ligaments, it isn't surprising that the general relaxing of aging tissue brings on such complaints.

Most women have the problem in a mild form and may only note that their underwear is wet from time to time. Others may have severe and uncontrollable urinary loss, and they become asocial and live hermitlike for fear of accidents or offending odor.

Hormone replacement therapy (as we saw in Chapter 2) can reverse thinning and atrophy of the bladder, urethra, and vaginal lining. Although treatment with estrogen can't reverse the already stretched and damaged ligaments, it can help restore the blood flow to them and possibly strengthen them. Hormone replacement is most beneficial as a preventive measure against muscle relaxation in the pelvic area, for it helps slow the loss of muscle tone. Given to a patient prior to surgery, it improves the surgical outcome and speeds healing.

Problems occur when stress on the uterus, bladder, or rectum becomes greater than the strength in the supporting tissue. Once this occurs, it may be difficult to correct these changes without surgery. Any of the pelvic organs, including the uterus, the bladder, the rectum, and even the vagina itself, can sag once their anatomic support is lost. Sometimes the problem is singular, involving only one organ; sometimes several together are involved. Here are a few examples of the kinds of problems women may face with pelvic relaxation.

Uterine prolapse. The uterine ligaments and muscles of the pelvic floor that support the uterus may be stretched or torn in childbirth. As these women age, their damaged muscles lose more tone and allow the uterus to descend into the vagina. This condition is known as uterine prolapse. (It occasionally occurs in nulliparous women also.)

The woman may become increasingly aware of a bearing-down discomfort as well as a mass within the vagina that may suddenly protrude from the vagina upon exertion. She may also have discomfort walking or sitting, and suffer from bladder problems. In first-degree prolapse, the uterus descends slightly from the apex of the vagina. In second-degree prolapse, the uterus descends further so that the cervix or neck of the uterus protrudes from the opening of the vagina. The most rare form, third-degree prolapse, occurs when the entire uterus is exposed between the patient's legs, having dropped outside the vagina.

Cystocele. In the front wall of the vagina, a layer of supporting tissue holds the bladder and urethra in place. If this supporting tissue is weakened, the bladder may drop down into the vagina, causing a bulge called a cystocele. A large cystocele acts as a reservoir and never empties completely, leaving stagnant urine in the bladder and providing an area for bacteria to multiply, causing chronic infection. Sometimes, unless surgical repair is done, a woman will suffer multiple recurrent urinary infections that never seem to clear up.

Enterocele. If the supporting tissues weaken in other portions of the vagina, other organs may be affected. When the uterus descends, abdominal contents such as the small intestine may bulge into the roof of the vagina, creating an enterocele. Women with an enterocele often complain of a dull ache in their lower abdomen when they are on their feet for prolonged periods of time. Occasionally a segment of the small intestine may actually get caught in the enterocele and cause a surgical emergency.

Many physicians do not understand the significance of this type of hernia and therefore frequently miss it during the pelvic examination. If surgery is performed for uterine prolapse and a significant enterocele is present, the enterocele must also be repaired. If it isn't, a vaginal prolapse can occur following surgery.

Rectocele. Weakened support on the back wall or floor of the vagina can allow the rectum to bulge into the vaginal canal, causing a rectocele. Passing stool may become difficult, and in severe cases, the patient may have to assist her bowel movements with manual pressure. She does this by inserting her hand into her vagina and applying pressure against the rectum from the vaginal side.

Once these conditions have developed, it may be difficult to reverse them without surgery, but there are exercises you can do to forestall or alleviate the problem. Some of the muscles in the floor of the pelvis are striated or voluntarily controlled, and they can be exercised and strengthened like other muscles in the body. The principal ones in this group are the levators, which raise the pelvic floor. Exercises to strengthen this set of muscles are often called Kegel's exercises, after the man who described them. I tell my patients to imagine they are urinating and need to stop the urine in the middle of the flow. By contracting and releasing these muscles one to two hundred times a day, it may be possible to strengthen them enough to relieve many of the symptoms of pelvic relaxation. That may sound like a lot of work and time, but the exercises can easily be done in ten to fifteen minutes.

The amount of time that the contraction is held is not critical; what *is* important is the number of times that the muscle is contracted. Therefore, the exercises can be done very rapidly. You can do them while driving your car and waiting for a red light to change, or while watching TV.

Causes of Urinary Incontinence

One of the most common symptoms of pelvic relaxation is undesired leakage of urine. Many physicians immediately consider this a reason to operate. But it is extremely important to find a doctor with some expertise, for there are many causes of urinary incontinence that do not require surgery. In fact, in some cases, surgery will only make the symptoms worse.

Although this problem may seem difficult to understand, it is really quite simple. Water (or urine) runs to the location of lowest pressure. Normally the pressure in the urethra* is greater than that in the bladder. This keeps the urine in the bladder until you are ready to void. When you urinate, a number of physiologic events take place simultaneously—the voluntary muscles in the pelvic floor relax while the smooth, involuntary muscles in the bladder wall contract. Thus the pressure in the contracting bladder becomes higher than in the relaxing urethra and urine flows out. The causes for urinary incontinence, therefore, can be divided into those that lower the pressure in the urethra and those that raise the pressure in the bladder.

An evaluation of urinary incontinence should give careful consideration to all the possible factors, including those that follow.

Cystitis

Perhaps the most important cause of increased bladder pressure is infection or cystitis. When the bladder becomes infected, the trigone or base of the bladder and the bladder

*The tube that carries urine from the bladder to the outside of the body.

wall itself become extremely irritated. This causes the bladder to contract, thus raising the pressure. For this reason, any evaluation of incontinence must begin with a laboratory culture to rule out the presence of infection. Often, appropriate antibiotic therapy is all that is needed to correct the problem. Because cystitis is usually accompanied by an urge to void and often by pain during urination itself, it is referred to as urgency incontinence.

Postmenopausal Atrophy

Occasionally older patients may feel sharp urges to urinate yet repeatedly have negative urine cultures in the lab. This may be due to an inflammatory change in the bladder lining that is often associated with postmenopausal vaginal atrophy. Applying vaginal estrogen cream to the vaginal tissues or taking estrogen by mouth will often alleviate both the atrophy and the leakage of urine.

Bladder Muscle Dysfunction

Another cause of increased bladder pressure is malfunction of the nerves and muscles in the bladder wall. In a condition called *detrusor hyperreflexia*, the irritable bladder muscles contract constantly in response to a cough or other minor stimulus. This causes constant involuntary emptying of the bladder, even when only a small amount of urine is present. Medications that sedate the unstable bladder muscles may cure this form of incontinence.

One of my new patients came to the office complaining about constant loss of urine. She had had a hysterectomy and bladder repair for incontinence some six months earlier. Her problem was so severe that she was confined to the house and forced to wear sanitary napkins all the time. Her gynecologist wanted to redo her surgery, but she was unwilling and afraid. Her worst problem was that her son was getting married. She desperately wanted to go to his wedding but felt unable to make the long trip and be in the wedding party. She was willing to be catheterized and wear a bag to collect her urine for the occasion, but I thought an antispasmodic medication to soothe her bladder might be worth a try. So I started her on one pill every twelve hours, and unbelievably, in two weeks she was completely cured of her incontinence. She has since been able to do anything, go anywhere, and no longer worry. Obviously she was a patient who had hyperactive function of the bladder muscle, which never would have been cured by further surgery. She merely needed a drug to stop the constant emptying of the bladder by the hyperactive muscle.

In other cases, the reverse problem can cause leakage of urine. When nerves associated with the bladder muscles are damaged from diabetes mellitus or severe neurologic disease, the bladder may not recognize the signal that it is filling. It therefore doesn't contract, and the result is "overflow" incontinence as the overdistended bladder spurts urine during stress. Patients with this condition, referred to as neurogenic bladder, should not be considered surgical candidates. Therapy is based on frequent voiding to keep the amount of urine in the bladder at a minimum.

Emotional Factors

Emotional factors have recently been recognized as a cause of incontinence. In psychogenic incontinence, a stressful event such as the loss of a family member or a traumatic divorce is the cause of the undesired leakage of urine. When this symptom first appears after an emotional event, time alone may be all that is necessary to heal the patient. Surgery for incontinence should be avoided during this period of adjustment.

Then there are those women who have giggle incontinence. Simply put, they have urinary leakage whenever they giggle, and the phenomenon has existed since they were little girls. The cause of giggle incontinence has never been established.

Finding the Causes of Incontinence

A careful examination should always be performed when urinary incontinence appears. Problems may sometimes be found in the neurologic system. Even atherosclerosis (hardening of the arteries) may contribute to problems in the bladder.

Urethroscopy

One of the most important parts of the examination is urethroscopy. By inserting a narrow tube with lights and a lense into the urethra, the doctor can actually see areas of infection or scar tissue. Repeated infections at the base of the bladder can cause chronic inflammation and narrowing of the urethra itself, which may be treated by urethral dilatation, or stretching of the urethra. This process should only be done after urethroscopy has shown that the urethra has indeed been narrowed by infection.

The procedure should be performed gently, using topically applied jelly to anesthetize the tissues. I have often been angered by the callous way women are treated in some urologists' office. The urethral dilatation should not be attempted until the anesthetic jelly has had ten to fifteen minutes to numb the tissues. More often than not, the jelly is applied and dilatation immediately follows before the tissues are anesthetized. This can be very painful. Sacrificing comfort is unforgivable when another five minutes would ensure a painless procedure. Dilatation should not be performed when there are signs of active infection, for this also increases the patient's pain and suffering, and may tend to spread the infection. Therefore, the patient should first be evaluated, then cultured and treated. When the area is no longer infected or inflamed, the urethra can be dilated if scarring and narrowing are confirmed by urethroscopy.

Dilating the urethra releases the obstruction to the outflow of urine from the bladder. It relieves the backup (as in a plugged kitchen drain), promotes the proper urinary flow to facilitate correct emptying of the bladder, and therefore aids healing of the bladder lining. However, I feel that too often the dilation procedure is performed without proper workup, evaluation, explanation, or preparation of the patient. Make sure that your doctor thoroughly evaluates your case and explains the situation to you before you agree to urethral dilatation.

There is now a trend away from excessive urethral dilations. Many women respond equally well to antibiotics for infection and, more importantly, to reassurance when they have external sphincter spasm. Many women find that when they are tense, they have a feeling of incomplete emptying of their bladder, marked frequency of urination—predominately during the day—and urethral discomfort. They find that their symptoms are often relieved by sitting in a hot tub for a while or in a sauna which allows them to become relaxed. Spasm of the external sphincter is a manifestation of stress and is one of the most common problems seen by physicians.

Often such a patient sees a urologist who performs a urethral dilation which overstretches the external sphincter and temporarily relieves the symptoms until the sphincter regains its tone in ten to fourteen days, and then, once again, the woman has her old symptoms back. This may begin a vicious cycle, with repeated urethral dilations, changes in urologists, and repetition of the treatment. However, as I mentioned in the chapter on urinary tract infections, most patients can find relief from the symptoms when they are reassured and taught to try to relax while voiding, and not to try to be in and out of the toilet as quickly as possible. For some women biofeedback may work well to help them relax when they void.

Therefore, it should be apparent that you should not require excessive urethral dilations. One or two should suffice, because the female does not need a wide caliber urethra in order to void adequately. It is important to realize also that there is a new syndrome called the "mutilated urethra syndrome," which is something created by the urologist who repeatedly dilates the urethra.

Urodynamics

Many medical centers now have sophisticated laboratory procedures known as urodynamics to test patients with urinary incontinence. These procedures include filling the bladder and testing pressures in the bladder, urethra, and sometimes the rectum as a way of discovering neurologic and muscular problems.

There is some controversy over which patients should undergo urodynamics. Certainly those who have had a previous operation that failed to cure their symptoms or who demonstrate any possibility of a chronic infection or muscular or neurogenic problems should be studied in this manner. Also, preoperative evaluation may help to pick out those patients who will respond well to surgery and may help eliminate those who will not.

Anyone considering surgical correction for incontinence should at least undergo a simple office procedure called a cystometrogram. In this procedure, the bladder is filled with sterile water or gas and the pressure of the bladder wall is measured at varying volumes, showing how well the bladder muscle reacts. If the pressures measured are abnormal, the patient needs more sophisticated testing.

Surgery for Incontinence

Once infection, bladder muscle abnormality, and psychological reasons have been ruled out, it is likely that the patient has a structural reason for her incontinence. Anatomic incontinence is the type most likely to be improved by surgery. However, it should be stated that *no* operation for stress urinary incontinence (or SUI, as anatomic incontinence is called) is 100 percent effective. Even with the most experienced surgeon and careful preoperative testing, failure rates of 10 to 20 percent are common. The Marshall test, a simple part of the pelvic examination, may identify patients who may not respond to surgical correction. The examiner places two fingers in the vagina on either side of the urethra at the base of the bladder and elevates this structure as high anteriorly as possible. If urine still spurts out when the patient coughs, then repairing these angles in the operating room is not likely to cure the problem.

The pressure in the urethra must be greater than that in the bladder to maintain continence. Normally the urethra and bladder are in a position where they both are subjected to normal abdominal pressure changes. Therefore, when pressure increases in the abdomen, it is equally transmitted to the bladder and urethra and thus the pressure difference between the two is maintained. This pressure difference and the angle between the bladder and urethra provide the normal obstruction to the outflow of urine.

In true anatomic SUI, the urethra has fallen down out of its axis so that the angle is lost. Then increases in abdominal pressure that occur with coughing or laughter or other stimuli are no longer transmitted to the bladder and urethra equally. Instead, the bladder receives most of the increased pressure. This causes bladder pressure to become higher than that of the urethra, and leakage occurs. The goal of the corrective operation is to elevate the urethra, bringing it back into the proper position so that once again it will be subject to the same pressure as the bladder.

If you are still confused, here is a mathematical example. Suppose the normal resting pressure is 10 in the bladder and 20 in the urethra. With a cough, the pressure within the abdomen goes up 60 points. In normal women, the 60 points will be transmitted equally, resulting in a pressure of 70 in the bladder (10 + 60) and 80 in the urethra (20 + 60), and continence is maintained. However, if the patient's urethra has dropped away from the correct axis, the pressure in the bladder will be 10 + 60, but only a portion of the pressure, say 30 points, will be transmitted to the urethra (20 + 30). Therefore the pressure in the bladder is now higher, and the patient leaks urine. If the urethral pressure is low at resting levels, even weak bladder contractions can result in loss of urine. Such low pressures are often due to poor muscle support or loss of estrogen.

Choosing the correct operation to repair the anatomy is critically important. Until recently, many surgeons simply performed the operation they themselves were most familiar with, sometimes totally disregarding the anatomic defect in the patient. With the advent of urodynamics and a better understanding of the defects that cause SUI, tailoring the correct operation to each patient is now common.

Surgical approaches to SUI fall into two basic groups. *Retropubic suspension,* such as the Marshall-Marchetti operation, is performed through an incision in the lower portion of the abdominal wall behind the pubic bone. Sutures placed at the junction between the base of the bladder and the urethra are anchored to the back of the pubic bone. This elevates the bladder and urethra and restores the proper angle between them. This operation takes approximately ninety minutes, and patients are hospitalized approximately one week.

The second type of operation for SUI is called an *anterior repair.* This is a vaginal operation which involves opening the roof of the vagina, elimintating the cystocele, and closing the supporting tissues and vaginal wall under the bladder. This pushes the defect upward from below rather than pulling it up from above, as with retropubic suspensions. Anterior repair takes approximately one hour and also involves about a week in the hospital. It, too, restores the angle between the urethra and bladder and therefore makes continence possible again.

The newest operative procedure for stress incontinence is a combination of both of the above. A small incision is made in the lower abdomen, and sutures are inserted between the anterior abdominal wall and the junction of the bladder and urethra. In this technique, a special needle is inserted down through the abdominal wall, behind the pubic bone, and into the vagina where trailing sutures fix the bladder and urethral junction and then are passed back up again onto the anterior abdominal wall and tied. The procedure also involves a small vaginal incision to identify and mobilize the area of the junction. Known as the Raz and Stamey operations, they are now being done on the west coast, and more recently have begun to be done by some east coast surgeons as well.

For these operations, the bladder must be drained. Edema or swelling around the operative site usually makes urination impossible during the first few days. One new postoperative technique is not to put a catheter into the swollen urethra, but rather to use a suprapubic drain. This technique has the advantage of creating less chance for infection and trauma in the operated area. Patients should not be discouraged if it takes time for the bladder muscles to work again after this type of surgery. Other patients are taught to do self-intermittent catheterization prior to surgery. Post-operatively, she performs this simple procedure and is able to leave the hospital, using this technique to empty her bladder while recuperating. Over time, there is little residual urine left in her bladder after voiding—as determined by catheterization—and she may discontinue the technique.

People frequently ask whether a hysterectomy is necessary in these operations, and there is considerable disagreement among physicians on this question. Many experienced surgeons feel that the uterus acts as a dead weight on the suture lines, thus adding to the stress that the repair must support. Removing the uterus may therefore improve the overall cure rate for these procedures, but the medical literature is currently uncertain.

Unlike most surgical procedures, the ultimate outcome of incontinence surgery depends a great deal on the patient herself. Obesity and cigarette smoking are the two most common factors that contribute to failure of the operation. The coughing resulting from chronic bronchitis acts as a pile driver on the surgical repair. Similarly, obesity increases the weight that the repair must endure.

If it is necessary that you have surgery, ask you doctor about using estrogen vaginal cream prior to the operation. As you now know, estrogen will make your tissues healthier and easier to operate on. It will also contribute to better healing. After surgery, doing Kegel's exercises (see p. 187) is always helpful.

The Pessary—A Nonsurgical Alternative

Sometimes patients may want to avoid surgery for medical or personal reasons. A few anatomic defects, particularly uterine prolapse, may be temporarily improved with a pessary. This is an applicance, usually made of soft rubber or plastic, which must be fitted into the vagina. By acting as a trampoline between the back of the pubic bone and the top of the vagina, a pessary can sometimes hold prolapsed organs within the vagina by purely mechanical means. The irritation it often causes to the lining of the vagina when it is used for extended periods of time makes it a poor permanent choice, except in older patients with medical problems. Pessaries can be removed easily for sexual relations. They should be cleaned and checked regularly.

To give some last words of advice then, if you are suffering from incontinence of any degree, get a thorough workup. Get rid of any infection that you might have, do your exercises, use some estrogen if you have no contraindications. If surgery is suggested, get a second opinion. In fact, it might be advisable to get two opinions in virtually all cases: one from a urologist, the other from a gynecologist. The urologist would be able to assess the stress incontinence and evaluate whether there is any bladder muscle dysfunction associated with it, and the gynecologist could evaluate for gyn abnormalities such as uterine prolapse. Some physicians, either gynecologist or urologist, with sufficient interest in the subject of female incontinence, may be able to do a complete evaluation. However, this is one area of women's health where it pays to be particularly cautious, because treatment, especially surgical treatment, may not be indicated in your case, even though it may be suggested and casually promised to cure all your troubles.

9

No More Unwanted Pregnancy at Age 40 . . . or 43 . . . or 45 . . .

If you're approaching your forties, you may well have some questions or worries about your birth control method. If it's the pill, you're probably apprehensive about its safety; if it's a barrier method, you may be weary of using it; and if it's an IUD, you may be troubled by scare stories in the media. Despite all this, you can actually be optimistic about your prospects of preventing pregnancy safely. Today there are more acceptable ways to avoid having a baby than ever before. In choosing among these many methods, you should consider not only their technology but also how each one fits your individual needs. Your health history, sexual activity patterns, and personal likes and dislikes can affect not only your effective use of the contraceptive but its safety, too.

Today's Over-35 Woman—A New Life-style

When a woman in or nearing her forties comes in to review her contraception method with me, I try to get a well-rounded picture of her life-style and lifelong health status. Recently this has been getting more complicated. Today's older women lead more complex lives than their mothers did. They also seem to have much greater diversity in their sexual habits, marriages, career plans, medical histories, and childbearing status than their predecessors. Thus their contraceptive needs are much more diverse.

Women's sexual habits have changed, along with their

attitudes about these habits. It's not rare at all now to find women in older age groups who are sexually active with multiple partners or who report a past history of such activity. Actually it may not have been so rare before, but today's openness about sexual matters makes information about them more available. And that information is important to the doctor who is prescribing contraception. Some contraceptives can help protect women with multiple sexual partners against infections; others may be of little help or actually unsafe for such women.

But women over forty today differ from their mothers in far more than sexual practices. Life-styles have changed drastically. In our mothers' generation, most women in mid-life were securely married and did not work outside the home. Often they had three or four children (the postwar baby boom) and definitely did not want any more. This picture of the mature woman has changed in significant ways. Many of my forty-year-old patients are divorced or remarried, and I'm seeing more in this age group who have never married. Moreover, mature women with only one child—or none—are increasingly common. So are women in their mid- or late thirties who still expect to bear a child. Working women with full-time jobs plus young children are also increasing in number. What is increasingly rare is the "typical" full-time mother with lots of kids and no career interest at all.

Jobs and careers make reliable contraception essential at later ages. Yet many women fear the pill and IUD, while rebelling at the prospect of having to use a diaphragm or foam "every time." Moreover, many women (rightfully) want to avoid the hazards of sterilization. Others want to avoid any contraceptive method that threatens their final years of fertility.

Sometimes it seems that women want their doctors to suggest a perfect birth control method—which simply does not exist and probably never will. The choice is between somewhat less effective but generally safe methods (the various barrier methods) and highly efficacious pills or IUDs, which have some serious known hazards.

Discussions of contraceptives in the media have emphasized the hazards. Thus although women today have a lot of information about contraceptives, this information is not always balanced. Reporters naturally tend to emphasize the negative or alarming features of their subjects, such as the risks of the pill or IUDs, and some women in my practice for whom one of these methods should be quite safe are reluctant to use them. News reports hardly ever mention that most methods of birth control are relatively much *less* hazardous than pregnancy itself.

That statement applies particularly to women over forty. With one possible exception, all methods of birth control are safer for such women than having a baby. The exception is the pill used by high-risk older women (for example, those who smoke). We'll explore those risks fully later in this chapter.

Another gap in the knowledge of many older women today relates to barrier methods of birth control. Their mothers were often experienced in using such contraceptives; after all, the pill goes back only about twenty years. But today I see thirty-five-year-olds who have been on the pill almost continuously since their late teens. They've heard about diaphragms and condoms but have absolutely no personal experience with them.

On the other hand, women today are much more conversant with surgical sterilization and abortion. Twenty years ago, people shied from even talking about these measures; now women often are willing to undertake them without fully understanding their risks. Possibly that unfortunate trend is in part attributable to physicians. It's easy for a busy doctor to fall into holding the simplistic view that a woman of forty who has some nuisance bleeding doesn't need her uterus anymore, or that tied tubes will be a blessing to a woman who doesn't want any more children. But in my view, this is an area of pregnancy prevention in which the risks have been played down.

Another difference among today's older women is one that I'm happier to observe: their willingness to have the man share the burden of preventing pregnancy. That trend still isn't as strong as I'd like it to be. Nevertheless, male sterilization and condom use are becoming more frequent.

This not only relieves the woman of taking all the responsibility but also of some physical risks as well (e.g., from the pill or surgical sterilization).

Guidelines for Choosing Contraception

For the mature woman who wants to make sure her contraceptive is right for her, I have three golden rules: Know Thyself, Tell Thy Physician, and Keep Thyself Informed.

Know Thyself

By Know Thyself, I mean that before keeping your appointment with your doctor, you should have a think session *with* yourself *about* yourself. And get your husband or sexual partner in on it if you can. He'll sometimes tell you things about yourself that you don't fully realize. (For example, your husband may remind you why you have three kids instead of the two you had planned: you forgot to take your diaphragm or pills along on that long weekend!) But he may also get interested enough in the whole contraceptive problem to give you more help than you had expected. He may even volunteer to look into vasectomy or the use of a condom.

Here are some of the questions you should ask yourself:

- *What are my birth control aims*? Do I want no children (or no more)? Or do I want to keep my options open— "maybe just one more" at age 39 or 40? These questions are important, because some birth control methods, as you'll see, may affect future fertility.

- *What are my sexual habits*? Do I have frequent or infrequent intercourse? Do I stick to one man or play the field? Are my present habits likely to persist or change? Answers to these questions indicate whether you need an exceptionally effective method (for example, if you have a lively sex life) and whether you need the protection that some contraceptive methods, such as condoms, offer against sexually transmitted disease.

• *What about my current health*? Am I totally fit, or do I have problems of *any* kind? Think hard about this, because problems ranging from high blood pressure to persistent vaginal infections may affect the safety and comfort of your contraceptive choice.

• *What about my past health*? Have I ever had an ectopic pregnancy, a diagnosis of venereal disease, or known exposure to such disease? As a teenager, did I have an infection in my reproductive tract that kindly Dr. So-and-so simply treated without explaining much about it to my parents? Have I ever had a heart problem, high blood pressure, or a stroke? Don't omit anything—only your doctor can really decide how any health problem may affect the safety of your contraceptive choice.

• *What are my feelings about contraceptives*? Do I hate the thought of taking precautions "every time" or would I prefer the methods that are medically the safest even if they are less effective and more trouble?

• *How would I feel about an unplanned pregnancy*? Would it be an emotional, professional, medical or marital disaster, or just an annoyance? Could I resign myself to it or, if not, would I be comfortable about being sterilized or having an abortion? These questions all bear on how effective your contraception must be to safeguard your peace of mind and health.

• *Am I a "together" person or a bit scatterbrained*? Will I forget to take or use an "every time" contraceptive—even now and then?

• *What problems did I have with previous contraceptives*? An unplanned baby? A pill-related illness? A discontented sexual partner? Pain or bleeding or vaginal irritation? Sometimes yes answers to these questions rule out certain contraceptives; sometimes they mean you should explore a different or newer version of the same contraceptive.

Tell Thy Doctor

Your next step is to be absolutely frank with your doctor about the answers to these questions. Otherwise, she or he cannot possibly give you sound counsel. You can get into real health trouble, for example, if you conceal a previous venereal infection, an adverse reaction to the pill, or an ectopic pregnancy. You might end up with a contraceptive that is really dangerous for you.

Therefore, don't be shy about talking about your past or present. Believe me, your doctor's probably heard it all before. And don't be shy either about expressing your preferences in contraceptives. Finally, don't promise what you can't deliver. If you're unmethodical or forgetful, you're not likely to change just because the doctor thinks barrier contraceptives are wonderful.

Keep Thyself Informed

You're doing so right now with this book. Good work!

An older woman's physiology differs from that of a twenty-year-old; her fertility drops as she ages. By forty, she's much less likely to conceive than at twenty or even thirty. She also may be having intercourse less often than she did. Such changes make some contraceptives unsuitable for her and others more suitable than they would have been earlier in her life. The following table shows the general effectiveness of the types of contraceptives available today. In this chapter, we'll explore the suitability of each for the older woman.

Effectiveness of Contraceptive Methods

Method	Failure Rates (per 100 women per year)
oral contraceptives	1 – 2
intrauterine devices	1 – 6
diaphragm	2 – 20
condom and foam combined	1 – 6

condom	2 – 36
foams, creams, jellies, and vaginal suppositories	2 – 36
rhythm, calendar method	1 – 47
temperature method	1 – 30
mucus method	1 – 30
douche	40 +
sterilization	1*
withdrawal	?
no method	60 – 90

*Per 1,000 procedures.

The Pill

The pill presents the greatest dilemma in contraception, especially to older women. If it's always been your method, you are probably addicted to its ease of use and its almost foolproof effectiveness. But you also know that the pill has life-threatening side effects in some women. Moreover, researchers agree that advancing age (as well as smoking) substantially increases the risks of such side effects.

Oral contraceptives bathe all the tissues of the body with powerful synthetic hormones. These hormones affect not only the reproductive system but other systems as well, including the brain, gastrointestinal tract, liver, and circulatory system. That's why they have a multitude of side effects.

The synthetic estrogens and progesterones in birth control pills differ from the natural estrogens and progesterone your body produces in their chemical structure, their effects on the body, and the way they are administered. For example, normal ovarian function produces a rise and fall of natural estrogen in the body, whereas birth control pills produce constant levels of synthetic estrogen for twenty-one days. The high doses of synthetic estrogens and testosterone-based progesterones used in birth control pills also have quite different effects than the low doses of estrogen and progesterone-based progestin derivatives used in hormone-replacement therapy described in Chapter 1. Although birth control pills now contain less synthetic estrogen than the earlier pills, nevertheless, the dose is still many times the normal. This is because the level has to be high enough to shut down the female reproductive system. Pills produce their desired contraceptive effect by preventing ovulation through shutting off the hypothalamus and pituitary glands, so that the ovary does not receive the hormonal message it needs to produce an egg. In addition, birth control pills exert other contraceptive effects: thinning the uterine lining (endometrium) and reducing its secretions, lowering the receptivity of cervical mucus to sperm, and altering fallopian tube function.

It is in the circulatory system, however, that the pill can have its most dangerous consequences, and that system is where an older woman may be particularly vulnerable. Birth control pills cause the blood to clot more easily. If a clot develops in the brain, it can cause a stroke; in the coronary artery, it can bring on a heart attack; and in a leg vein, it can cause an inflammation called phlebitis. Some women on the pill experience a rise in blood pressure which can strain the heart or damage the arteries.

Pill-related problems can also cause liver abnormalities such as benign tumors, jaundice, abnormal production of proteins, and changes in cholesterol and triglyceride levels. In addition, gallstone development in pill users may be more frequent than in nonusers, although a recent large English study disputes this fact. Less serious problems from birth control pills include nausea, weight gain, vomiting, breast tenderness, appetite increase, and the annoying recurrence of the common yeast vaginal infection called *Candida* or *Monilia* vaginitis.

Women Who Should Not Use the Pill

Some women, because of their current health status or a history of certain health problems, are especially vulnerable to serious risks if they take oral contraceptives. First, no woman who is pregnant or suspects she is pregnant should be taking the pill. It should *not* be used for the purpose of causing abortion; it's not effective and may simply damage the fetus.

Second, if a woman has or has *ever* had any of the following conditions, she cannot take the pill.

1. heart attack (myocardial infarction)
2. stroke (cerebrovascular disease)
3. blood-clotting disorders (thrombophlebitis or thromboembolism)
4. angina pectoris (pain in the chest associated with a heart condition)
5. cancer of the breast or sex organs, or suspected cancer of these areas
6. unusual vaginal bleeding that has not been checked and diagnosed by a doctor
7. liver tumors or seriously impaired liver function.

Another set of medical conditions, some of them more common in older women, makes pill use highly inadvisable, but do not absolutely rule it out if you have or have ever had any of the following:

1. breast nodules, or an abnormal mammogram
2. family history of breast cancer
3. diabetes
4. high blood pressure
5. high cholesterol or triglyceride level
6. cigarette smoking
7. migraine headaches
8. heart, kidney, or liver disease
9. epilepsy
10. depression
11. fibroid tumors of the uterus
12. gall-bladder disease
13. menstrual periods that are grossly irregular

As far as I am concerned, smoking alone is enough to prevent me from prescribing the pill even for younger women. To understand why, look at some figures.

The table that follows shows that death attributed to pill use among nonsmokers in the 25-to-29 age group are 1.6 per 100,000—lower than the 12.1 deaths per 100,000 attributed to pregnancy and childbirth. For pill users aged 25 to 29 who smoke, however, the risk increases to 6.1 in 100,000. And as women grow older, the risks of smoking and oral contraceptive use go from bad to perilous, as you can see in the table. Finally, at age 40 to 44, deaths attributable to pill use by smokers skyrocket to nearly 61 per 100,000—almost as high as the risks of childbirth in that group (68.2 per 100,000).

But I'm not enthusiastic about the pill even in the nonsmokers' category after the mid-thirties. As the table shows, the mortality rate in this group jumps sharply after age 35.

MORTALITY ASSOCIATED WITH PREGNANCY AND CHILDBIRTH, LEGAL ABORTION, ORAL CONTRACEPTIVES (BY SMOKING STATUS), AND IUDs, BY AGE*

| Age (Years) | Pregnancy and Childbirth† | Legal Abortion** | Oral Contraceptives‡ | | IUDs‡ |
			Nonsmokers	Smokers	
15–19	10.4	1.0	0.6	2.1	0.8
20–24	9.5	1.4	1.1	4.2	0.8
20–29	12.1	1.8	1.6	6.1	1.0
30–34	22.8	1.8	3.0	11.8	1.0
35–39	43.7	2.7	9.1	31.1	1.4
40–44	68.2	2.7	17.7	60.9	1.4

*Source: Christopher Tietze and Sarah Lewit, "Life Risks Associated with Reversible Methods of Fertility Regulation," *International Journal of Gynaecology and Obstetrics* 16: 456–459.
†Per 100,000 live births (excluding abortion).
**Per 100,000 first-trimester abortions.
‡Per 100,000 users per year.

Minimizing Risks for Older Pill Users

Sometimes an older woman will insist on continuing the pill, or for some reason, she may need to do so. If the following statements apply to you, it may be possible for you to use the pill after your mid-thirties under close medical supervision.

1. Your medical history and current health are free of any factors that would make the pill especially risky. (See list page 207.)
2. You have had no serious side effects from the pill previously.
3. You are a nonsmoker.
4. You are willing to have frequent medical checkups.
5. You are aware of risks of the pill and are willing to chance them.

These are musts. In addition you should:

6. Require the highest efficacy contraception for health or other reasons.
7. Be unable or unwilling to use barrier methods or an IUD.

If you are afflicted with heavy menstrual bleeding or severe menstrual pain and you meet the criteria in the list, the pill may be an adequate choice of contraception for you. This is a medical reason providing one motivation for using the pill but not a necessary condition for its use.

If you are an older pill user, there are three things you can do to lessen the known risks of using the pill.

First, if you smoke—quit. Smoking and birth-control-pill use are analagous to drinking and driving—they don't mix safely. Moreover, smoking *alone* will raise your chances of premature death more than taking the pill. Doing both will be several times more dangerous than the sum of their individual risks.

Second, make certain you're taking a pill containing a low dose of estrogen. I am appalled by the number of patients coming to see me who are taking high-dose pills (80 micrograms or more of estrogen). In fact, such oral contraceptives still constitute over 20 percent of birth-control-pill sales. But, fortunately, the trend has been toward prescribing pills that contain 30 to 50 micrograms of estrogen. Check with your doctor to find out if you are on—or can switch to—the low-dose pill.

You and your doctor may also want you to try one of the new biphasic or triphasic oral contraceptives which have graduated progestogen hormonal doses which are patterned to more or less mimic the natural menstrual cycle. Because the progestogen is given in increasing dose, the overall effect is that the total dose of the progesterone-like substance is less than in some of the constant-dose formulas.

You can even get pills with no estrogen at all; in fact, these have been suggested specifically for the over-thirty-five woman. These pills are usually called progestogen-only minipills, but because the pregnancy rate with them is significant, they defeat the purpose for which they were intended.

Third, you might request that a blood test called an *antithrombin III* be done. Although no guarantees can be made, it may weed out those women with blood-clotting tendencies who would be at increased risk from the pill. However, the test is not universally accepted, and your own physician will be able to tell you if it is worthwhile in your own particular case.

Women using oral contraceptives must return frequently to their physicians for checkups. I ask my patients who are on the pill for the first time to come back in two months and thereafter to come back every six months. Each time, I take their blood pressure and examine their breasts; I may repeat lab studies yearly, including blood sugar, lipids, and liver profiles. The patients and I review their mental and physical state and decide whether to continue the medication or to change to a different form of contraception. Including an annual examination and a six-month examination, the cost of oral contraception is $175 to $220 per year. Actually, in my practice, I have had no patients over the age of thirty-five on oral contraceptives for some years. I do, however, have many younger women on oral contraceptives.

Interestingly, there seem to be some health benefits for women under thirty who do not smoke and who take oral contraceptives. Recent studies have shown that such women have a reduced incidence of a number of problems and hospitalizations. For example, the pill results in less than one pregnancy per 100 women per year. It decreases menstrual pain and blood loss and, therefore, it also decreases iron-deficiency anemia in menstruating women. Furthermore, some researchers feel that half of all cases of benign breast disease are prevented in women on the pill. (There is no evidence to date that taking the pill lowers the subsequent incidence of breast cancer.)

Ovarian cysts are also prevented, because the ovary does not function to produce eggs for the duration of oral-contraceptive therapy. The incidence of ectopic pregnancy is also decreased, for there is no egg present to be fertilized and get stuck in the fallopian tube. Researchers have also noted a decreased sensitivity to rheumatoid arthritis for women on the pill. Such women also have a decreased risk of hospitalization for PID, which may be due to the pill's effect on cervical mucus, making it thicker and more tenacious, thus probably preventing organisms in the vagina from reaching the uterine lining and traveling up into the tubes.

Oral contraceptives may also decrease several types of female cancer. Women who use them have a decreased risk of uterine and ovarian cancers compared to women who never took the pill. The decreased risk of uterine cancer is most probably the result of progesterone in the pill and the hormone balance that it provides. The decreased risk of ovarian cancer may be due to the fact that the pill stops the trauma of monthly ovulation to the ovary. (Of course, this is only speculation.) So although oral contraceptives have received a lot of bad press, there may be advantages for those women under thirty who are in good health and do not smoke.

If you are undergoing major surgery, try to schedule it far enough ahead to enable you to go off the pill for a month beforehand. Women having such operations who are taking the pill have an increased chance of forming postoperative thromboses (blood clots). Emergency surgery should be preceded by the administration of drugs to prevent such complications.

Intrauterine Devices

An intrauterine device or IUD is a small plastic object placed in the uterine cavity that is thought to prevent pregnancy by keeping the fertilized egg from implanting in the uterus. It provides uninterrupted contraception until it is removed. IUDs come in various shapes and sizes and are of two basic types. The "inert" type does not release medication into the uterus but simply produces a mechanical effect on it. The newer types of IUDs release a contraceptive substance.

To be effective, inert plastic IUDs must have a size and shape that creates a foreign-body reaction in the lining of the uterus, causing it to become slightly irritated. This irritation produces more white blood cells in the uterine environment than usual. Scientists theorize that this condition discourages implantation of a fertilized egg.

IUDs containing contraceptive substances are smaller because they do not depend on size and uterine irritation for their effect. In fact, these IUDs would be only 80 to 85 percent effective as contraceptives without their medication. With their medication, however, they are between 97 and 98 percent effective. They are generally more effective than inert IUDs, particularly the smaller sizes of inert IUDs. They are also easy to insert and less hassle for many women to use than larger IUDs.

The first medicated IUDs that were generally available relied on copper for preventing pregnancy. Copper interfers with implantation of the egg, increases the number of white blood cells in the uterine cavity, and may interfere with sperm mobility.

A newer IUD, Progestasert, contains a small amount of the hormone progesterone, which is natural and identical to the hormone your ovary makes. Progresterone released in a tiny daily amount from the IUD causes the uterine lining to be slightly out of phase and not suitable for implantation. It may also make the cervical mucus more sticky, so that sperm—or bacteria—cannot easily pass into the uterus. Theoretically,

Progestasert users might be found to have a lower risk for PID. The small amount of progesterone released by this IUD does not affect ovarian function, for its low levels cannot be detected in the bloodstream. Thus it does not cause the side effects produced by the synthetic hormones in oral contraceptives.

The following table shows how effective the various IUDs are in preventing pregnancy. Some of the data are from the manufacturers' technical information for physicians, and some come from research studies. Actually different studies on the same IUD often yield different results. In general, however, you can see that the progesterone and copper IUDs are a bit more effective as contraceptives than the non-medicated IUDs.

IUD Type	Pregnancy Rate/100 Women						Expulsion 12 mo		Medical Removal 12 mo	
	At 12 mo		24 mo		36 mo					
	N*	P*	N*	P*	N*	P*	N*	P*	N*	P*
Lippes Loop										
Size A	5.3		9.7				23.9		12.2	
B		3.4		6.3				18.9		15.1
C		3.0		4.8				19.1		14.3
D		2.7		4.2				12.7		15.2
Copper-7	1.7	1.9	2.6	2.9	3.4	3.4	8.0	5.7	13.6	10.9
Progestasert	2.6	1.8					7.4	3.1	15.1	11.2
Tatum-T	2.1	3.0	4.5	4.9	5.8	6.0	8.0	7.8	13.9	10.9
Saf-T-Coil†										
Size 25 S**	—	—					—	—	—	—
32 S**	—	—					—	—	—	—
33 S		2.4		3.1				18.3		15.6

*N = nulliparous women (women who have not had children); *P = parous women (women who have had children).

†The Saf-T-Coil is no longer being manufactured. Production stopped in July 1982 because of low demand for this IUD.

**Good data on small sizes of Saf-T-Coil are not obtainable. They must be assumed to be poorer than the above data given for the largest size (33 S), which is used in women who have borne children.

As you can also see, no IUD has a pregnancy rate as low as the pill, but in older (less fertile) women, this may not be as important as in younger women. Moreover, a woman using an IUD who is worried about only 97 to 98 percent effectiveness—which is not to be sneezed at—can use a spermicidal foam at mid-cycle to increase protection during her fertile days.

Despite the unfavorable recent publicity, IUDs are highly effective and safe for *properly selected* patients, and older women are often ideal candidates for their use. All in all, IUDs are much safer for many women in these age groups than the pill (see table on page 208). The following guidelines can help you evaluate the IUD for your own use. You will, of course, need to consult your physician to determine whether an IUD is right for you.

These conditions *must* be met to consider using an IUD:

1. You must have an anatomically normal uterus.
2. You must not have any history of VD, PID, or ectopic pregnancy or certain other medical problems (see Risks of IUDs following) that contraindicate use of IUDs.
3. You must know the risks of IUD use and be willing to take them.

In addition, if most of the following statements apply to you, you may be a good candidate for IUD use:

4. You require a contraceptive method that doesn't interfere with or delay intercourse.
5. You want or need to avoid the pill or sterilization.
6. You are willing to put up with minor (often temporary) bleeding or spotting between periods.
7. You have a stable, monogamous sexual relationship.
8. You have excessive menstrual bleeding problems or cramps or both that the progesterone IUD might alleviate. (Excessive menstrual bleeding is a reason for considering the progesterone IUD but not for general IUD use. In fact, the Copper 7, Tatum T, Saf-T-Coil, and Lippes Loop make bleeding and cramping worse.)

Risks of IUDs

Like birth-control-pill users, IUD users have to be carefully screened to eliminate women at high risk for complications. The conditions in the following list tell the doctor *in advance* that a particular woman should *not* use an IUD, or should not use it at a particular time of her life. Some of these contraindications apply to all IUDs and some only to specific IUDs; your doctor will have this information.

1. existing or suspected pregnancy
2. abnormalities of the uterus resulting in distortion of the uterine cavity
3. unusual or unexplained uterine bleeding
4. cancer or suspected cancer of the reproductive tract
5. acute pelvic inflammatory disease (PID) or a history of PID
6. infected abortion or infection of the uterus following childbirth in the past three months
7. acute infection of the cervix (insertion must be delayed until infection is controlled)
8. previous ectopic pregnancy
9. significant anemia (would not be a contraindication for a Progestasert IUD)
10. chronic steroid therapy (which causes susceptibility to infection from organisms that might be introduced at insertion)
11. Wilson's disease or allergy to copper (pertains only to copper-bearing IUDs)
12. some types of valvular heart disease
13. leukemia

These contraindications show why you must be absolutely frank with your physician in discussing your contraceptive choice. Only with full information on your health history, an examination, and certain tests can he or she decide if an IUD would be safe for you.

As with other contraceptives, there is always some risk. With IUD use, the dangers to life and health are infection, accidental pregnancy, and uterine or cervical perforation. The great majority of IUD users do not have these complications, but everyone contemplating IUD use should know about them.

Some years ago, a number of women using the Dalkon Shield died of infections that developed after they had accidental pregnancies. (The manufacture of the Dalkon Shield IUD has removed it from the US market.) These infections were attributed to the string on the IUD, which was made of multiple filaments enclosed in a sheath that created a pathway for bacteria to ascend from the vagina into the sterile uterine cavity. For this reason, IUDs that are currently available use only one-filament strings, which are safer. Nevertheless, the Dalkon Shield episode damaged confidence in all IUDs, and their use in the United States fell from 1,670,504 in 1971 to 775,161 in 1974. *If you are still using a Dalkon Shield, have it removed whether or not you are having any problems.* If you are not sure if you have a Dalkon Shield, ask your doctor!

In addition, recent reports indicate that even users of the one-filament IUDs have more infections of the reproductive tract (PID) than women using *no* contraception or women using non-IUD contraceptives. (The use of contraceptives other than IUDs—even the pill—seems to give some protection against infection.) The hormones in the pill are thought to cause cervical mucus to become thickened. This mucus then serves as a mechanical barrier to bacteria, preventing their entry into the uterus. In different studies, the increased incidence of PID with IUD use varies widely. At least one authority in the field, Jack Lippes, believes that PID is more closely related to the 400 percent rise in gonorrhea that has occurred in the past few years than to IUD use. Obviously this question needs much more investigation.

In 1982, physicians became aware of another infection called actinomycoses. It seemed to affect primarily those women who used a plastic nonmedicated IUD that had been in place for more than two years. Women using copper-containing IUDs had low rates of infection.

There is growing evidence that calcium deposits on IUDs

may play a role in infection. Calcium seems to accumulate gradually on an IUD over a period of months and years. Calcium crusts provide a cozy niche for bacteria and fungi to hide from the body's normal defense mechanisms. Currently the Food and Drug Administration recommends replacement of IUDs every three years, but Dr. Waldemar Schmidt recommends replacement every two years because of calcium deposits. Schmidt feels that copper-containing IUDs offer some protection because of their mild bacteriostatic action, but this protection also diminishes with time as the copper dissolves off the device.

In my own office practice, gritty calcium could almost always be felt over the surface on nonmedicated IUDs after removal. On the other hand, copper and progesterone IUDs show little or no similar buildup. This may simply be due to the fact that medicated IUDs are removed routinely in one to three years' time.

I don't advise IUD use for women who have health histories of gonorrhea or PID or life-styles that indicate susceptibility to PID. These women, as various studies have indicated, seem to be in the younger, childless age groups and often have multiplicity of sexual partners. But I believe women who have no unfavorable health history and who are in stable, monogamous relationships can safely use IUDs, and so far I've had good results with my carefully selected patients.

One of the most serious consequences of pelvic infection is that damage to a woman's fallopian tubes may make her unable to have a child. Of course, preservation of fertility is of paramount importance in the younger woman, but in the older woman, fertility is usually of little importance, so this factor is not as critical. Indeed, it may hardly be considered by the woman over forty who is considering the use of an IUD.

Nevertheless, all IUD users should know the symptoms of PID: new development of menstrual disorders (prolonged or heavy bleeding), abnormal vaginal discharge, abdominal or pelvic pain, dyspareunia (painful intercourse), and fever. The symptoms are especially significant if they occur following the first two or three cycles after insertion of your IUD. If you develop these symptoms, make an immediate appointment with your doctor. Fortunately a broad-spectrum antibiotic is usually effective against PID, but if the infection does not respond in twenty-four to forty-eight hours, the IUD should be removed and treatment continued.

Accidental pregnancy occurs in 1 to 6 IUD users per 100 women per year. A pregnant woman with an IUD in place should have it removed; its presence increases the chances of spontaneous miscarriage and septic (infected) abortion (particularly in the second trimester). If the device cannot be removed and the woman wishes the pregnancy to continue, fetus and mother remain at risk to infection.

Some studies indicate that IUDs, especially the Progestasert system, are associated with higher risk of an ectopic pregnancy—a pregnancy that develops outside the uterus—than other forms of birth control (including other IUDs, barrier methods and the combination pill). The Progestasert IUD is not thought to *cause* ectopic pregnancies because its users do not have any higher ectopic rates than women using *no* contraception; the question is whether it simply does not prevent them. The situation is confused by the fact that the Progestasert system, unlike other IUDs, had its large-scale testing done in patients only after the ectopic pregnancy rates had more than doubled in the US population as a whole (for all women, not just IUD users). Nevertheless, the Progestasert system has had its package insert changed to make physicians and patients aware of the problem, and further studies are now underway.

Perforation is the third danger of IUD use. In this situation, the IUD breaks through the wall of the uterus into the peritoneal (abdominal) cavity. Such perforation occurs in less than one tenth of one percent of users, and almost always happens at the time of insertion, when it may be accompanied by sudden pain or bleeding. If perforation occurs, an IUD containing copper should be removed immediately; it can cause the formation of intraabdominal inflammation and adhesions. Nonmedicated and progesterone-containing IUDs— although they should be removed as soon as is convenient—

usually cause compartively little reaction. Often their removal is accomplished by laparoscopy.

Having now considered the risky side of IUD use, let's look at its advantages, especially for older women. In general— in properly selected patients—these far outweigh its dangers.

Benefits of the IUD

Older women without the specific risk factors discussed earlier should seriously consider IUD use. Efficacy of the medicated types approaches that of the pill; yet none of the IUDs has the generalized hormonal effects of the pill. Thus they offer some of the safety features of barrier methods (spermicides, condoms, diaphragms) without their higher pregnancy rates or inconvenience.

IUD use actually requires even *less* attention than the pill, which has to be taken daily. In fact, no other means of birth control demands so little of the woman as an IUD. Once it is inserted, all the woman has to do is check for its presence monthly and report any side effects to her physician. This ease of use is one important reason why most of my patients are delighted with their IUDs and wish they'd tried this method of contraception before.

There are, however, exceptions. Some women have problems (for example, cramping or intermenstrual spotting) with their device and hate it. Others tried an IUD early in their reproductive lives and couldn't tolerate it. When these women have a health record that is good, I don't hesitate to tell them to give the IUD another try. The newer IUDs are easier to insert than the older ones and more comfortable to wear. But also the woman herself has probably changed over the years, may have had children, and may well be able to tolerate IUD use now.

Indeed, research studies confirm that older women are more successful in using IUDs than younger women. Part of this excellent success rate may be due to the fact that more over-thirty-four-year-old women have borne children, making them better able to tolerate IUD use, but even childless older women seem to do well on IUDs.

Moreover, because IUDs provide effective birth control for between one to five years (depending on type), the older woman can consider them a semipermanent means of birth control that easily bridges the time span until she becomes menopausal and permanent birth control is assured. They avoid the risk of tubal ligation, a permanent procedure, and its possible consequences of menstrual pain and heavy irregular bleeding.

Which IUD?

Since there are so many different devices on the market, you should learn all you can about them and participate in the selection of the one you receive. Beware of physicians or clinics offering only one type of IUD to all their patients. No device is suitable for every woman; each has advantages and disadvantages.

One of the important ways IUDs differ is in their effect on menstrual bleeding. Inert IUDs are generally larger than medicated IUDs and tend to produce more menstrual pain and bleeding than usual. The copper IUDs also increase menstrual bleeding, but to a lesser extent than the Lippes Loop or Saf-T-Coil. The Progestasert system is the only IUD that actually *decreases* menstrual blood flow below its usual levels. It can also alleviate menstrual pain. Also, older women begin to have monthly cycles in which ovulation does not occur. Without ovulation, no progesterone is produced by the ovary, and the uterine lining grows thicker than normal, often leading to heavier menstrual flow and hyperplasia. The progesterone-containing IUD replaces the normal hormonal balance that she often lacks, and that's one reason why the Progestasert IUD may be particularly well suited for women over thirty-five. It also obviates the need for oral synthetic progesterone that doctors frequently prescribe for heavy menstrual bleeding. If she has no contraindications, I think that this particular IUD is probably one of the best methods the mature woman can select for birth control.

Nonmedicated IUDs require changing at least once in five years. Left in for longer than five years, they may weaken and break or collect a gritty coat of calcium that can irritate the uterine lining and cause increasingly heavy bleeding. The calcium may also provide crevices for bacteria and fungi to grow in.

Copper devices have been reported to become partly calcified after two years. Their removal is suggested at three years to prevent loss of contraceptive effect. In any case, medicated IUDs require more frequent replacement than inert IUDs because the contraceptive substances they utilize become depleted. Thus, the Copper-7 or Tatum-T must be replaced every three years and the Progestasert system every twelve to fifteen months. In addition, some evidence links insertion with flareups of PID, although studies showed that PID was less frequent after second insertions than first insertions.

Although IUD replacement every year or two has the disadvantages of expense and inconvenience, it also has distinct medical advantages. It gets the woman into the doctor's office regularly, thus assuring that she'll have the pelvic exam and Pap smear that are especially important at later ages. It may also decrease the chance of infection that accompanies IUDs when they remain in the uterus for many years. The annual cost of IUDs is approximately $25 to $120, depending on how often it needs to be replaced.

IUD Insertion

Once you and your physician have selected an IUD, it should be inserted during the menstrual flow. At that time, the physician is sure that you are not pregnant. Also, the opening to the uterus is enlarged, making the insertion easier and less painful, and the slight spotting that normally occurs with the insertion of an IUD will not be noticeable while you are menstruating.

Years ago, it was necessary to dilate the cervix to insert a coiled or bent IUD. That was an extremely painful procedure. Modern IUDs are made of a biologically inactive material that returns to its original shape after being straightened. This property allows the IUD to be straightened for easy insertion; once it is inside the uterus, it returns to its initial conformation.

Insertion of the IUD takes just two to three minutes. Several steps should be meticulously followed. One is sounding—inserting a slender, solid rod into the uterus to measure its depth and the direction and location of its opening. Some physicians omit doing this, but it is a critical step because if the cervical opening is too small or the uterine cavity is less than 6.5 centimeters in depth, the risk of pain, expulsion, or perforation is high. *No IUD should be inserted if the measurement is less than 6 centimeters*. Sounding also acquaints the physician with any oddities of the uterine cavity and forewarns of dangers or difficulties prior to actual insertion. In my opinion, insertion of an IUD without such knowledge is malpractice. Ask the person inserting your IUD if he or she will be sounding your uterus—and ask for the measurements, too, if you like.

Most women feel some cramps during insertion of the IUD. These subside in a few minutes and usually disappear completely in about half an hour. Some women, however, may experience discomfort for a few hours.

A woman having an IUD inserted should expect her current period to be slightly heavier or to last somewhat longer. For the next two or three cycles, she may note between-period spotting, or her next period may come early (the full flow probably will come on time, but she may spot two or three days early). On the other hand, no change may occur. Birth control protection begins the day of insertion. You should return to the doctor's office after your next menstrual flow to make sure the device has not been dislodged and no other problems have arisen. In addition, remember to check once a month, after your menses, that the string or tail of the device is still present. You can do this simply by inserting a finger high into the vagina and feeling the tiny thread that extends about an inch from the opening of the cervix. (Don't pull on the string!) Feeling the string is not always as easy as it may sound, because it is fine, and when warmed and moistened by the body, it is fairly imperceptible.

Side Effects and Removal

Pain and bleeding are the most common side effects of IUDs. Bleeding in users of unmedicated large devices such as the Lippes Loop C or D sizes or Saf-T-Coil, which approximately double menstrual blood loss over preinsertion levels, may be heavy enough to cause anemia. That is somewhat less likely with the Copper-7 or Tatum-T devices; they cause some increase in menstrual blood loss but not as much. On the other hand, the Progestasert system actually *reduces* the volume of menstrual bleeding an average of 40 percent below preinsertion levels; thus it could actually benefit women with iron-deficiency anemia. In many women, it also relieves menstrual pain. The intermenstrual spotting that this IUD sometimes causes tends to be less frequent in older women.

Menstrual pain cause by some IUDs can often be alleviated with drugs that inhibit the synthesis of prostaglandins (natural, hormonelike substances in the body). As I reported in the August 1979 issue of the *Journal of the American Medical Association,* antiprostaglandins, which I used in menstrual cramp studies, successfully alleviated pain caused by IUDs. The increased menstrual flow that occurs with some IUDs also can be decreased by taking these drugs (Ponstel, Anaprox, Motrin, or Dolobid) during the one to three days of maximal flow.

As for PID, you should not be at much risk if you have been properly selected for IUD use. Nevertheless, be sure you are familiar with its symptoms, as described earlier. If you develop any of them, make an immediate appointment with your doctor.

Removal of an IUD is even quicker and simpler than insertion. It takes only a few seconds and causes little or no discomfort. The doctor just pulls on the string and it slides out. This can be done at any time of the month, but if a new device is to be inserted during the same office visit, the visit should be scheduled to coincide with menstruation. Menopausal women should have their IUDs removed within six months of cessation of their periods, because after that, the devices become more difficult to remove.

If you want to become pregnant, you must, of course, have your IUD removed. How soon after that you can become pregnant depends on your own fertility; having used an IUD will not cause any delay in your ability to conceive. That's good news for women who want a baby, but it's a warning to most older women who do not desire a pregnancy that they should switch to another contraceptive method immediately after IUD removal. Otherwise they could end up with one of those "change-of-life" babies that we hear so much about.

IUD Advantages
1. Once it is inserted, an IUD requires little attention or concern.
2. It is one of the most effective contraceptive methods.
3. Since it acts locally in the uterus, it produces fewer side effects than the pill and is safer.
4. It does not interfere with spontaneity or sensation during intercourse.

IUD Disadvantages
1. It can cause heavy menstrual bleeding and cramping, and anemia (except for Progestasert).
2. It can contribute to pelvic inflammatory disease.
3. It can become displaced in such a way—by perforation or embedding—as to cause serious trouble to the user.
4. It requires the supervision of a physician.
5. It may permit the occurrence of an ectopic pregnancy.

Further IUD developments may eliminate some of these disadvantages. The devices have already been produced in most of their possible shape configurations, but medicated IUDs are only at the beginning of their evolution. For example, a longer-lasting progesterone IUD is being evaluated, and some devices may contain medications other than progesterone that reduce bleeding and cramping (possibly a small amount of antiprostaglandin). Other possibilities include medications (for example, copper and zinc) that will reduce the occurrence of herpes and other viral or bacterial infections. IUDs may also become delivery systems that provide intrauterine therapy to women who benefit from locally placed medication, as some do now from progesterone. Biodegradable IUDs intended to dissolve at a slow, predictable rate are also currently being tested. These would obviate the need for later removal.

In the future, then, even more choices will be available to women who are suitable for and receptive to IUD use.

Barrier Contraceptives

Barrier contraceptives include spermicides (foams, creams, jellies), condoms, and diaphragms and contraceptive vaginal sponges. A barrier method might be right for you if most or all of the following statements apply:

1. You need or strongly desire to avoid using the pill or an IUD.
2. You are willing to take precautions every time you have intercourse.
3. You are a methodical and responsible person.
4. Your sexual partner(s) is willing to use—or cooperate in the use of—intercourse-related methods.
5. You have previously used a barrier method successfully.
6. You would not consider a pregnancy catastrophic (because of willingness to have either another child or an abortion).

Though not as efficacious as birth control pills or IUDs, barrier methods are unquestionably safer from a health standpoint. With the possible exception of spermicides, they act locally only by putting up a mechanical barrier that prevents the sperm from reaching the ovum. Thus the egg is never fertilized, and normal uterine pregnancy—as well as ectopic pregnancy—is prevented.

The Pill and the IUD vs. Barrier Methods

Frequency of sexual intercourse is another factor to consider in deciding on a barrier method versus a pill or an IUD. I don't like to give pills or IUDs to women who have infrequent intercourse. Under these circumstances, the risk-benefit ratio is not favorable, and such women are better off using a barrier method.

In 1955, condoms and diaphragms constituted the chief contraceptive method of 52 percent of couples in the United States. By 1975, their share had fallen to 15 percent, mostly because women were switching to the pill. A countertrend began around 1978, as stories about the pill's serious side effects persuaded many women to go back to the older methods.

If you are in a stable relationship, as many mature women are, it is sometimes nice to share the responsibility for birth control. For example, right after your period, you might use only foam. In mid-cycle, during your fertile time, condom and foam combined would be a good method; and then before your period, your partner could use condoms. Or you might use foam just before and after your period and a diaphragm for the middle portion of your cycle. You should be willing to change with your life circumstances; remember that only sterilization is forever. And also remember that although women still bear the major responsibility for birth control, men are becoming more and more receptive to sharing it. If your partner hasn't reached that stage yet, maybe you can help him to do so.

Efficacy of the Barrier Methods

Great controversy surrounds the efficacy of barrier methods. The table on page 204-205 shows the enormous variation in reported failure rates with these contraceptives and compares their efficacy with that of other methods. For example, diaphragm use is reported to result in 2 to 20 pregnancies per 100 women per year and condoms from 2 to 36 pregnancies. How can we explain such differences? More to the point, what in the world are you to think about using one of these methods if you've been accustomed to the practically fool-proof pill?

One wit has explained the great variation in barrier-method failure rates by saying, ''The greatest reason for contraceptive failure is failure to use the contraceptive.'' That's why I gave you the commandment Know Thyself at the beginning of this chapter. If you are an impulsive, forgetful, or inconsistent person, don't assume your nature will change because you have switched to a barrier contraceptive. More than likely it will work fine every time—except for that one occasion when you or your partner doesn't use it. Or you may get away with skipping it once or twice, become lulled into a false sense of security, take another chance, and then find yourself pregnant.

Even with faithful use, the consensus seems to be that barrier methods are less effective than the pill or the IUD.

So if you decide on a barrier method—despite its more demanding use requirements and its lower efficacy—you must think about what you are prepared to do if you become pregnant. If you are healthy and would only be moderately put out by an unplanned pregnancy, well and good; you'll probably decide to have the baby. Or if you don't want the baby but have no qualms about abortion, the problem may be minor to you. (At least one authority has cited statistics indicating that barrier methods backed up by legal abortion are among the safest methods of birth control.)[1] But if you (or your partner) loathe the thought of abortion and would consider a pregnancy catastrophic, you should probably rely on a surer method. My recommendation in this situation would also be a vasectomy for your husaband or an IUD for you—provided you wouldn't have any undue risks with such a device (see p. 215). I would be less enthusiastic about recommending even a low-dose pill. It is important to note, however, that most reports indicate that barrier methods used faithfully will prevent pregnancy more than 90 percent of the time, and that by combining foam with condoms, nearly 100 percent protection can be obtained.

Also, at the age forty or over, you are considerably less fertile than you used to be. Thus barrier contraceptives may entail a much lower risk of pregnancy for you than for a twenty-five-year-old. With a 100 percent commitment to using them every time and exactly according to instructions, the chances are that you won't get pregnant.

Spermicides

Vaginal spermicides are made up of a sperm-destroying agent dispersed in an inert, bulky base that is heavy enough to block the opening of the cervix and prevent the entrance of any sperm that are not killed by the agent. They are available in many forms from many manufacturers. There are foams, creams, jellies, suppositories, and even foaming tablets. They can be purchased in almost every drugstore without a prescription and range in price from three to six dollars.

When used alone, spermicides are somewhat less effective than when they are used in a diaphragm or in addition to a condom. But they provide good protection, and for most women, using foam alone seems a lot easier than having a diaphragm fitted in a doctor's office. The jellies and creams, being more viscous, are usually used with a diaphragm for effective protection. Any spermicide can be used in conjunction with a condom.

To get proper protection from any spermicidal foam or cream, the spermicide must be placed deep in the vagina, near the cervix. Foams and creams come with plastic tamponlike applicators for this purpose. (Refill packages containing the spermicide alone are available at a lower cost.) All spermicides must be inserted not more than sixty minutes before intercourse and should be reinserted for each subsequent intercourse. There should be an interval of two or three minutes between insertion and intercourse. After intercourse, you should not douche or wash out the spermicide for at least six hours.

Suppositories and foaming tablets work in exactly the same way as foams but require a longer interval between insertion and intercourse—about ten minutes for foaming tablet, fifteen minutes for suppositories—because they need additional time to disperse. These tablets and suppositories are no more effective than foam, but they are easier to carry, because they are small. Some creams especially designed to be used without a diaphragm come in individually wrapped disposable tamponlike applicators, which are easy to carry in a purse.

Spermicides protect not only from pregnancy but also seem

to protect against infection. Laboratory tests show that these products inhibit the growth of the organisms that cause gonorrhea and syphilis. In a clinical study, regular users of Delfen cream had fewer cases of gonorrhea than nonusers. This protection, although it is far from foolproof, is important, for gonorrhea is thought to be a major cause of pelvic inflammatory disease and subsequent sterility. According to one estimate, as many as 80,000 young women in the United States become sterile each year as a result of gonorrhea infections. Spermicides also protect against less serious vaginal infections, such as the well known *Trichomonas* and *Monilia* (*Candida*). Moreover, they break down the protective envelope that covers the common Herpes virus, rendering it less able to cause genital infections. For those women who sleep with more than one partner, foam alone may offer some degree of protection against disease. *Combined foam and condom offer the best protection against veneral disease— except for saying no.*

Advantages of Spermicides

1. Spermicides are up to 95% effective when used correctly and faithfully.
2. They provide some protection against sexually transmitted disease because of their bactericidal (bacteria-killing) and viricidal (virus-killing) activity.
3. They do not interfere with the pleasurable sensation of intercourse.
4. They provide lubrication.
5. They produce no serious side effects in users. (Some men and women have an allergic reaction to certain spermicides, which can usually be remedied by switching brands.)
6. They are easily portable.
7. They are available without consulting a physician.

Disadvantages of Spermicides

1. Their use requires planning.
2. They can interrupt the spontaneity of sex.
3. Men object to the taste during oral sex.

4. Creams and jellies tend to drip and leak from the vagina. Foams are less messy, tend to leak less, and are generally more esthetically pleasing.

There is a possible additional disadvantage of spermicides that is much more serious than any of these. I did not include it in the list because it has not been definitely proved. Nevertheless, at least one study has implicated sperm-killing creams, jellies, and foams in birth defects and increased rates of spontaneous abortion. Jick and colleagues from the Boston Collaborative Drug Surveillance Program reported an increased incidence of limb-reduction deformities, tumors, chromosomal abnormalities, and congenital misplacement of the urinary opening to the undersurface of the penis (in the April 3, 1981, issue of the *Journal of the American Medical Association*). The frequency among infants whose mothers had used spermicides was 2.2 percent; for those women not using spermicides it was 1.0 percent. The study concluded: "If spermicides induce some of the congenital disorders described by this study, the effect might be produced by an action on sperm, ova, or the embryo itself. Obviously, spermicides damage sperm directly; should a damaged sperm produce conception, abnormalities could result. Alternatively, spermicides might be absorbed into the bloodstream and cause direct damage to the ovum before conception. Another possible mechanism would be the direct deleterious effect on the embryo." Rabbit and rat studies have shown that spermicides are absorbed from the vaginal wall into the blood and general circulation; absorption studies in humans have not been published to date.

You must remember that most women who routinely and correctly use these products do not get pregnant. The data therefore apply only to those women who have failed with the method.

Although women who use barrier methods have prided themselves on using the safest and most "natural" methods, it is possible that they have been fooled. Before you become alarmed about this side effect of spermicides, remember that the data from the study have been disputed recently, and follow-up studies must be done, for the ramifications of possible absorption into the woman's circulation are serious. In fact, Dr. Huggins of the University of Pennsylvania School of Medicine in Philadelphia reported on the outcome of pregnancies in women who were former diaphragm users and had unplanned pregnancies due to diaphragm failure. He found that the rates of spontaneous abortion, stillbirth, and total malformation were little different from those of women who used other means of birth control, but there were increased number of babies born with neural tube defects such as spina bifida to women who accidentally became pregnant while using the diaphragm. (All diaphragms are used with spermicides.)

Condoms

Would you believe that 35 percent of condoms are now purchased by women? That is the figure given by some manufacturers. Other indicators of this trend exist: more and more women's magazines are carrying advertising for condoms, and manufacturers are now selling these contraceptives in economy packages of 36, a size that women reportedly are more inclined to buy than men. To me, this trend seems healthy in two ways. It shows a growing confidence among women in asserting their right to cooperation from their partners in birth control; and it indicates a mature attitude in the men who are willing to accept this responsibility. But it's also physically healthy in this era of frighteningly large rises in occurrence rates of sexually transmitted diseases. Few authorities have challenged the condom's unmatched advantages in preventing these infections.

The condom provides this protection because it prevents direct contact between male and female genitalia while permitting normal intercourse. It is a thin sheath made of latex or lamb intestinal membrane that covers the penis and prevents sperm from entering the vagina. (Incidentally, condoms are also called rubbers, sheaths, safes, prophylactics, and sometimes by the trade name of the manufacturer—for example, Trojans, Ramses, or Fourex.) Until modern times, the condom was the only effective means of contraception. No one knows when it was first used, but the ancient Romans were fashioning condoms out of the intestines and bladders of animals for the prevention of venereal disease. In the 1500s, the Italian anatomist Fallopius recommended their use for the same purpose.

In improved and more varied forms, the condom remains one of the most reliable and safest contraceptives available. Many studies have shown that when properly and consistently used, it is 97 percent effective in preventing pregnancy. (Unfortunately, as shown in the table on pages 204-205, some actual user figures indicate that failures are common—probably because people do not follow directions.)

During wartime, American soldiers have received condoms as part of their prophylactic kit to protect them from veneral disease. This use intensified the association of this contraceptive with prostitution, and down through the years, the condom has become the scapegoat for our prudish attitudes toward sex. With our new sexual openness and freedom, that attitude is changing. A Supreme Court decision made in the 1970s has eased restrictions on condom sales and display and advertising. Open display of condoms is now reportedly the practice in more than half of the drugstores in the United States. Indications are that, partly as a result of this promotion, a decline in the popularity of condoms that started with the introduction of the pill has now been reversed. Or as one observer phrased it, condoms became "vastly popular," beginning in the mid-1970s.

Condoms may even offer protection from cervical cancer by preventing sperm from coming into contact with the cervix. Some researchers suspect that the potent chemicals (histones) that sperm contain are a factor in causing cervical cancer, particularly among young teenage women whose cervical structure is not yet stable and is thus vulnerable to injury.

Condoms are sold not only in drugstores but sometimes in vending machines in men's lavatories. They come lubricated or nonlubricated; with or without a small reservoir on the end to hold the ejaculate; perfectly smooth, ribbed, or knobby;

colored or plain. The most recent advance in condoms is the addition of spermicidal substances which thinly coat the inside as well as the outside of the condom. They cost between one and two dollars, depending on the features chosen, for a package of three. They are usually individually wrapped and are easily carried in a wallet or purse. They can be used only once. Latex condoms are one third cheaper than those made from animal membrane. Therefore, depending on the type chosen, the annual cost of contraception with condoms will be between $60 and $250, which makes them one of the more expensive methods of birth control.

To use a condom, place the rolled condom at the tip of the erect penis and unroll it down the entire length of the penis. An unlubricated condom may break because of friction during intercourse when normal vaginal lubrication is not sufficient, but prelubricated condoms may contain too much lubricant. If you are lubricating your own, as many people prefer, you should not use Vaseline or cold cream, which weakens the latex rubber. K-Y jelly, Surgilube, Personal Lubricant, or Transi-Lube may be used, as they are water soluble, wash away easily, and will not affect the latex.

The penis should be withdrawn promptly after ejaculation while the ring of the condom is firmly grasped to prevent spillage. Check the condom after use to be sure it has not ruptured. If it has broken, you should immediately fill your vagina with a contraceptive foam or douche with lukewarm water, and since neither of these methods is reliable, you may also want to consult your physician. The condom should be discarded in a waste paper basket; never flush it down the toilet because it can clog the plumbing.

When it is properly used, the condom has a small rate of failure resulting from manufacturing defects, such as pinholes or weakness in the sheath, from which ejaculate can leak. Consequently it is sometimes recommended that foam be used in conjunction with the condom, especially at mid-cycle.

Advantages of the Condom
1. The condom is easy and convenient to use.
2. It prevents infection.

3. It is quite effective if properly used.
4. It produces no side effects except in the case of rare allergies to latex rubber or lubricants.
5. It does not require a physician to prescribe or fit it.

The major dissatisfaction with the condom is that it can reduce sexual pleasure.

Disadvantages of the Condom.
1. It interrupts the spontaneity of sex, since it must be put on immediately before intercourse.
2. Men and some women find that it reduces their sensitivity and pleasure.
3. Users are aware of its presence, and some women as well as men dislike this fact.
4. Prompt withdrawal is necessary to avoid spillage.
5. Fear that the condom may slip or break can result in less energetic lovemaking.

Interestingly enough, many couples find that these characteristics are sources of satisfaction for them. They report that the placing of the condom over the penis, when it is done by the woman, is very sexy; the decrease in sensitivity results in prolonged intercourse; and awareness of its presence provides peace of mind.

Diaphragms

The diaphragm is a circular, dome-shape device made of latex rubber stretched over a thin metal ring. (The latex rubber is of much heavier gauge than that used in the condom.) After adding a spermicide, the user inserts the diaphragm through the vagina to cover the cervix. The main function of this contraceptive is to hold the spermicide in place against the cervical opening. It is ineffective when used without spermicide.

In my view, there's little to be gained by trying to sort out the widely varying figures on diaphragm effectiveness. You can find almost any figure you want in the literature. Thus I have to rely on my experience with patients. And I have found—as have many of my colleagues—that some women use the diaphragm successfully forever and some have no luck at all. I know that some of the failures are due to negligence, but it's also possible that inherent flaws in the method contribute. For example, such imponderables as the amount of change in the size of the vagina during sexual intercourse may contribute to unforeseeably poor fit of the device.

They are several styles of diaphragms, which differ mainly in the type of metal ring that is used. *All of them must always be used with a spermicidal jelly or cream.* The diaphragm is reusable and, with proper care, will last for twelve months. A tube of spermicidal jelly or cream costs between $6 and $8 and usually will provide enough spermicide for ten applications or more. The diaphragm itself can be purchased at any drugstore for $12 to $15. Thus the annual cost of using a diaphragm is between $120 and $170. Diaphragms are sold in plastic cases that make them easy to carry in a purse or leave in a drawers.

The woman who wants to use a diaphragm must be fitted for the proper size by a physician or paraprofessional. She must also be trained to prepare, insert, and care for it. I require two visits with a patient to teach her to use her diaphragm properly. During the first visit, I fit the diaphragm by trying a number of different-size rings (the rims of the diaphragm only), and then I teach my patient how to use it. I try to find the largest possible size that is comfortable for her, because the vagina tends to expand with sexual excitement; using the largest possible correctly fitting size helps ensure that the diaphragm will not be displaced during intercourse.

One teaspoon of spermicide is placed in the center of the dome of the diaphragm and more is spread around the edges. The diaphragm is then inserted, either by using an inserter or the fingers alone. It must be placed in the proper position behind the symphysis pubis, in the notch behind the pubic bone that nature has provided to hold it in place. If the diaphragm is too small and does not fit snugly, it will slip far back into the vagina. If it is too large, it will hurt. And in either case—too small or too large—it will not provide good contraception. Unfortunately, diaphragms are sometimes poorly fitted; in most such cases, they are fitted too small. I am sure that this, along with forgetting to use it, accounts for the majority of "diaphragm babies."

Once she has been fitted and given instructions, my patient goes home and practices putting in the diaphragm. When she is confident that she is doing it correctly, she returns to the office, either wearing it or ready to put it in by herself in the office. This visit is especially important not only because we check the diaphragm together to make sure that she knows how to place it and how to make sure it is correctly positioned, but because I also recheck to make sure that the size of the diaphragm is right. Even though I talk to my patients and try to relax them on their first visit, many of them cannot relax completely and have increased vaginal muscle tone. By the second visit, when a woman has had time to experiment with her new diaphragm and become accustomed to inserting it she can relax. Therefore, I occasionally find that the patient should use a diaphragm in a size larger than was first prescribed. Proper fit is critical, for without it, displacement of the diaphragm may occur, most likely at the height of sexual excitement when the inner two thirds of the vagina expands. It may also occur more commonly when the woman is in the superior position.

When the diaphragm is inserted properly, fitting snugly behind the pubic bone, it is not possible to feel the back rim of the diaphragm. By inserting the entire second finger or second and third finger into your vagina, you can feel your cervix deep in the vagina—it feels like the tip of your nose—and make certain that the rubber dome of the diaphragm is covering the cervix and holding the sperm-killing cream or jelly in place. If your cervix is not covered by the diaphragm, you have no protection. When my patient has learned to place her diaphragm correctly and to double-check its position, then and only then she has my okay to use it.

The diaphragm can be inserted up to six hours before sexual relations, but the spermicides lose their effectiveness if coitus is delayed for more than two hours. However, simply inserting more spermicide into the vagina, without removing the diaphragm, will provide contraceptive protection. Additional spermicide must be added for each successive intercourse, and the diaphragm must remain in place for at least six hours after the last intercourse (which often is overnight). When intercourse occurs in the morning and the diaphragm is left in during the day, spermicide may leak from the vagina, making it necessary to wear a sanitary pad throughout the day.

Here are a few more tips on diaphragms:

- *Inspect a new diaphragm.* If you see anything that indicates that it is not perfect, return it.

- *Inspect your diaphragm very carefully each time before it is used.* Hold the diaphragm near a light source and pull it gently away from its rim to make sure there are no holes. If a tiny hole exists, the light will shine through. Also, if there is puckering near the rim, this could mean thin spots, Some women carefully fill their diaphragm with water. They then inspect it for tiny water drops leaking through.

- *Removal.* The diaphragm must be left in place at least six hours after the last intercourse. Remove your diaphragm by inserting your index finger up and over the top of it, usually slightly to the side. Next, turn the palm of your hand downward and backward, hooking the index finger firmly on top of the inside of the upper rim of the diaphragm, breaking the suction. Pull the diaphragm down and out. This avoids tearing the diaphragm with the fingernails. The diaphragm should *not* be removed by trying to catch the rim from below the dome. (See diagram in photo insert section.)

- *Washing.* After each use, the diaphragm should be washed in warm water and Ivory soap. Detergent soaps, cold cream soaps, and soaps containing petroleum should not be used because they weaken the rubber.

- *Drying.* After washing, the diaphragm should be dried thoroughly with a towel.

- *Dusting.* The diaphragm should only be dusted with cornstarch. Scented talcs, body powder, baby powder, and other products should not be used because they weaken the rubber. More important, there are some new studies hinting that talc, which can be contaminated with asbestos, may be dangerous to your health. When applied to a diaphragm or even a sanitary napkin, it may make its way into the body (see page 156, Chapter 6). Therefore, keep a little dish of cornstarch in a bowl in your bathroom and, using a large cotton ball, dust it on your diaphragm.

• *Storage*. The diaphragm should be placed in its plastic case for storage. It should not be stored near a radiator or a heat source or in a drawer with open fingernail polish remover. With time and use, you may note that the rubber on the diaphragm will darken.

Your diaphragm should be refitted every year. This is important because the size or type you need may change. It also must be rechecked:

• if you have gained or lost more than 10 pounds

• if you have had an abortion or a baby

• if there has been any vaginal or pelvic surgery

The diaphragm should not be left in the vagina longer than necessary. Though it is rare, cases of toxic shock syndrome have been reported to have occurred with diaphragms left in place for over twenty-four hours.

Unless you are willing to follow these procedures consistently, you'd be much better off using a less demanding form of contraception. But I believe that if you follow them carefully from the beginning, they will become an almost automatic routine after a few weeks.

Advantages of the Diaphragm:
1. The diaphragm is 90 to 98 percent effective *when properly used*.
2. It usually does not interfere with the sensation or pleasure of intercourse. (Some couples would disagree with this.)

3. It is much less likely than the pill or IUD to cause health problems.
4. It may provide a degree of protection against sexually transmitted disease because of the bactericidal activity of the spermicide used in conjunction with the diaphragm.

Disadvantages of the Diaphragm:
1. It requires planning.
2. It is not always readily available. (It is easily carried in its case in your purse, but if you leave it at home, you may not be able to obtain a replacement in a hurry.)
3. It can interfere with the spontaneity of sex.
4. Not all women can use a diaphragm, because of anatomic peculiarities.
5. It is less effective than an IUD or oral contraceptives.
6. If it is not properly fitted, it may contribute to recurrent bladder infections.
7. Some men and women may be allergic to the rubber or the spermicide and may complain of a burning sensation. Changing to a plastic diaphragm or a different brand of spermicide usually corrects the problem.

Contraceptive Vaginal Sponges

A nonprescription vaginal contraceptive sponge, named Today, containing a spermicide has recently been marketed. It has undergone testing since 1976 and has been shown to be 82–90 percent effective. Dr. Tyrer of the Planned Parenthood Federation of America put its failure rate at 18 percent for the first year of use and 10 percent after that. Costing one dollar per throwaway sponge, it is one of the more expensive contraceptives. However, it adds another contraceptive choice for women who wish to use, and possibly alternate, barrier methods.

Surgical Methods of Birth Control

Sterilization procedures are conventionally thought of as vasectomy for the man and tubal ligation for the woman. In addition, hysterectomy is sometimes—I believe unjustifiably—performed with sterilization as a major reason.

I am cautious about "female" surgery in particular because I believe that often women don't fully understand its risks. The people who should be educating them are not doing a thorough enough job. That applies to some of my physician colleagues; it also applies to TV and the print media. How many stories have you read or seen on TV about the dangers of the pill and IUDs? How many have you seen on the life and death risks of tubal ligation and hysterectomy? I'd give odds that you've heard overwhelmingly more pill and IUD horror stories than surgical horror stories. Therefore you may be astonished to learn that hysterectomy is considerably riskier to life than one year of use of either the pill or the IUD (see table, page 252-253).

Sterilization Procedures

Sterilization provides extremely effective permanent contraception. It should be considered nonreversible, and so it is only for people who have decided not to have any—or any more—children. When one is performed on a woman, a sterilization operation (tubal ligation or some hysterectomies) constitutes major surgery. As in any other major surgical procedure, there are associated complications as well as some fatalities. For men, however, the sterilization procedure (vasectomy) is infinitely simpler and safer. *It has no death rate,* no serious medical complications, and is a minor doctor's-office procedure after which the man can walk home. The only dangers are some psychological problems that may occur in a small minority of men.

Thus if a couple decides on a surgical approach to birth control, I advise them that the man should have the procedure, because he is the partner at least risk. There can be no question about this: every time a man turns down a vasectomy, his partner becomes subject to a tubal ligation (or even a hysterectomy) that carries very *definite* risks to comfort, health, or even life.

As I said in *No More Menstrual Cramps,* I have always

been fascinated by the fact that the research establishment warns about *theoretical risks to men while it accepts the proven* dangers to women of sterilization or some methods of birth control as inevitable. We know of the many adverse effects of the pill—including death—and we know that some women die every year during sterilization surgery. Yet these deaths are minimized by the male-dominated medical profession. Tubal ligation is promoted as "Band-Aid" surgery, even though it is a major operation that is usually performed in a hospital under full anesthesia. To me, this attitude epitomizes the sexism of medicine.

For women considering sterilization, therefore, I routinely recommend that their husbands have a vasectomy instead. I am amazed at the number of women who nevertheless choose to undergo operations; they are willing to risk their lives so that their husbands will not have a moment's discomfort. Some of these women are overwhelmingly concerned for their spouses or feel terribly beholden to them. Others fear that their husbands will not be able to endure even a minor operation or will become interested in other women after being sterilized or will become impotent. Perhaps the best way of overcoming these fears is to learn more about vasectomy.

Vasectomy

Vasectomy is a safe, 99-percent effective procedure that has only one permanent physical effect: it thereafter prevents the man from fathering children. It is *not* castration and therefore does not in any way interfere with normal male function during intercourse. In fact, many men report an increase in their sexuality following vasectomy. The only thing missing is about one drop of fluid from the ejaculate that would have contained millions of sperm. Neither partner can notice its absence; no one can tell that the man has had a vasectomy unless his seminal fluid is examined under a microscope to observe the absence of sperm.

Despite these positive features, no unwilling man should be talked into a vasectomy. For one thing, the procedure must be considered irreversible, though occasionally it may be undone.

Therefore, the man should have a vasectomy only if he is certain he does not want to father any more children. In addition, a small minority of men—about 5 percent—have psychological problems following the procedure, which often manifest themselves in impotence. One might guess that an unwilling patient would be more likely to have such difficulties, because these problems do not have any physical cause.

On the other hand, 95 percent of men who have had a vasectomy do not hesitate to recommend it to other men. That probably explains why the procedure has been growing in popularity; as many as 750,000 men in the United States now elect it each year.

Vasectomy is much simpler and safer than any sterilization procedure for women. The male sex organs, being located outside the body, are easily accessible. Consequently male sterilization, unlike female sterilization, does not require abdominal incision.

In performing a vasectomy, the surgeon makes a small slit in the skin of the scrotum (the skin sac that holds the testicles) to expose the vas deferens. The vas is a tube that transports sperm from the testicle, where it is manufactured, to the prostate gland, where it is added to the ejaculate. Just as there are two fallopian tubes in women (one for each ovary), there are two vas deferens in men (one for each testicle). The vas are cut, tied, and clamped or otherwise obstructed so that sperm can no longer pass. This procedure is exactly analogous to female sterilization during which the fallopian tubes are obstructed so that the egg cannot pass on to the uterus.

A vasectomy takes about twenty minutes. It is usually performed in the physician's office under a local, dental-type anesthetic injected in the skin of the scrotum at the site of each of the two incisions. The cost is usually $200 to $300.

I do not believe there has ever been a vasectomy-associated death in the United States. Minor complications such as pain, swelling, or occasional infection of the incision site may occur, but these result in only minor and temporary discomfort.

With so much to recommend it, one may wonder why

vasectomy is not even more popular. One reason is that there are so many misconceptions about vasectomy, perhaps resulting from the early history of the procedure. About fifty years ago, it was used primarily to sterilize criminals, mental defectives, and those with hereditary diseases. In addition— on the basis of extremely doubtful evidence—some people have speculated on possible adverse effects. For example, after vasectomy, the sperm that continue to be manufactured are absorbed by the body, and men who have had a vasectomy may develop antibodies to sperm. This phenomenon has never resulted in any adverse health problems in men, but some researchers warn of vague possible effects on body organs. For example, a researcher noted that vasectomy caused an increase in atherosclerosis in ten monkeys. (The ten monkeys are referred to again and again in the medical literature and created a quiet panic among the medical community. I feel that such flimsy evidence provided a much-wanted excuse for many men to avoid the procedure.) However, a recent report in *Medical World News* (December 20, 1982) began, "A vasectomy isn't good for monkeys, but it doesn't seem to hurt men."

In a well-controlled study of 6,000 men, Dr. Diana Pettiti found no statistically significant difference between the sterilized and non-sterilized men. Even after ten years, men with vasectomies were no more prone to heart or stroke problems than other men their age.

In another nineteen-year study, Alexander and Jick followed 29,250 men of whom 4,830 were vasectomized. By the seventeenth year of the study, the rates of heart attack were nearly identical. Another study by Perrin followed 5,000 men and found no significant difference between the two groups. Therefore, the conclusion should be clear that to date, unless you are a monkey, there is no increased risk of death from atherosclerosis resulting from vasectomy. There is, however, freedom from worry, from the use of mechanical barrier methods, and, for the man, there should be pride in having taken responsibility for such an important matter. Furthermore, you as a woman have probably taken most of the risks and responsibilities of birth control before and have gone through the discomfort of pregnancies and dangers of delivery. I feel that turnabout is fair play. I hope that he does, too.

Tubal Ligation

Many women, weary of the anxiety or inconvenience that birth control causes, yearn to get rid of the whole problem permanently. Thus when tubal ligation is suggested, they look upon it as the perfect solution—a safe and carefree end to pregnancy worries. To correct that overly optimistic view, I'm going to emphasize some troublesome problems this surgery can cause.

Tubal ligation is accomplished by cutting, tying, burning (cauterizing), clipping, or otherwise blocking the fallopian tubes so that the egg produced in the ovary cannot come into contact with sperm, and thus fertilization cannot take place. The fallopian tubes, lying deep in the abdominal cavity, must first be exposed by the surgeon; all techniques for exposing them require that the abdomen be opened.

Four types of tubal ligation are performed to block the tubes: laparotomy, laparoscopy, vaginal tubal ligation, and postpartum tubal ligation. They range in cost from about $650 to $1120. All the procedures seem simple and safe enough, but things do not always go well. The overall complication rate for tubal ligation has been reported to vary from 0 to 7.4 percent,[2] depending on the procedure used and the surgeon. Serious complications in a recent study of 3,500 women undergoing sterilization by laparoscopy were reported as 1.7 in 100.[3] The complications included "Unintended major surgery" when the abdomen had to be reopened to correct a surgical error; rehospitalization for infection, bleeding, or pregnancy; and fever lasting more than two days.

Sometimes the surgeon has difficulty finding and isolating the two tiny fallopian tubes. Sometimes he mistakenly seals a ureter, blocking the flow of urine into the bladder, causing serious problems and requiring immediate corrective surgery. The surgical instruments used may perforate the bowel or a blood vessel in the abdomen. Use of cautery can inadvertently burn the intestine, resulting in serious infectious complications. Or the heat from the cauterization may spread to adjacent tissue and destroy or decrease the nearby blood supply to the ovary. Less disastrous slips or misidentifications might result in the cauterization or clipping of one of the supporting ligaments of the uterus. If this error goes unnoticed, a fallopian tube is left open and the woman is not protected from pregnancy.

Some other complications—such as a blood clot in the lung, bleeding from a damaged blood vessel, and cardiac arrest—can be fatal. Fortunately these are quite rare. Nevertheless, some women die each year as a direct result of tubal ligation;[4] a number of the deaths are due to complications when a general anesthetic is used. But whether the over-all mortality is 1 in 10,000 cases or 1 in 25,000, as given in various publications, these are deaths that need not have occurred.

When it is properly performed, tubal ligation should guarantee 100 percent effective birth control. The actual effectivenss is somewhat less than 100 percent, because the seal may not completely block the tube or may be applied to the wrong tube. Or the tube may repair itself later on. For these reasons, one or two pregnancies occur per 1,000 "sterilized" women at the end of one year. Should pregnancy occur, there is an increased possibility of tubal pregnancy.

In addition, the scientific literature is currently reporting that women who have undergone tubal sterilization, especially with cautery technique, subsequently have higher hysterectomy rates. By destroying tissues and vessels, the cautery type of tubal surgery interferes with the blood supply of the ovary, which may affect its function; its hormonal output may decrease, making ovulation irregular. The result is an abnormal pattern of uterine bleeding that becomes a basis for increased rates of hysterectomy.

I see so many women who have had a tubal ligation who complain of heavy monthly bleeding, irregular cycles, and long periods of flow. These complications often occur six months to two years after tubal ligation; women must be forewarned that such difficulties may lie ahead.

The alteration in ovarian function may also be the basis for increasing numbers of reports that tie tubal ligation to the subsequent development of premenstrual syndrome.

Despite its hazards, tubal ligation is being recommended more and more widely. My own view is that its risks outweigh its benefits. For example, a woman who is in her late forties has only a few years of fertility left; moreover, her ability to conceive during those years is less than when she was young. For these reasons, a spermicide, a diaphragm, or an IUD will take care of her contraceptive needs until her menopause. The younger woman in her late twenties or early thirties will benefit by having an excellent means of preventing contraception, but her ovarian function may be compromised, leaving her with years of abnormal bleeding ahead.

Laparotomy. In this oldest sterilization procedure, the surgeon makes a three- to five-inch incision in the abdomen to expose the fallopian tubes. He then either removes a section from each tube and ties the ends with surgical thread, or he seals them with electric cautery, bands, or clips. The method the surgeon uses to seal the fallopian tubes is important, in terms of both safety and effectiveness. The most common method is the Pomeroy technique: the surgeon lifts each tube to create a loop, ties the base of the loop firmly together with suture, and cuts off the top of the loop. In about a week, the suture is absorbed and the two scarred ends of the tube pull apart, leaving a gap between them.

Some surgeons do variations of this procedure by using a different suture material or by blocking the fimbria (the fingers of the fallopian tube that receive the egg from the ovary). Once the tubes are blocked, the incision is closed with stitches.

Laparotomy usually requires a general anesthetic and takes about thirty minutes. Patients spend about four days in the hospital, and full recovery may take six weeks. Of all the sterilization procedures, this one has perhaps the highest rate of failure—up to 2 percent subsequent pregnancy rate; it costs more, and has a high rate of complications. Still, it is the procedure of choice when a woman has a history of previous complicated abdominal surgery with adhesions resulting from infection—for example, from a ruptured appendix.

Minilaporotomy. This simplification makes the laparotomy easier and quicker to perform. An instrument is inserted into the uterus through the cervix and is used to push the uterus up against the abdominal wall. The surgeon then makes a small (about one inch) incision in the skin above the uterus, exposing the fallopian tubes. (Sometimes the surgeon may use a retractor, which operates somewhat like a small speculum, to help him locate the tubes.) He ties or severs the tubes and closes the incision. This procedure takes twenty to thirty minutes. It can be done under local anesthesia, but often a general anesthetic is used. In many countries, the patient goes home from the hospital the same day, but in the United States, women remain in the hospital for a couple of days. It takes about two weeks at home before the patient feels normal again.

Laparoscopy. This technique is commonly called Band-Aid surgery, because the incision required is so small (about ½ in.) that it can be closed and covered by an adhesive strip.

The laparoscope is a long tube that is slightly thicker than a pencil, which is inserted into the abdomen. Using fiberoptic technology, cold light is transmitted through the instrument to illuminate the operative field inside the abdomen. Like a hollow flashlight, the laparoscope enables the surgeon to see the internal organs and to insert operating tools through the hollow bore of the instrument.

The surgeon first makes a small incision near the navel. Through a long, thin needle inserted into the incision, about 2 liters of an inert, harmless gas (carbon dioxide or nitrous oxide) are pumped into the abdominal cavity. The gas helps prevent surgical accidents by pushing the intestines away from the uterus and the fallopian tubes. The laparoscope is then inserted through the incision, and the fallopian tubes are individually isolated and sealed. (Some surgeons make a second small incision at the pubic hairline to insert the operating instruments.)

The most common method employed during laparoscopy is

cauterization, using electricity. The cautery, or coagulation forceps, is passed through the laparoscope to grasp the tube; then current is applied in short burst to burn and seal it. Lately, because of the dangers of cautery, clips and rings to seal the tubes that can pass through the laparoscope are often being used. The silastic ring (or Falope ring), for example, can be slipped over a tubal loop, which the surgeon forms in the same manner as in the Pomeroy technique. The new Hulka clip simply clips the tube closed. In theory, these procedures have the advantage of being easily reversible, because no portion of the fallopian tube is removed or severely damaged as with cautery.

After the tubes are sealed, the instruments are withdrawn, the gas is released, the incision is closed with one stitch, and a small adhesive bandage is applied. The procedure takes about thirty minutes and is usually done under general anesthesia. The hospital stay usually lasts one day, and the patient is back to normal in two or three days. Many patients complain about pain, which usually eases after twenty-four hours, but some women report discomfort for one or two weeks.

Vaginal tubal ligation. In this procedure, the surgeon exposes the fallopian tubes by making the incision deep in the vagina in order to open the abdominal cavity. An instrument called a culdoscope, which has a light source, may be used to view the tubes. The operation takes about thirty minutes, and the hospital stay usually is one day. After two or three more days, the patient feels normal but should refrain from having intercourse for about a month to allow the incision in the vagina to heal. This procedure is declining in popularity; it has more potential than other procedures for infection, because the doctor is operating though an incision in the nonsterile vagina, and for bleeding.

Postpartum tubal ligation. A tubal ligation can be performed right after childbirth. At that time, the woman is already in the hospital, the uterus is still enlarged, and the fallopian tubes are much easier to locate. The surgeon makes a one- to two-inch incision below the navel, isolating and sealing the tubes. It takes about thirty minutes. An additional day or two may be added to the hospital stay, but the patient usually feels normal in about the same time it would take to recover from the childbirth alone.

Many doctors feel the postpartum period is an ideal time for a tubal ligation if a woman wants one. Surgery at this time, however, can be technically more difficult and dangerous because of the greater size of the pelvic organs and their greater vascularity. Increased blood flow through the enlarged blood vessels, for example, increases the danger of hemorrhage. And should anything happen to the patient's newborn baby, she may regret her decision for immediate tubal ligation.

Though I don't think many older women need a tubal ligation, occasionally I can see its necessity. If all or most of the following statements apply to you, tubal ligation may be an appropriate way to end your birth control problems:

1. Your husband refuses to have a vasectomy.
2. Using pills or the IUD is too risky because of current health status or history.
3. You have had failures with barrier methods (condoms, spermicides, diaphragms) or have an aversion to their use.
4. The prospect of pregnancy is disastrous for you.
5. Your general health is good.

If you do decide to have a tubal ligation, try to have it done as safely as possible. For example, make sure that both you and your surgeon know what type you prefer. Your physician will, of course, have veto power over your choise. Nevertheless, you should have some opportunity to select the procedure you want, unless there is a medical reason why it is not right for you. If your doctor simply doesn't perform the type of surgery you want or has had very little experience with it, find another doctor or at least get another opinion on the best procedure for you.

My own medical judgment is that, of the various ligation methods, your risks will be least with a laparoscopy using a Falope ring. Avoid cautery if possible, although a recent improvement in the technique permits more careful control of the electrical current, decreasing the risk of inadvertent burns. If your surgeon intends to use cautery, ask if he is using this newer "bipolar cautery" technique.

Laparoscopy became a commonly taught procedure in the late 1960s and since that time has been an important part of the training of the obstetrician/gynecologist. If your gynecologist is older, he may well have learned the technique in postgraduate courses; these tend to be short and less thorough than the training a surgeon receives during residency. Therefore, it might be advisable to choose a doctor who received his training after the procedures became part of the regular training program, or a doctor who teaches the procedure to residents, or a doctor who has done at least two hundred procedures.

If you choose tubal ligation, you must have a Pap test and a pelvic examination first. If, by some misfortune, you turn out to have uterine or cervical cancer or huge fibroids, it would make little sense to have a tubal ligation when hysterectomy might well be the better choice.

On a more personal note, because the procedure usually is irreversible, elect tubal ligation only when your life is fairly stable. Most requests to have tubal surgery reversed come from women who underwent tubal ligation just after they got divorced; later they remarried and wanted a child.

Future means of tubal ligation may be safer than current ones. Researchers are trying to find ways of blocking the tubes that do not require surgical penetration of the abdomen or the vagina. A new procedure that shows promise uses an instrument called a hysteroscope. Similar to the laparoscope, it is inserted into the uterus through the small opening in the cervix (the os) instead of through an incision in the abdomen. Once the hysteroscope is inside the uterus, the surgeon can locate the two openings where the fallopian tubes attach to the uterus and seal them by inserting a plug, injecting a silicone-rubber sealant, or injecting a scarring agent.

Advantages of Tubal Ligation
1. Tubal ligation is a one-time procedure with a one-time cost.

2. It is nearly 100 percent effective.
3. It does not interfere with spontaneity during intercourse.

Disadvantages of Tubal Ligation

1. Tubal ligation is usually permanent and should be considered irreversible. Even when reversals can be made, subsequent pregnancy rates are poor.
2. It may interfere with the blood supply of the ovaries and lead to abnormal hormone production, lack of ovulation, unusual bleeding patterns, and a need for later surgery, including hysterectomy.
3. The full implications won't be known for at least another decade.
4. The surgery may have serious complications such as hemorrhage, peritonitis from bowel burns, infection of the wound, and others. Even without complications, it causes postoperative pain.
5. Should the procedure fail and pregnancy occur, there is an increased risk of tubal pregnancy.

Abortion

The issue of abortion has special relevance to the older woman. The health risks and disruption of mid-life tranquility that a late pregnancy can cause are serious concerns for her. Yet an older woman may be particularly vulnerable to unwanted pregnancy. She is likely to have switched fairly recently to a less reliable and less familiar contraceptive method than the pill; or if she has been using the rhythm method of contraception, her irregular mid-life cycles will put her in real jeopardy. And, regrettably, some women tend to get a little careless in their forties, mistakenly believing that they are past their fertile years.

In these pages, I'm not going to discuss the ethical side of the highly charged abortion issue; neither am I going to describe the procedures in any detail. This chapter is, after all, on the subject of pregnancy prevention, not pregnancy termination. Yet birth control failure is often what causes the abortion issue to be raised, so I do want to provide at least some rudimentary guidance on the risks of abortion and how to minimize them.

Some women are not really sure of their feelings about abortion, and they often put off examining those feelings until they experience an unwanted pregnancy. That can lead to either panic or procrastination. Panic can result in a hasty—and perhaps subsequently regretted—decision to abort or not to abort; procrastination can cause delay in getting an abortion that will make the procedure more risky than necessary. My first advice on the subject, therefore, would be to sort out your own feelings and those of your husband on this subject. Then apply the results of this thinking to the contraceptive you are using or about to start using. If terminating a pregnancy goes deeply against your emotions or your ethics, then you should be using a highly effective contraceptive (IUD) or a combination method such as a spermicidal foam for you and a condom for your husband.

The woman whose deeply held religious convictions forbid contraception, abortion, and sterilization is of course in a difficult position. For her, a late baby may be less traumatic than an abortion.

To women who would consider an abortion, I say: learn all you can about it—its risks and how to minimize them. Minimizing risks means having a legal abortion and having it done as early as possible in your pregnancy at a reputable clinic or hospital, or in the well-equipped office of a physician experienced in the procedure.

Life Risks to Women from Pregnancy or Prevention of Pregnancy*

	Chance of Death in a year
Preventing pregnancy	
Oral contraception (nonsmoker)	1 in 63,000
Oral contraception (smoker)	1 in 16,000
Using IUDs	1 in 100,000
Using barrier methods	None†
Using "natural" methods (e.g. rhythm)	None†

Undergoing sterilization:	
Laparoscopic tubal ligation	1 in 10,000
Hysterectomy	1 in 1,600
Vasectomy	None
Pregnancy	
Continuing pregnancy	1 in 10,000
Terminating pregnancy	
Illegal abortion	1 in 3,000
Legal abortion:	
Before 9 weeks	1 in 400,000
Between 9–12 weeks	1 in 100,000
Between 13–16 weeks	1 in 25,000
After 16 weeks	1 in 10,000

*SOURCE: Adapted from R. A. Hatcher, G. K. Stewart, F. Guest, N. Josephs, and J. Dale, "Contraceptive Technology 1982–1983," 11th edition, Irvington Publishers, New York.

†However, if method fails, then pregnancy or abortion risks must be considered.

In the table, you can see that legal abortion is *much* safer than illegal abortion; even late legal abortion is safer than illegal abortion. In fact, if abortion is performed by twelve weeks, it is ten times less risky than continuing the pregnancy. Early abortion is also considerably more safe than tubal ligation, and it's far safer than hysterectomy or using the pill if you smoke. Delaying an abortion greatly increases its danger. When the abortion is performed at less than the ninth week of pregnancy, the risk of death is only 1 in 400,000. After the sixteenth week of pregnancy, the risk to life shoots up to 1 in 10,000, the same as the overall risk of childbirth and tubal ligation. Knowing your own mind about abortion will allow you to move fast if you must have one and thus avoid the hazards of a late procedure.

Abortion risks also rise with age.

Mortality Associated with Legal Abortion by Age*

Age (Year)	Mortality per 100,000 first-trimester abortions
15–19	1.0
20–24	1.4
25–29	1.8
30–34	1.8
35–39	2.7
40–44	2.7

*SOURCE: Christopher Tietze and Sarah Lewit, "Life Risks Associated with Reversible Methods of Fertility Regulation," *International Journal of Gynaecology and Obstetrics* 16: 456–459.

The death rate from abortion for women in their forties is 2.7 per 100,000. The death rate for giving birth when in your forties is 68.2 per 100,000. While a total of 136 women died between 1972 and 1978 because of the consequences of legal abortions,[5] many times that number died as a consequence of childbirth.

Your physician or local medical society should be able to guide you to reputable abortion facilities in your area. The cost of first-trimester abortions ranges from $150 to $300. Before you have an abortion, ask what technique will be used. If you're in the first sixteen weeks of pregnancy, you should have a vacuum curettage unless some reason exists to contraindicate this procedure.

Vacuum curettage, which utilizes suction to abort the pregnancy, can be done under general anesthesia in a hospital or clinic or with local anesthesia in a doctor's office; it empties the uterus completely in just a few minutes. It has almost replaced sharp curettage (scraping the uterus with a sharp instrument), an older technique that required greater dilation of the cervix and often use of a general anesthetic. Sharp curetting also carried a greater risk of excessive bleeding, incomplete removal of the products of conception, and infection.

There's one quite simple technique that I think too few

women are aware of that can often eliminate the need for abortion. That's the insertion of a copper IUD as a "morning-after" measure. It usually will prevent development of a pregnancy if inserted within three days of unprotected intercourse. This procedure simply prevents implantation and certainly provides a better solution to unwanted pregnancy than abortion or the "morning after" pill containing DES, with its unacceptable hormonal risks. So if you've neglected to use your diaphragm or spermicide, give your doctor a call right away and ask about the "morning-after" use of this contraceptive. You need not continue using it permanently once it has served this purpose, but you may decide you want to anyway.

Abortion techniques used later than about the sixteenth week of pregnancy principally involve the introduction of substances into the uterus that produce fetal death. These procedures are more difficult and dangerous than those done earlier in pregnancy. Therefore, do not wait until they are necessary.

What I recommend even more strongly is that you avoid the need for abortion. That way you have no difficult decisions to make, no regrets, and no abortion complications. Those complications are rarely fatal, but they are definitely unpleasant. They can include infection, unsuccessful abortion, intrauterine blood clots, cervical or uterine trauma, and hemorrhage. You should avoid exposure to these hazards even once, and certainly you won't want to risk them repeatedly. I feel compelled to say this because with abortions now reaching the 1.5 million per year level, it seems evident that some women must be substituting them for effective birth control. And with all the options available today, that is unnecessary.

Hysterectomy

By rights, a chapter on birth control should not even include a section on hysterectomy. But the older you get, the more likely you are to encounter a physician who will recommend it. Sometimes he will make this recommendation at least partly on the basis of your not wanting any more babies "at your age." I am very much against this and other nonurgent reasons for this major operation. It has a death rate of 1 per 1,600[6]—far higher than any method of birth control—and requires six to eight weeks for recovery. Serious complication and death rates are high—ranging from ten to a hundredfold greater than for patients having a tubal ligation, depending on the group studied. Yet I meet women every day who would not dream of taking the lesser risks of pill or IUD use but do not hesitate to have their uterus removed.

Birth Control Without Contraceptives?

In *No More Menstrual Cramps*, I discussed coitus interruptus and the rhythm method, which some couples employ to try to prevent pregnancy without using contraceptives. In all honesty, I cannot recommend either one as reliable, but I shall discuss them because some readers will want to know about them.

Coitus Interruptus

In coitus interruptus, the couple uses no contraceptive during intercourse; instead, the man withdraws before ejaculating. Needless to say, failures with this "method" are high: the man may forget to withdraw, may decide not to, or may not time his withdrawal effectively. And even if the man does withdraw as planned, sperm may leak from the penis prior to ejaculation or seminal fluid may contact the woman's external genitalia, which can result in pregnancy. For all these reasons, couples using this method should expect it to fail sooner or later. While the lower fertility of older women makes coitus interruptus somewhat less risky than it is among teenagers, that's the most I can say for it—and that's not much. Moreover, couples accustomed to using conventional contraception would certainly be unwise to switch to this method in mid-life, when there are so many more reliable ways to prevent conception.

Natural Family Planning

Natural Family Planning, which involves abstaining from intercourse during the woman's fertile period, is used by many couples because it is the only means of birth control sanctioned by the Catholic church. Some women have used rhythm with varying degrees of success for many years, but as they grow older, they should become extremely cautious about it. Menstrual cycles often change or become irregular in the mid-thirties or forties, and the fertile period becomes much harder to predict.

During each menstrual cycle, a woman can conceive only during a stretch of about five days. This fertile time begins shortly before ovulation (the release of an egg by the ovary), which occurs about fourteen days *before* menses. The egg will live for only two days unless it is fertilized, but sperm usually live for three days in the woman (although they have been known to survive for up to a week). Thus during the five successive days when there is an opportunity for a live egg and a live sperm to be at the same place at the same time, a couple having unprotected intercourse has an excellent chance of producing an heir.

Since it is impossible to predict the very day when ovulation will occur, we must identify a longer period of time— usually about six to eleven days—during which a couple may avoid pregnancy by abstaining from intercourse. There is no consistently accurate way at present to determine the fertile time of the month for a particular woman, but it can be estimated by one of three methods, or can be estimated by using all three methods together:

1. calculating the fertile period by recording menstrual cycle dates (the "calendar" or "rhythm" method)
2. recording body temperatures daily (the Basal Body Temperature method)
3. observing changes in cervical mucus, which can be coupled with noting changes in the texture of the cervix.

For the older woman, the calendar method is likely to prove unreliable, so I shall discuss the other two methods first.

Just before you ovulate, your temperature may drop slightly, and it will rise sharply immediately afterward. This change in temperature—between 0.5 and 1 degree Fahrenheit—gives a pretty accurate indication that ovulation has occurred. You can note this change by using a special basal thermometer (cost, about $6) to take your temperature, preferably rectally, *at the same time every day* immediately upon awakening, before you even get out of bed or smoke a cigarette. Since a nonfertilized egg will survive for only two days after ovulation, intercourse should be safe three days after the temperature rises. Changes in temperature indicate that ovulation has occurred but do not signal the beginning of ovulation, so to be perfectly safe, a couple should abstain from intercourse from the onset of menses to three days after ovulation.

The problem with this method is that the change in body temperature is so small that you can easily miss it. In addition, other factors such as taking your temperature at a different hour or getting a cold can cause body temperature changes that confuse the issue.

Because of these uncertainites, users should try to confirm the accuracy of the temperature observations by observing changes in the cervical mucus each month. Immediately after menstruation, the cervical mucus is absent or scanty, but as the time for ovulation approaches, the amount of mucus increases and becomes cloudy and sticky. Before and during ovulation, the mucus becomes thinner, clear and very slippery, much like raw egg white; and after ovulation, it becomes cloudy and sticky once more and decreases in amount. The chemical composition of the mucus also changes in both acidity and glucose content during these periods. Thus it is possible to determine the time of ovulation by observing the mucus or by testing it with litmus paper for acidity or with a test tape for glucose content. The dry period after menstruation would be considered safe, as would the dry period before menstruation. However, not all women experience these changes during every cycle, and any vaginal infection will affect the mucus. Thus the cervical-mucus pattern is not a reliable indicator of the fertile period in nearly a third of all women. Nevertheless, it may be of help if it is used in addition to temperature observations.

An older woman whose cycles are still regular may be able to use the calendar method to help determine her fertile period. It requires keeping a record of menstrual cycles for six to eight months and then calculating the unsafe period on the basis of that record. Ovulation occurs fourteen days, plus or minus two, before menses, and three additional days must elapse to ensure that any sperm present in the woman have died. Thus counting the first day of flow as day one, by subtracting nineteen from the number of days in the shortest cycle you have recorded, you can determine the first unsafe day of your average cycle. By subtracting ten from the number of days in your longest cycle, you can determine the last unsafe day. For example, if your shortest cycle was twenty-six days and your longest was thirty-one, days 7 through 21 are unsafe for you, and you should not have unprotected intercourse during this time. With this method, however, the first irregular cycle may result in mistimed intercourse and pregnancy. Thus it is highly chancy.

Advantages of Natural Family Planning
1. It is the only method the Catholic church permits its members.
2. It is inexpensive.
3. It uses no devices during intercourse which might interfere with sensation.

Disadvantages of Natural Family Planning
1. It is one of the less reliable contraceptive methods and should never be used by a woman who must not become pregnant.
2. It requires periods of abstinence.
3. It requires organization and motivation.
4. It cannot be used effectively by a woman who has irregular cycles or vaginitis.

5. It provides no protection against sexually transmitted disease.

Contraceptives of the Future

Many new ideas for contraception are currently being developed. Most will not be available for many years, at least not in the United States. However, as research continues, there will be a wider array of methods so that couples will have a better choice in selecting a suitable and appropriate contraceptive. Here are some of them.

New Hormonal Delivery Systems (Implants of Hormones Under the Skin)

Implanting a capsule containing progestogen without estrogen under the skin is a means of delivering low-dose progestogen therapy. The capsule gradually releases the hormone through its wall. The capsules contain enough progestogen to maintain a contraceptive blood level for three to four years. Because the capsule can be removed at any time, the method is reversible. This method is now being tested in Europe.

Contraceptive Vaginal Rings

Vaginal delivery of hormones may have some advantage over taking them orally. When you take birth control pills, the hormones first pass through the liver in high concentration. The liver must then break down a large load of synthetic hormones. Changes in liver function result from high concentrations of these synthetic hormones. This also accounts for liver tumors that are found in some women taking oral contraceptives. (Such tumors are very rare but may be dangerous and life threatening if they rupture.)

In contrast, absorption through the vagina puts the hormones directly into the bloodstream, from which they can reach their target organs without having to pass through the liver. The contraceptive vaginal ring releases the hormones against the vaginal lining at a fixed rate. For monthly birth control, it is used much like a birth control pill, with the woman leaving it in place for three weeks and removing it for a week. When the woman no longer wishes birth control, she removes the ring permanently. To date, approximately 15 percent of users have complained either about vaginitis, vaginal irritation, or menstrual problems.

New IUDs

One new IUD being tested contains levonorgestrel, a synthetic 19-nortestosterone-derived progestogen. This IUD is said to thicken the cervical mucus by its progesterone-type activity. The cervical mucus then acts as a barrier against both bacteria and sperm. Postcoital tests have shown no penetration by sperm. Further documentation may show this method to have protective effects against pelvic infection. Using this IUD also seems to reduce menstrual bleeding and decrease intermenstrual spotting. To date, pregnancy rates have been zero with this device. Women have complained of pain or lack of menstruation in approximately 12 percent of cases.

Barrier Methods: Cervical Caps

More than one cervical cap is available today, but all are still in experimental stages. A custom-molded cap with a one-way valve that permits a unidirectional flow of blood or mucus from the cervix is being studied for its efficacy when it remains in place for several months to years. The possibility of its causing vaginal and cervical irritation is being scrutinized. Because the cap does not allow flow back into the cervix, birth control is achieved. It is held in place by suction and surface tension. Trials in this country, however, have been cut short because of an excessive pregnancy rate. This may be the fault of the cap or the fault of the physicians, who simply need more experience in fitting them. Doctors participating in this research are receiving more instruction before new trials again get underway.

Other valveless cervical caps have been available from Europe for some years. They come in several sizes, and the best possible fit over the cervix requires trying several sizes, much like fitting a diaphragm. These caps must be used with a spermicide and can be left in place for up to twenty-four hours after intercourse, according to the manufacturer's instructions. However, the Harvard Medical School Family Health Care Program warned that unwanted pregnancy rates were greater than 10 percent. Also, women complained about cap displacement during intercourse as well as discomfort to their partners. One of my concerns is that because of the toxic shock problem, I would be somewhat reluctant to insert a device that will remain in the vagina for any extended length of time. Also, because these caps have no opening to allow access of menstrual flow, it is theoretically possible for the flow to back up in the uterine cavity should it inadvertently be left in place when menstruation begins. This is entirely possible, as some women have been instructed to leave this device in place for up to seven days.

Other barrier type devices under development include a disposable diaphragm with a controlled-release spermicide. The nonoxnol-9 spermicide diffuses out of the diaphragm after insertion. The diaphragm can be worn and is effective for up to 24 hours by early estimates. The time-release feature would eliminate the need for additional applications of spermicide if intercourse is repeated. As the device is currently envisioned, it will be fitted by a physician and then purchased via a refillable prescription. The possibility of developing a one-size-fits-all device will also be explored.

There is also a new contraceptive controlled-release suppository being developed. After an initial burst of spermicide, the suppository will release spermicide continuously over a 16-hour period.

And so as more research is performed, there will be more and hopefully better choices in contraceptives available.

10

Medical Laboratory Tests—
What Do They Mean?

Laboratory tests, an important part of medical practice and a vital addition to your physical examination, are used for two different reasons: to help diagnose disease, either suspected or unsuspected; and to check the progress of a patient or her treatment. Most physicians test two body fluids, the blood and the urine.

Whereas women in their teens and early twenties may need little more than a blood count and urinalysis for their physical examinations, women over thirty-five should have complete blood chemistries as part of their routine annual testing. As you get older, lab tests become more important, because it is more likely that disorders may be found or that unsuspected abnormal processes have begun without either you or your doctor being aware of them.

Measurements made in the lab can determine either the quantities or the types of substances present. These measurements are then compared with a normal "reference range." "Normal" values vary and are influenced by age, diet, environment, sex of the patient, and by the method used for the measurement by the individual lab. For this reason, it is important that you not compare your lab values with those of your friends. Even I must constantly check reference ranges from my lab, for they may change from time to time as the lab changes its methods of testing. You should also be aware that reference ranges are based on values found in 95 percent of the population. That leaves 5 percent of the normal population that may have laboratory values above or below the stated "normals." So just because a lab value is outside the range of "normal," it does not automatically mean that the patient has disease. On the other hand, the patient may have perfectly normal lab results and be terminally ill. You've probably heard the joke about the patient who died in spite of his completely normal chart.

The range of normal for many tests is quite wide, but most individuals' test levels lie within much narrower bounds. Thus past test results are important in evaluating a patient's current status.

Blood Tests

My patients have blood drawn at the time of their initial or yearly physicals. Afterward, I give them a list of the tests that will be run on their blood and tell them to call in for their results in two or three days. After scanning the list, the usual question is, "Can you really get all that information from those three little tubes of my blood?" The answer, of course, is a definite yes.

It is to your own advantage to understand the type of information that can be obtained from lab tests and, perhaps more important, to know why it is necessary to get such information. Some of this information gathering falls in the realm of preventive medicine, because early diagnosis before symptoms are present or numerous gives the doctor a real edge in instituting effective therapy. It is possible that early measures will prevent a full-blown problem from occurring.

In other cases, lab findings identify an existing problem. For example, the finding of anemia will often settle the question of why the patient has been feeling draggy for the past few months. Or a viral blood count will tell me that the patient needs bed rest and that antibiotics have no place in her treatment. Other tests, the blood chemistries, often give clues about conditions that I may not have thought about or that patients have been unwilling to admit. For example, abnormal liver function tests may tip me off to the fact that my patient recently began drinking excessively. Many patients never mention such a fact. The clues are there, though, on the lab slip. They become an invaluable starting point for discussion with the patient, for these early signs of liver damage become an important impetus for the patient to change her habits. Usually with several weeks off alcohol, on vitamins, and with a good diet, the abnormal findings revert. Therefore, when routine testing is done, it is possible to catch subtle changes and advise the patient or treat her before permanent and irreversible damage takes place.

If your blood is not handled properly, your laboratory values will not be accurate, so it is important to have some knowledge of just how the blood should be processed in your doctor's lab, especially if the blood is drawn there and then shipped out to a laboratory. Tests are done on both the blood cells and on the serum or liquid in which the cells are carried, so the blood sample must be prepared two different ways. For the blood cell counts, whole blood is mixed with an anticoagulant to prevent the cells from clumping together. For the serum analyses or blood chemistries, the blood cells must be separated and discarded. To do this, your doctor's office must be equipped with a centrifuge. This simple machine spins the tube of blood after it has clotted for twenty to thirty minutes. Spinning for fifteen minutes separates the red blood cells from the serum, concentrating them at the bottom of the test tube. It is important to do this, for if the red blood cells remain in contact with the serum for extended periods of time, they break and may spill substances such as potassium, magnesium, and enzymes known as LDH and SGOT into the serum. Therefore, lab test results of the serum may be abnormal, due not to the patient's illness but to poor lab technique. Blood sugars pose another such problem. Enzymes in the red blood cells break down or digest glucose if the red cells are left in contact with serum too long. This results in apparent low blood sugar level. To avoid false results, then, the cells are centrifuged and the serum is poured off and transported to the lab while the red cells are discarded. Some labs supply gel barrier tubes, which allow the red blood cells to pass through a layer of gel during centrifugation. The serum is then physically separated from the red cells by this inert barrier, and the laboratory technician does not have to pour off the serum manually.

I give the following letter to every new patient and to every patient who returns for her yearly physical. Because of new laboratory technology, all these tests can be done at relatively little expense—under $25. I consider that quite a bargain.

Dear Patient,

The following tests will be done on your blood:

3 thyroid tests

9 liver function tests

3 kidney function tests

a blood sugar level

a cholesterol level

a high density lipoprotein level

a cholesterol/high density lipoprotein level ratio (this indicates risk of heart attack)

a blood triglyceride level

a test for syphilis

a test for anemia and red cell size and number

a white blood cell count and differential

a test for body salts, sodium, potassium, chloride, calcium, phosphorus, magnesium, and iron.

It is important that you call the office regarding the results of all lab work done for you. Please call at the time indicated below.

Most patients are eager to know how their blood chemistry is doing and so willingly undergo the process of drawing blood. However, once in a while, a patient comes in who is extremely anxious, really hates needles, or has veins that are just plain lousy. I myself have tiny veins, and doctors have always had problems getting blood from me. I especially remember the time I needed blood drawn in order to get my marriage license. It took three different visits to the medical school health clinic and three different doctors to get my blood. So patients like these get special TLC (tender loving care) in my office.

The Complete Blood Count (CBC)

The complete blood count, or CBC, is one of the most informative and frequently ordered of the routine tests. It has four major components: the red blood cell count (or the hematocrit, which is now replacing it), the hemoglobin level, the white blood cell count, and the differential cell count or, in laboratory language, the "diff." In addition to the standard tests of the CBC, I usually do a "sed (sedimentation) rate" on my patients and sometimes a platelet count.

A CBC can be done on blood obtained from just pricking your finger. More often, however, a greater amount of blood is drawn from your arm. The part of this blood to be used for the CBC is prepared in a separate tube with an anticoagulant. The rest is usually centrifuged and used for the blood chemistry analyses.

You almost certainly have had a CBC sometime in your life. Let's see just what the tests are and what it means when your doctor says your CBC is normal.

The Red Blood Cell Count

Red blood cells (rbc's) or erythrocytes contain hemoglobin. This is a pigment that is capable of carrying oxygen from the lungs to the cells and carbon dioxide, a waste product, away from the cells, back to the lungs for exhalation. When the number of rbc's falls below the number necessary for carrying out these functions efficiently, the patient is considered anemic. Other disorders are characterized by too many red blood cells.

Women have fewer red blood cells than men. Adult women have about 4.0 to 5.5 million rbc's in a microliter of blood, whereas adult men have approximately one-half million more than that per microliter. (To picture a microliter, visualize a liter (or about a quart) of liquid divided into one million droplets; each drop would be one microliter.) This difference is believed to be due mainly to the effect of the male sex hormone, testosterone, on red blood cell production. The hormonal effects become evident at puberty; boys who have not reached puberty and therefore do not have adult levels of testosterone have red cell numbers equal to those of girls. With puberty, their counts rise above the female levels.

Another factor that sometimes contributes to sex-related differences in rbc numbers is menstruation, although unless the flow is excessive, menstrual blood loss does not seem to contribute significantly to the difference. Still, because young menstruating women tend not to have high levels of hemoglobin, I counsel them not to donate blood when the Red Cross or other blood drives solicit volunteers. However, my advice to postmenopausal or hysterectomized women is that they are the ones who *should* volunteer their blood. Adult male patients especially are prodded to donate.

One of the reasons that I feel so strongly that men and older women should donate blood is that I believe that lowering their hemoglobin and iron stores will benefit them. There is some evidence that men (and postmenopausal women) may be more subject to heart attacks because of their increased iron stores and sluggish blood. Men, unlike menstruating women, have no way to rid their bodies of excess iron. Donation provides such an outlet. My husband has donated four gallons of blood over the years.

This is also one of the reasons that men and non-menstruating women should not take more than minimal supplements of iron. The minimum daily requirement of iron for these groups is 15 mgs daily, and they should not take more. I am often perturbed by advertisements of geriatric vitamins which contain mostly iron and little else, as I consider these supplements dangerous to health of men and non-menstruating women. Many of the highly advertised commercial products for older people contain 50 mgs of iron. I personally feel such products should be banned, but since that is very unlikely, I am trying to alert the public to their dangers.

Anemia. Some 20 million Americans suffer from anemia, most types of which are characterized by inadequate amounts of red blood cells. The anemic patient may be generally tired and pale and may not be able to pinpoint the onset of her decrease in energy. I once had a patient who was severely anemic, but because her anemia had developed over a long period of time, she never realized how little she had been able to do until she began to get treatment. Until that point, she was convinced that her lack of energy was a symptom of advancing age.

Red blood cells develop in the bone marrow (as do white blood cells) for about 6 days and then are released into the blood, where they circulate for about 120 days until they die and are replaced. Consequently direct damage to the bone marrow from toxins, poisons, or cancer that invade the bone may cause anemia. Toxic wastes, insecticides, and even some prescription drugs can affect the bone marrow. Sometimes the red blood cells that are produced are destroyed too quickly, as in hemolytic anemias. The more common anemias, however, are caused by blood loss through heavy menses or bleeding into the intestinal tract, or by iron, vitamin B_{12}, or folic acid deficiencies.

Some patients develop iron-deficiency anemia from an undiagnosed ulcer of the stomach or duodenum that is bleeding little by little or from a cancer of the intestine that leaks in similar fashion. Other patients may have an insufficient intake of iron or inadequate absorption of it due to digestive disturbances. Children, especially those whose diet consists largely of milk, are the commonest victims of iron-deficiency anemia. Menstruating or pregnant women and growing teenagers make up the bulk of the rest of the iron-deficient population. Adult males and postmenopausal women rarely have iron deficiency, unless their diet is unusually poor. If they do have iron-deficiency anemia, it is usually a clue that they may be bleeding somewhere in the body.

Anemia is actually a late development in iron deficiency. Many women are iron deficient but are not anemic. When the anemia finally appears, iron levels have usually dropped very low. The red cells tend to be pale and smaller than normal. Noting the appearance and size of the red cells and determining the serum iron will help diagnose anemia, but there is another test called a ferritin test that helps in making the diagnosis by differentiating between iron-deficiency anemia per se and anemia from chronic disease, inflammation, or infection. This serum ferritin test is a reliable indicator of iron stores. If you are iron deficient, since anemia is a late development in this disorder, it is necessary to take your iron supplement not only until your hemoglobin and red count are normal again but until your iron stores are replenished. Although you may feel better, as your hemoglobin rises within a few weeks, it may take several months until the iron stores are normal again. So continue to take your iron for as long as directed by your physician.

Some patients have vitamin B_{12} deficiency, and that leads to pernicious anemia. Their complexion appears somewhat lemon yellow. Instead of red cells that are too small, the red cells of these individuals are too large. Patients who have had part of their stomach removed for ulcers or other disease are more prone to this type of anemia because they lack intrinsic factors in stomach secretions that are necessary for B_{12} absorption. Such patients will not be able to absorb supplementary B_{12} in the form of tablets and will have to take it by injection. Strict vegetarians may also lack B_{12} after a year or so on an all-vegetable diet, and therefore people who eat no animal products should be advised to supplement their diet with B_{12} tablets.

Another anemia, often confused with pernicious anemia, results from inadequate folic acid. Persons with poor diet, alcoholism, or chronic intestinal problems can acquire this problem sometimes within a matter of months, especially if colitis develops. The problem for the physician lies in distinguishing between B_{12} and folic-acid deficiences. Both anemias produce cells that are oversize and therefore cannot be differentiated from a blood smear or by individual size measurements. To diagnose folic-acid deficiency, the levels in both the serum and the red blood cells must test low, since it is the amount of folic acid in the red cells that reflects the level of folic acid in the body tissues. It is imperative to order measurement of B_{12} and folic-acid levels, for if the wrong therapy is given, the patient will not improve and, in fact, the disease will progress, sometimes to the point of permanent neurological damage.

As you see, except in certain genetic disorders such as

sickle cell disease and thalassemia ("Cooley's" or Mediterranean anemia), anemia is generally regarded not as a disease in itself but as a symptom of some underlying problem such as diet. or blood loss. Often, treatment of the underlying problem is essential to the resolution of the anemic process.

Therefore, if you or your physician suspects that you are anemic, it is important to do more than just take vitamins or iron indiscriminately. Not all anemias have the same cause, and if you learn that you are anemic and simply decide to take iron without further investigation, it is entirely possible that your anemia may worsen and in time become severe. Your physician must not only determine the specific type of treatment for the anemia but must also rule out other problems of which anemia may be a symptom.

High red blood cell count. Erythrocyte counts may rise above normal in response to certain situations. For example, if you travel and stay at a high altitude where the rarefied atmosphere is relatively low in oxygen, the decreased oxygen level is sensed by the body. Your bone marrow then increases production of red blood cells to compensate for the lowered oxygen tension.

In a pathological condition known as polycythemia vera which occurs in a small percentage of older adults, production of not only red cells but also of white blood cells and platelets increases. The result is greater viscosity and sluggishness of blood flow, creating symptoms that may include difficulty in breathing (because of the reduced rate of blood flow) and flushed appearance of the skin.

Patients who are dehydrated also may appear to have an increased red cell count. This *apparent* increase is actually due to a decrease in plasma volume, so that the relative volume occupied by the cellular elements seems higher. A dehydrated patient, therefore, may seem to have adequate red cell parameters when she actually has a borderline or mild anemia.

Pregnancy creates a relatively unique situation in which, despite an increase in production of erythrocytes, the erythrocyte count and related values seem to fall. (Of course, in some cases, they actually do fall; the criteria for determining true anemia of pregnancy vary, and laboratory data must be carefully interpreted by a physician.) The paradox arises because plasma increased within the blood vessels at a faster rate than that of the red cells. Thus the increase in red cells is low relative to the increase in fluid, resulting in what is sometimes called a dilutional anemia.

Hematocrit

The hematrocrit is also known as the packed cell volume, or PCV. It is the percent of a column of whole blood that is occupied by erythrocytes after the blood has been spun in a centrifuge at a specific time and speed, so that the red cells are backed at the bottom of the column. In men, the column of packed cells usually occupies 40 to 54 percent of the column of blood; in women, 37 to 47 percent. The technique for counting erythrocytes directly is a very rough one, replete with potential error; consequently the hematocrit is often used in place of the erythrocyte count.

Hemoglobin Level

This test determines the relative proportion of hemoglobin in your blood. Regardless of the number of red blood cells present, if you don't have enough hemoglobin in them, your body won't receive sufficient oxygen and anemia will result. Hemoglobin needs iron to combine with oxygen, which is why an iron deficiency will eventually lead to anemia. The normal range for hemoglobin levels are 12 to 16 grams per deciliter for women and 14 to 18 grams per deciliter for men.

Using the hemoglobin level, the hematocrit, and the red blood cell count, your doctor or lab can mathematically compute the size and amount of hemoglobin in your average red blood cell. These computations include the mean corpuscular volume (MCV), mean corpuscular hemoglobin (MCH), and mean corpuscular hemoglobin concentration (MCHC). These help in classifying the anemias morphologically; that is, according to whether one's cells are too small (microcytic), too large (macrocytic), contain too little hemoglobin (hypochromic), or are ball shaped rather than disc-shaped. These data often can be correlated with the etiology, or origin, of the anemia, and enable the physician to proceed along a logical course of exploration of the problem by pointing her or him in a direction appropriate to the possible problem. The indices may also be used to determine whether a patient is responding to therapy, as they will normalize upon appropriate treatment in the more common forms of anemia.

Erythrocyte Sedimentation Rate (ESR)

This simple test determines how fast red cells settle out of the blood. Blood that has been treated with an anticoagulating agent is placed in a slender tube in a vertical position in a rack. At exactly one hour, the level at which the red cells have settled is noted. In general, the more slowly the red cells settle, the better; the faster they settle, the greater the chance of disease. Red cells fall more rapidly when the globulin or fibrinogen levels are high, because these substances tend to make them stickier and heavier.

A high "sed rate," therefore, can alert the physician to a possible hidden infection or inflammatory process such as arthritis, although it cannot tell what the process is or where it is located. An elevated rate may also help document that the patient with vague complaints and few physical findings really has underlying disease. Finally, ESR provides a way to follow the progress of patients with arthritis, colitis, or similar problems. I routinely do sed rates on all patients.

White Blood Cell Count

The normal range of white blood cells (wbc's) per cubic milliliter is somewhere between 4,000 and 12,000, depending upon your laboratory. Unlike rbc's, which remain in the blood vessels throughout their life span, the wbc's merely transit in the blood to the places in the body where they are needed to fight infection or maintain immunity. Higher counts are usually seen in patients who have bacterial infections such as strep throats, appendicitis, or bacterial pneumonia, as well as in stress, pregnancy, leukemia, and other special conditions.

The white blood cell count is an important factor in some diagnoses. For example, whether or not to proceed with surgery in a patient with suspected acute appendicitis is often based on the patient's white blood cell count. Or a pneumonia patient's improvement can be followed as her count decreases and finally drops to normal levels. Patients with viral illness, however, usually have a wbc that is in the low to normal range. If my patient is seemingly ill with fever and swollen glands, I often prick her finger and get a blood count. If it is low and her differential (another test that we will get to next) shows an increase in lymphocytes (a certain type of white blood cell), I may culture her throat but will send her home without any antibiotic therapy, because she most likely has a viral illness that an antibiotic, which fights bacterial infections, will not affect. By contrast, if her white count is elevated and her polys (another type of white blood cell) are increased on her differential, then I will culture her throat and sometimes treat her with antibiotics immediately, not even waiting for her culture to be completed.

Some patients have low white counts due to cancer, chemotherapy, radiation, or other disease states. These patients often show a decreased ability to fight bacterial infection.

Differential White Blood Cell Count

The purpose of this test is to note the physical appearance of both red cells and white cells and, more especially, the relative numbers of the six different types of white blood cells. This is done by counting one type of cell, and comparing those figures with the normal range. Abnormalities in the relative quantities or in the appearance of the various types of cells can provide important clues to the patient's disorders.

The differential is done on a drop of blood which is spread into a thin layer by pushing one glass slide over another. The blood smear is allowed to dry and is then stained. Under the microscope, the smear is fairly colorful. The red blood cells stain red, and the white cells usually have a light blue background and centers (nuclei) that take on a purple hue.

Taking a quick look at the all-over picture (or, in medical parlance, "eyeballing the slide"), I look first at the number of white cells that are visible in each microscopic field to get some idea once again of the patient's total white cell count. I then quickly scan the appearance of the red cells. In women who are anemic, the red cells may appear pale, with clear central areas. Sometimes in anemic patients, the red cells on the slide may take on a variety of odd shapes and sizes—some smaller, some larger, others not completely round. In other illnesses, such as pernicious anemia, the cells appear to be pale and oversized, while in spherocytosis, the cells appear to be ball-like and smaller than normal in diameter.

I usually scan the slide to make sure that there are adequate numbers of platelets around, especially if the patient is complaining of bruising too easily or other bleeding problems. Then I set out to do the white blood cell differential.

I should admit at this point that I no longer routinely do smears on patients myself. Instead I have them done at the lab I use. However, when I need to know the answer now and not ten hours later, I do it myself. All doctors are taught the procedure in medical school, and I had additional experience working in a hospital lab for a summer. I have always had these testing facilities available in my office because I feel that it is important, especially for the rare case late at night when my patient has a sore belly and I suspect appendicitis.

The six different types of white cells are: polymorphonuclear cells, known as polys; lymphocytes, known as lymphs; eosinophils, known as eos; basophils, known as basos; monocytes, known as monos; and bands, which are young polys. Interestingly, each of these types of cells has an individual function in fighting various infections and inflammations or may be associated with allergic responses. A few easy examples: bacterial illnesses are usually associated, as you know, with an increase in the total white blood cell count, but this usually also involves an increase in the relative number of polys seen on the slide in relation to the other cells. Also in acute bacterial illness, young band cells may be thrown out of the bone marrow early to help fight the infection. On the other hand, in a viral illness, the relative proportion of the lymphocytes is increased. If you have an allergy or have picked up an intestinal parasite, the eosinophil count will be higher than normal, and that will give the doctor a clue that further testing may be necessary. Infectious mononucleosis is often suspected by the technician who sees a change in the usual appearance of the lymphocytes.

Platelet Count

The third "formed element" of the blood is the platelet, which is actually a fragment of a large cell that resides in the bone marrow. Platelets play an important role in blood coagulation and help maintain the integrity of the blood vessels. Although a platelet count is not usually included in the CBC, I sometimes order it. In fact, my patients have been known to request it, especially if they have been bruising easily.

If you get a cut, the platelets seal the break in the blood vessle, stopping the outflow of blood. The platelets also interact with the blood vessel walls and with the clotting factors present in the blood, to ensure normal blood clotting. Drugs such as birth control pills may increase clot formation in some susceptible women. The clot may then break loose from where it originally formed and travel to the brain, causing a stroke, or to other parts of the body, causing other difficulties. This particular problem, though it is rare, is more likely to occur in the older woman who smokes and takes oral contraceptives.

At the other extreme, some medications (as well as a number of rather rare inherited disorders) interfere with the normal clotting function of platelets and may result in easy bruising or in bleeding into the gastrointestinal tract or in the skin. One of these medications is aspirin. Others are known as blood thinners, such as coumadin or heparin, and are used in some patients who have recently experienced a heart attack. Aspirin chemically inhibits the platelets' metabolism, interfering with their ability to stick to other platelets. Recent studies have shown that men at high risk of heart attack are benefited by small doses of aspirin. Men who have followed such a regimen have fewer recurrences of new heart attacks than men who do not take aspirin. Women have shown less significant statistics, but fewer women suffer heart attacks, so the statistics are not as easy to come by. Dr. Simon Handley at the Queens Medical Center in Nottingham, England, showed that 40 milligrams of aspirin (one-half of a baby aspirin) taken every 48 hours might avert heart attacks in men, although other investigators use higher doses.

Blood Chemistry

Blood chemistry tests which analyze the chemicals in your blood serum also yield a great deal of precise information about your body's general health, some of which is unavailable by any other means. Of course, not all of the hundreds of substances in your blood are tested each time you have an exam—separate tests or standard groups of tests are ordered, depending on your needs.

The introduction of automated instruments that permit many tests to be done quickly on a small amount of blood was a great advance in laboratory medicine, saving time for both the patient and the laboratory technologist and reducing the expense of testing. These tests are performed as blood and chemicals are mixed continually and rapidly in an intricate complex of small tubes by machines called continuous flow analyzers. You may hear your physician ask for an "SMA 12" or "SMA 6" profile. "SMA" stands for Technicon's Sequential Multiple Analyzer. The SMAs are autoanalyzers that can perform 6, 12, 24, or more tests on your blood at once, depending upon the particular instrument. These same tests can also be done separately by hand or by other machines. The important thing is that they be done by experienced personnel and interpreted in terms of your own physical examination by your physician. Laboratory tests without physical examination (and the reverse!) tell only half the story.

Glucose Level

Regardless of methodology, there are some tests that will be requested by most physicians as part of a routine examination.

One of the most frequently ordered tests is the "blood sugar," or glucose level. Proper utilization of glucose by the tissues is regulated largely by insulin (a hormone secreted by the pancreas), as well as by a number of other hormones such as cortisone and the thyroid hormones. High levels of blood glucose (called hyperglycemia) may indicate poor insulin supply or insulin "resistance," hallmarks of diabetes mellitus.

Your blood-sugar level changes during the day, depending on food intake, exercise, or medications. Therefore, you should understand that when you have a blood-sugar test, it reflects your blood-sugar level only at that instant in time. If you are fasting, your blood sugar should be within a certain range of normal. However, if you have eaten that day, it is important that your physician know when you ate last and what you ate. In this way, your blood-sugar level can be better interpreted.

Low levels of blood glucose may arise from inadequate diet, or from excess insulin produced in response to stress, or, in sensitive (hypoglycemic) individuals, to glucose or carbohydrate intake. Lightheadedness, mood changes, and faintness may be indicative of hypoglycemia. But this condition is difficult to detect on the basis of a single blood sample (except in cases of so-called fasting hypoglycemia or in insulin overdose, which may occur in diabetic patients). If she or he suspects either hypoglycemia or diabetes mellitus, your physician may request that you take a "glucose tolerance test" (GTT).

Glucose tolerance test. To assure an accurate glucose tolerance test, I tell my patients to increase their carbohydrate intake prior to their test by eating extra carbohydrates, including three desserts a day for the three preceding days. This helps accustom the pancreatic insulin secretions to a sugar load and is especially important in patients who have been on a low carbohydrate diet. Unless this priming is done beforehand, the pancreas may respond sluggishly to the stress of the large sugar load given during the glucose tolerance test, yielding a falsely positive result.

After an overnight fast, your blood will be drawn for a

fasting glucose level. Then you will be given a measured amount of glucose, usually in the form of a soft-drinklike beverage, and your blood and urine will be tested for glucose (and sometimes insulin) first at half-hour, then at hourly intervals, usually for four to five hours. In this way, your body's ability to handle the "glucose challenge" is assessed. You may react to the glucose in the soft drink by producing too much or too little insulin or insulin that is secreted too late, and this will be reflected in your glucose levels. The underlying cause of any hyperglycemia or hypoglycemia can then be pursued and proper diet and medication prescribed.

Glucose tolerance tests are important in the diagnosis of diabetes mellitus. But there are times when the results of a GTT may not be reliable. For example, after a heart attack or other major body stress, the glucose tolerance is more than likely to be falsely positive. The test should also not be done when infection is present or following the fracture of a major bone. In women, there is a phenomenon known as gestational diabetes: a woman who has never had diabetes may be given a GTT during her pregnancy and be informed that she has diabetes. However, there are metabolic changes in normal pregnancy that alter blood sugar levels, and tests during this period must be assessed with the knowledge that the woman is pregnant. Pregnant women with borderline GTTs should be restudied after giving birth to determine their status, for there is actually an increased incidence of diabetes in women who have a history of gestational diabetes. And for women who develop true diabetes with pregnancy, special care must be taken to avoid complications, since the children of such women show an increased incidence of abnormalities.

Women at risk for diabetes. While we're on the subject of diabetes in women, let me pause for a moment to tell you some interesting recent research findings concerning women, weight problems, and diabetes. There is now evidence that women who are fat primarily in the upper body are eight times more likely to develop diabetes than normal women. Ahmed H. Kissebak at the Medical College of Wisconsin also found that this fat distribution pattern may relate to why some women lose weight easily when dieting, whereas others whose weight is centered primarily around their hips, buttocks, and thighs have a much harder time losing weight.

The explanation may lie in what biopsies have shown. Fat cells removed from women with lower-body obesity were of normal size, but there was a marked increase in their number. Excessive numbers of fat cells may be produced by overeating during childhood. In contrast, women with upper-body fat had normal numbers of fat cells, but the size of the cells was larger than normal. This type of obesity is thought to be produced by overeating during adult life. Because the fat cells in upper-body obesity are enlarged beyond normal, the surface of the cells contains fewer insulin receptors than usual. The body then produces more insulin to compensate for the lower number of receptors. In individuals who have family histories of diabetes or who are otherwise genetically susceptible, such obesity leads to the development of adult-onset diabetes. However, with weight loss and the consequent reduction in size of the fat cells, the symptoms of diabetes can be eliminated. Losing weight in such cases should, therefore, also be able to prevent the usual complications of the disease.

Discussing Kissebak's study, *Science* magazine offered some enlightening conclusions about obesity and weight loss:

Since about 40% of U.S. women are obese, the results suggest that 10% of all women are upper body obese, and the risk of their developing diabetes is about eight times normal. The results also suggest that as many as 6 million of these women already have subclinical diabetes.

The study also explains some women's diet woes. It is a relatively easy matter to shrink enlarged fat cells by dieting, so that women who are predominantly upper body obese can lose weight effectively by sticking to a diet. It is much harder, however, to shrink or kill normal-sized fat cells, so that women who are predominantly lower body obese find it very difficult to lose weight, even when they adhere to a diet faithfully. A woman who is obese over all her body, furthermore, might find that her upper body will be reduced dramatically by dieting while her lower body will remain large.

The results are not directly applicable to men, who tend to have only one pattern of weight distribution. They gain weight around and above the waist, giving rise to the common potbelly. Maturity-onset diabetes is generally more common in obese men than in obese women, but Kissebak's results indicate that the incidence is higher still in upper body obese women. The observation that the upper body obese women have higher levels of male hormone suggests that the hormone may stimulate the deposition of fat in a pattern similar to that in man. Testosterone, furthermore, has previously been found to increase the incidence of diabetes, and that may be a contributing factor in these women.[1]

New glucose tests. For the patients with diabetes, home monitoring of blood glucose can now be accomplished in selected patients—those who are willing and able to perform fingertip punctures on themselves and who can then use a "dipstick" similar to those used in routine urine testing to assess blood glucose levels. Small machines are available for more accurate at-home quantitation of glucose levels. These machines are at the time rather expensive, but they are infinitely important, especially in pregnant women with diabetes or in some cases of "brittle" childhood diabetes.

A new test, done in the laboratory by more sophisticated techniques, gives an "average" of blood sugar control over the preceding two months. It is called a glycohemoglobin test and is best suited for monitoring the diabetic patient who is being treated with diet, insulin, and/or oral hypoglycemics. By periodic monitoring of glycohemoglobin levels, the physician has a good idea of the effectiveness of the patient's therapy. This test may sometimes be used as an adjunct to the oral glucose tolerance test, for there is a highly significant correlation between the glycohemoglobin test and the peak response of the glucose tolerance test.

Blood glucose levels are significant not only for patients

who are hypoglycemic for various reasons or who are suspected of having diabetes mellitus, but also for patients with many other conditions. Thyroid disease, other endocrine dysfunctions, liver disease, medications including oral contraceptives, and pregnancy all affect the body's ability to metabolize carbohydrates. The glucose determination is, therefore, a routine and highly useful test.

Serum Proteins

The total protein, albumin, and globulin levels are another set of measurements that give something of an overview of the body's function in that they indicate its ability to produce or lose protein. This ability is intimately tied with other aspects of metabolism, including those related to carbohydrates and lipids.

The "total protein" is composed of two major sets of proteins: albumin, which carries other molecules such as hormones through the blood and is essential in maintaining water balance in the body; and the globulins, most of which function in the immune system and include the best-known antibodies of the group, the *gamma* globulins.

Low levels of albumin may indicate inadequate intake of foods, poor liver function over a long period of time (albumin, like most of the proteins, is synthesized in the liver), or loss of protein through the kidneys or gastrointestinal tract. High albumin levels are relatively rare and most often are a reflection not of increased production of albumin but of increased water loss (i.e., dehydration) which will make the levels of the protein *relatively,* although not actually, high.

High globulin levels may indicate increased production by cells in the liver (different from the cells that produce the albumin), and so may reflect liver disease. More often, high globulin levels reflect excess activity of the antibody-producing cells of the body, the lymphocytes. This occurs when the immune system is stimulated, as in infection, inflammation, or malignancy. Low globulin levels may reflect other disorders of the liver, or immune deficiency or suppression occurring in certain diseases or as the result of the administration of agents designed to suppress the immune response, such as high doses of cortisone or chemotherapeutic agents used in treatment of malignancies.

Cholesterol and Fat Problems

It used to be easy. You ordered a cholesterol level on your patient and told her the number—whether it was high, normal, or low—and that was that. High numbers were bad, low numbers were good as far as heart disease was concerned. But it's not so easy anymore—just ordering a cholesterol isn't good enough. We have learned that other factors are just as important as cholesterol in predicting heart disease. Now I order high-density lipoproteins (HDL) and cholesterol/high-denisty lipoprotein ratios, and just to keep it fairly simple, let's stop there.

There is an inverse relationship between HDL and coronary heart disease. That means that low levels of HDL are bad and lead to an increased risk of coronary disease, whereas increased HDL levels create a protective effect. In easier terms, high HDL is good. Therefore, to determine your risk of heart attack, it is important to know both your cholesterol and your HDL level. That's because even if your cholesterol is high, if a large proportion of it is carried in the HDL fraction, then you are in little danger of having coronary heart disease.

HDL is a protein that carries cholesterol away from the arterial wall and brings it to the liver for breakdown and excretion. This process assures that the artery accumulates less cholesterol. However, if the cholesterol is high and the HDL value is low, then that patient is at high risk for developing coronary heart disease.

Other associations listed below support the conclusion that HDL is inversely related to coronary heart disease (CHD) risk.

Clinical Relationship Between HDL and CHD

HIGH Levels of HDL and LOW Incidence of CHD	LOW Levels of HDL and HIGH Incidence of CHD
persons with family history of notable longevity (familial hyper-HDL)	persons with family history of premature CHD or peripheral vascular diseases
long-distance runners, cross-country skiers, and persons with high levels of physical activity	patients with familial hypercholesterolemia (primary type II hyperlipoproteinemia)
premenopausal females	postmenopausal females
Eskimos of rural Greenland	premenopausal females receiving long-term contraceptive medications (slight increase in CHD)
members of Zen macrobiotic communes in Boston who are vegetarians and fish-eaters	patients with Tangier disease (genetic HDL deficiency)
newborn babies	patients with diabetes mellitus, particularly those who are obese and physically inactive
animals that are resistant to CHD, such as dogs and rabbits	

Dr. Charles Glueck at the University of Cincinnati College of Medicine studied families with a history of longevity, whose members have reached their eighties and nineties in very good health, without serious cardiovascular disease. One characteristic of these people is an unusually high plasma level of HDL, generally more than 75 milligrams per deciliter.

The concept that elevated plasma concentrations of HDL exert a protective effect against CHD also is in accord with the relative immunity to CHD of premenopausal women, whose HDL concentrations are about 30 percent to 60 percent higher than those of their male counterparts in the same age groups. The fact that women have higher HDL levels than men may explain why women have lower rates of CHD than men.

It has been further proposed by Miller and Miller that the development of arteriosclerosis might be more successfully prevented by increasing plasma HDL, and hence the clearance of cholesterol from the arterial wall, than by conventional attempts to reduce cholesterol.

Determining HDL levels detects patients who may be a risk for CHD. This is important because: (1) patients with low HDL levels are usually asymptomatic; (2) CHD is very prevalent; (3) CHD is a life-threatening disease; (4) early intervention could prevent or delay heart attack in persons shown to be a risk.

To elevate plasma HDL levels, it may be useful to exercise and to follow a diet that emphasizes eating vegetables, cereals, fish, little if any meat, and no foods that contain large amounts of saturated fats (hot dogs, potato chips, etc.).

Dr. Donald S. Fredrickson, director of the National Institutes of Health, suggests that before a person found to have a high blood level of cholesterol is placed on a stringent low-cholesterol diet or treated with cholesterol-lowering drugs, analysis should be made of the HDL. If high HDL is what accounts for most of the cholesterol, then treatment may be unnecessary and undesirable.

Therefore, you can see that by knowing your cholesterol as well as your HDL level, your physician can give you your very own coronary-risk profile. I hope you will wind up in a low-risk group. If you don't, then you should begin to alter your diet to improve your risk factors, and there is no better time to begin than right now.

The table that follows shows how the physician interprets your results. Let us assume your percent HDL/cholesterol is 25. That would be good and would place you in a below-average risk group for developing coronary disease. The lab's computers also may work out your cholesterol/HDL ratios. Either method will give the desired information.

Percent HDL Cholesterol

	Male	Female
Protection Probable	Greater Than 28	Greater Than 28
below average CHD* risk	23–28	23–28
average CHD risk	16–22	18–22
high CHD risk	7–15	9–17
CHD risk dangerous	less than 7	less than 9

Cholesterol/HDL Ratio

	Male	Female
Protection Probable	Less Than 3.5	Less Than 3.5
below average CHD risk	3.5–4.4	3.5–4.4
average CHD risk	4.5–6.4	4.5–5.5
high CHD risk	6.5–13.4	5.6–10.9
CHD risk dangerous	13.5 or greater	11 or greater

*Coronary heart disease

Triglycerides

Triglycerides come from fatty foods in our diet and are also manufactured in the liver when we ingest excessive amounts of sugars or alcohol. Stored as fat, triglycerides are an important energy source but also make up many of the bulges that women hate. Because triglycerides show up in the bloodstream after a meal, lab measurements are not accurate unless a twelve- to fourteen-hour fast precedes the blood test. An overly high triglyceride level can be counteracted in some patients by placing them on a low-cholesterol diet as well as eliminating sugars and alcohol and adding exercise to the daily routine. Some people, however, have genetic susceptibility to triglyceride problems which are not caused by overweight or faulty diet habits, and these people especially should be encouraged to follow the special diet instructions.

Low triglycerides are associated with fewer cardiovascular problems.

Kidney Function Tests

BUN (Blood Urea Nitrogen) and creatinine. Kidney functions can be evaluated through two common tests, the BUN and the creatinine level. The BUN is somewhat less reliable because it is subject to variation due to factors such as a high-protein diet, exercise, dehydration, or problems such as heart failure. The BUN represents the final product of protein breakdown in the body. Urea is actually produced in the liver, dissolved in the bloodstream, and carried to the kidneys for elimination.

Elevations in BUN can signal major problems with kidney function and early stages of kidney failure. However, high levels may in some instances indicate a large protein overload from hemorrhage, where the breakdown of blood results in huge amounts of protein to be processed, or from infections, cancers, diabetes that is out of control, and other conditions that lead to massive protein breakdown in the body.

Creatinine levels are also based on elimination of protein by the kidney. Creatinine is a waste product produced from the metabolism of high-energy compounds in muscle. Its level in the blood in any individual remains fairly constant regardless of diet or exercise, unless the kidneys are damaged. Blood levels of creatinine rise later in kidney disease than do levels of urea nitrogen, but because creatinine levels are not so subject to external influence, they are generally considered a more reliable index of kidney function. Since even one healthy kidney is sufficient to keep creatinine levels within normal limits, an elevated creatinine level is a serious problem because it indicates malfunction of both kidneys.

Creatine phosphokinase (CPK). Creatinine is produced from a compound called creatine, by a reaction involving an enzyme called creatine phosphokinase (CPK). CPK levels provide a sensitive index of muscle damage—indeed, almost too sensitive, because sometimes an injection, a fall, or a minor wound may raise the CPK levels of the blood when muscle tissue is traumatized.

The most frequent use of tests for CPK is in detection of myocardial infarction (MI). Even very small amounts of damage to the heart muscle will elevate the serum CPK levels. These evaluations generally occur within six hours of MI and peak within eighteen hours, thus being an earlier index of heart attack than other enzymes. Again, interpretation of CPK levels must be done with caution, in light of the many interfering factors. Not a routine test, the CPK level is reserved for those patients with a suspected myocardial infarction.

Uric acid. Uric acid levels increase in the serum in both mild or severe kidney disease that produces some diminution of kidney function. Uric acid is an end product of the metabolism of substances called purines, which are present in nucleic acids such as DNA. Some people suffer from a hereditary problem that results in overproduction rather than underexcretion of uric acid. This is known as gout. Such patients can be treated with medications that inhibit uric acid production or enhance its excretion, and they are generally placed on a diet lacking in purine-containing substances, especially organ meats such as liver and sweetbreads. Excess uric acid production also occurs in leukemias and malignancies.

Buildup of uric acid is responsible for kidney stones and for joint swellings in some patients with gout. Such stones and swellings contain actual deposits or uric-acid crystals. Some medications, especially certain diuretics and vitamin C (ascorbic acid), can cause high serum uric acid values. If you are taking any of these medications, remind your physician, as he or she may wish to retest your uric acid levels after you stop taking medication.

Test of Disorders of the Liver

SGOT, SGPT, LDH, GGT. Enzymes are substances that speed chemical reactions in the body. Abnormalities of the liver enzymes can help pinpoint what problems exist and where they are coming from. For example, alkaline phosphatase is an enzyme that increases if there is obstruction of the bile ducts of the liver. This is because it is concentrated along the network of bile drainage tubes that lead from the liver into the bile ducts. When blockage of these ducts occurs due to disease or stones or gall-bladder disorders, the alkaline phosphatase level rises. (Alkaline phosphatase is also manufactured in bone tissue, and in growing children it is normally elevated due to bone cell activity.)

Two transaminases, serum glutamic-oxalacetic transaminase (SGOT, now known as aspartate aminotransferase or AsT) and serum glutamic-pyruvic transaminase (SGPT, now know as alanine aminotransferase, or AlT) also reflect liver disorders. (Sorry about these confusing names!) SGOT and SGPT are especially indicative of damage to liver cells themselves, although bile duct disorders also result in their elevation. SGPT tends to remain high longer than does SGOT in liver disease and seems to be more specific for that organ than is SGOT, which is also markedly elevated following a heart attack. SGOT and SGPT are intimately involved in the breakdown of protein into energy. Therefore, these enzymes are found in any tissue where such activity is needed, such as muscle, lung, brain, and so on.

LDH, or lactic dehydrogenase, is an enzyme that converts lactic acid to pyruvic acid and plays a role in sugar metabolism. Because of its general activity, it, too, is found in various tissues besides the liver, especially the heart and muscles. Because LDH is so ubiquitous in the body, its elevation must be interpreted with caution. Even vigorous exercise can contribute to LDH elevations.

Gamma glutamyl transpeptidase (GGT) is another liver enzyme that serves as an indicator of liver cell damage or bile duct obstruction. It is a particularly good index of excessive alcohol intake, whether or not liver damage has occurred. Heavy alcohol intake is followed within eighteen to twenty-four hours by an increase in serum GGT levels, which decline only several weeks after intake stops. GGT is the clue I mentioned at the beginning of this chapter that can be used to detect the "covert alcoholic" and to open discussion with her about getting help with alcohol abuse. In some ways, this test provides monitoring of the alcoholic in the same way that glycosylated hemoglobin can be used in diabetes monitoring.

One liver test is not enough to make a specific diagnosis.

More often, it is the pattern of tests that points to a probable cause. For example, a postsurgical patient who has dined on raw clams might gradually begin to feel fatigued, somewhat nauseated, and achy; she might lose her appetite and then experience fever, chills, and headache. Her physician notes that she looks somewhat jaundiced or yellow and has a tender and enlarged liver. Her lab tests will most likely be abnormal in a pattern consistent with hepatitis—for example, her SGOT, SGPT, and bilirubin will be elevated; her urine may be positive for bilirubin; and her blood count will show a picture indicative of viral infection with a low white count and an increase in lymphocytes. Together, such a history and abnormal tests would be immediate clues to the doctor that he was dealing with a case of hepatitis. Then further tests would be ordered to document the type of hepatitis: infectious—type A or serum hepatitis—type B. The patient's stage of illness or recovery can also be monitored.

Bilirubin. Bilirubin is a product of the breakdown of hemoglobin, part of the body's normal processing of dead red blood cells. In its first stage, a nonwater-soluble form called indirect bilirubin is carried in the bloodstream to the liver, which converts it into a water-soluble form called direct bilirubin. This passes from the liver through the bile ducts into the intestinal tract, where most of it is eliminated in the stool. Bilirubin is what accounts for the characteristic brown color of feces. A small part of the direct bilirubin is reabsorbed from the intestine into the bloodstream, and because it is water soluble, it can now be handled by the kidneys and eliminated in the urine.

The blood test for total bilirubin thus measures both forms—the indirect bilirubin on its way to the liver and the direct bilirubin, which has been processed by the liver.

An abnormal level of total bilirubin can indicate problems in the liver or bile ducts, or red blood cell breakdown, and, by testing the individual levels of direct and indirect bilirubin, the cause can be found. For example, if the indirect bilirubin level is high, then red cells probably are being broken down at a greater rate than normal; or it may be due to a liver that cannot process the normal amounts of hemoglobin breakdown because its function is impaired.

However, it may be that the bilirubin has been processed by the liver but cannot make its way into the intestine because of obstruction due to gallstones, tumor, infection, or other problems. So more and more direct bilirubin is rerouted into the bloodstream. Without the usual amount of direct bilirubin, the feces become light and are usually referred to as clay-color in cases where blockage of the ducts is complete.

The usual level of total bilirubin (and this may vary with your lab) is 1.2 milligrams, with direct bilirubin being 0.4 milligrams and indirect 0.8 milligrams. Jaundice, the development of yellow color in the skin and the whites of the eyes, can be noted when the total bilirubin is 2.5 milligrams or greater. The color of the skin, of course, is due to the elevated level of bilirubin. Even in the lab, the serum portion of the blood of these patients appears to be notably different from the other specimens because of its deep yellow hue.

Just one note: sometimes people (usually babies) become orange-yellow due to consuming excess amounts of carotene. Carotene is found in carrots and other yellow vegetables. While it imparts a somewhat shocking orange shade to the skin, these people have no yellowing of the whites of their eyes. This becomes an important clue to the cause of the "orange suntan." Therapy, in this case, is just to cut down the intake of yellow vegetables.

Amylase and Lipase

Amylase is a starch-digesting enzyme which is related to the digestive function of the pancreas. If you have acute abdominal pain or symptoms that suggest pancreatic problems (more likely to occur in heavy alcohol consumers), a serum amylase level test should be ordered. Sometimes an elevated amylase may be one of the few clues to pancreatic cancer. The enzyme can also be elevated by irritation of the abdominal organs surrounding the pancreas and by disorders of the salivary glands, such as in mumps.

Levels of lipase, an enzyme that aids in fat digestion, are more specific to pancreatic disease. But because lipase is difficult and time-consuming to measure, the lipase level is not a very useful test in an emergency. However, a combination of the lipase and amylase tests often proves to be most helpful in establishing a diagnosis of pancreatic disease.

Body Salts

Sodium, potassium, chloride, and bicarbonate are salts (known as electrolytes) present in blood and body fluids and are essential for all functions of the body. Sodium and potassium ions are positively charged, whereas chloride and bicarbonate ions are negative. Thus when they are present in the proper proportions, these four electrolytes are primarily responsible for maintaining the overall electrical neutrality of the body.

Potassium. This is the major mineral component inside the body cells and is vital for the transmission of nerve impulses for muscle responses, including those related to the heart. High or low levels of potassium are dangerous, as they may lead to abnormalities of heart rhythm or contractions.

Prolonged diarrhea, vomiting, or sweating are common causes of electrolyte imbalance. Patients taking diuretics of certain types are especially prone to loss of potassium and may be asked to eat fresh bananas, oranges, or dried apricots to replenish their body losses, or a potassium supplement may be prescribed.

Patients with low potassium values are often symptomatic and complain of muscular weakness, muscle cramps (especially in the legs), and fatigue. Cardiac patients, particularly those on multiple cardiac drugs as well as diuretics, must have their potassium levels monitored carefully.

Sodium. In addition to having functions closely intertwined with those of potassium, sodium is involved in maintenance of water balance (hydration) of the body. Excessive sweating in the summer may lead to sodium loss. Conversely, excessive sodium is associated with fluid retention. (You may have experienced this after eating in a Chinese restaurant where mono*sodium* glutamate was included in the food.) Therefore, sodium-restricted diets are often prescribed for patients with high blood pressure, as the increase in amount of fluid within the vessels supposedly increases blood pressure. Similarly, premenstrual fluid retention can, in some women, be ameliorated by reduced salt intake in the premenstrual week.

Table salt is sodium linked with chloride—and speaking of table salt, most of us use ten times more than is needed by the body. The puffy ankles that result are not due to an increase of fluid in the blood vessels but to an increase in salt and water surrounding the cells outside the bloodstream. This occurs because the body must keep the concentration of sodium within narrow limits, and if too much sodium is consumed, then water must be retained to assure normal salt concentration. With reduction in salt, water will also be lost. It follows that weight will also be reduced, and that is why most dieters are advised to follow a low-salt diet or are sometimes encouraged to take diuretics. But, of course, the loss of salt and water is not what is really important; loss of fat is. Another caveat to dieters is that the vital regulation of salt balance is a complicated process, accomplished by several interacting hormones. Dieters who have abused their bodies with crazy eating patterns would do well to remember that the deaths among people who followed the liquid protein diets or had anorexia nervosa were often due to derangements of body salts that led to fatal heart rhythm irregularities.

Bicarbonate. This salt is produced by red blood cells from carbon dioxide, a waste product of the body's cells. Usually it is taken by the red cells to the lungs, where it is eliminated and exchanged for oxygen. Therefore, bicarbonate can either be removed from the bloodstream by the kidneys or blown off in the lungs as CO_2.

Sometimes a woman who is nervous or anxious for one reason or another begins to hyperventilate and blow off too much carbon dioxide. The more anxious she is, the more she tends to overbreathe, because she feels that she cannot get enough oxygen into her body. As the process continues, feelings of numbness and tingling occur in the hands and feet, and there is a sense of suffocation. If it goes on for too long, there may be spasms of the hands and feet and she will finally faint as Mother Nature takes over to counteract the excess breathing. The problem is that the person is breathing so much that the body fluids become too alkaline from too great a loss of carbon dioxide. Treatment is simple: the patient should simply place a small brown paper bag over her nose and mouth and breathe into and out of it. In this way, she is forced to rebreathe some of her own exhaled carbon dioxide, and soon the body is back in equilibrium. It is a frightening feeling for those people, however, and they should be reassured that it is a nervous problem and not a sign of disease.

Chloride. Chloride and sodium ions are the most numerous of the electrolytes, and chloride levels are closely tied to those of sodium. Chloride is particularly concentrated in the hydrochloric acid of the stomach's digestive juices but is generally found in the same tissues as sodium and potassium. Abnormally low levels of chloride could signal serious conditions such as Addison's disease; high levels could indicate excessive water loss or hyperventilation, as just described.

Magnesium. This trace metal is important in enzymatic reactions. Its blood levels may be low due to diarrhea, malnutrition, alcoholism, or vomiting. Patients on large amounts of diuretics who have to take potassium supplements should also have their magnesium levels checked for deficiency.

Zinc. Deficiency of zinc is rare but interesting because it is sometimes associated with loss of taste. One of my patients was able to enjoy food again only after being treated for this deficiency. Like magnesium, this trace metal is involved in many enzymatic reactions.

Lithium. This salt is normally measured only in those patients on lithium therapy for manic-depressive illness. Because it is toxic, the levels must be carefully monitored. Monitoring is even more critical in the patient who is on diuretics or has any kidney abnormality. The line between the effective dose and the toxic dose is fine, so that people on therapy are usually monitored regularly.

Calcium, Phosphorus, and Parathyroid Disease

Since the invention of automated laboratory equipment, doctors routinely have multiple lab tests performed on most of their patients. As a result, they have discovered hyperparathyroidism in a number of cases where it was unsuspected and patients were asymptomatic. The disease is thus sometimes jokingly referred to as SMA disease (after the SMA machinery that made the diagnosis).

At least one person in 100,000 is estimated to have this problem. However, since I have picked up 3 cases in the last three years, the prevalence is probably higher. There may be no early symptoms, or they may be as vague as weakness and fatigue after only small amounts of exertion, arthritislike symptoms, and personality changes. If they are carefully evaluated, some of these patients will be found to have hypertension, mild kidney failure, decrease in bone density, and excess calcium loss in the urine.

The tipoff on the SMA is an elevated calcium level. When I find this, the first thing I do is repeat the test twice. In that way, I feel laboratory error will be ruled out. Once it is established that calcium and phosphorus abnormalities exist, the next blood test to be done is for parathyroid hormone levels. With this information, as well as with the calcium and phosphorus levels, the doctor can tell if a parathyroid abnormality exists.

Unfortunately, the reason for abnormal calcium is not always so straightforward. Bone is the largest body reservoir of calcium and phosphorus. There is a delicate but constant exchange between the calcium in your blood and the calcium deposits in your bone. Calcium is also intimately involved in transmission of signals through nerves and muscles, in blood clotting, and in permitting substances to enter and leave cells. Therefore, normal levels of calcium are essential for life. Phosphorus is a component of phospholipids, which make up cell membranes. It is also part of the energy mechanism of the body. The levels of both calcium and phosphorus are regulated by a number of organs, including the thyroid gland and four small glands that surround it known as the parathyroids.

Their activity maintains the normal concentrations of these minerals.

Calcium and phosphorus are absorbed from foods in the small intestine. To complicate matters, this absorption is also dependent upon the presence of vitamin D, whose production is stimulated by parathyroid hormone. The kidneys excrete or reabsorb calcium and phosphorus, and their activity is also affected by parathyroid hormone. Because calcium and phosphorus levels are influenced by all these intertwining factors, abnormalities in their levels may reflect disorders of any one of these systems. It may also be due to inadequate or excessive intake of vitamin D or to defects in its production from vitamin D precursors present in the body. (A certain amount of exposure to sunlight is required for conversion of vitamin D precursors to the active form of vitamin D. That is why a moderate amount of sunshine is good for us.)

Excess activity of the parathyroid glands results in high levels of serum calcium and low levels of serum phosphorus, while the converse is true of decreased activity of these glands. When the parathyroid glands are overactive, calcium is drawn from the bone—the body's major source and store of calcium and phosphorus. In the postmenopausal female, this may present a second insult to bone strength along with the loss of her hormonal support and make her especially prone to fracture. In addition, because of excess calcium in the urine, calcium stones may form in the kidneys.

It would also follow that low calcium levels could be due to low parathyroid function, kidney disorders, intestinal malabsorption, or vitamin D deficiency.

A thorough workup is essential for the patient with documented high calcium levels, because sometimes these are associated with malignant tumors of the lung, kidney, or ovary.

If the problem is parathyroid disease, then doctor and patient must decide whether or not to do surgery. The subject is very complicated and beyond the scope of this book, but if any such surgery is contemplated, I feel that it is essential that it be done by an experienced head and neck surgeon, who usually is available at large medical centers.

Hormonal Tests

A multitude of hormonal tests are available to help the physician diagnose women's endocrine problems. While the function of the parathyroid glands is assessed indirectly by means of calcium and phosphorus measurements, the function of a number of other glands can be determined more directly, by measuring the blood levels of the hormones they secrete and of those that regulate their secretion. Many of these tests are time-consuming and most are expensive, but they enable us to pinpoint diagnoses for problems that a decade ago went unlabeled. For example, we can determine estrogen levels that give us insight into ovarian function. Or we can measure progesterone levels that document whether or not a woman has ovulated and when, and if her ovaries are functioning well enough for her to become pregnant and remain pregnant. A marked rise in the follicle stimulating hormone (FSH) level is one of the most sensitive tests used to document the onset of menopause. The measurement of hormones by laboratory tests is extremely complicated, but there are a few topics that I think are especially interesting to women, and they follow.

FSH and LH. As you saw in Chapter 1, one of the most intricate hormonal feedback systems of the body is that which regulates the female reproductive system. If there is a question about the proper functioning of your ovaries, your doctor may take measurements of ovarian hormones and the pituitary hormones FSH and LH.

A marked rise in FSH levels is one of the most reliable indications of ovarian failure, whether it is due to premature, natural, or surgically induced menopause. Therefore, if you want to know if your menopause is starting or your menses is simply late by a month or two, request an FSH test. Conversely, loss of menstruation accompanied by low or normal FSH levels can suggest the influence of stress, weight loss, or emotional problems. A relatively high LH and FSH ratio is one indicator that helps establish the diagnosis of polycystic ovarian disease.

Prolactin. Prolactin is a hormone secreted by the pituitary. It exerts its effect directly on the body rather than through an intermediary endocrine gland. Among other things, it stimulates and causes secretion of milk. Prolactin is also present in men; abnormally high amounts may be associated with loss of sex drive, impotence, and breast enlargement.

Prolactin determinations are called for in women with unexplained loss of menstruation, milk secretion from their breasts that is not associated with pregnancy and childbearing (a condition known as galactorrhea), hypothalamic-pituitary disease, or infertility. (Eight percent of infertile women have prolactin abnormalities, and indeed I believe that all women having a workup for infertility should have a prolactin level test done.)

Classically, elevated levels of prolactin are associated with amenorrhea as well as galactorrhea. Prolactin levels also provide information about various menstrual abnormalities. The test is best done on blood drawn in a fasting state in the morning, as soon as possible after awakening.

Abnormal production of prolactin may be caused by overactivity of the pituitary or by an actual tumor of the pituitary. Such tumors may be tiny and nearly microscopic or as wide as an inch or two. Adrenal disorder, hypothalamic disorders, hypothyroidism, and ovarian problems may be associated with abnormal production of prolactin. Many drugs also increase prolactin production, including tricyclic antidepressants; narcotics; phenothiazines; reserpine (Serpasil) and alpha methyldopa (Aldomet), which are antihypertensives; some antihistamines (Meclizine, Tripelennamine); and estrogens. Stress of any kind, including psychological stress, can lead to an increase in serum prolactin concentrations. Nipple stimulation will also elevate results. Treatment, either by surgery or radiation or with a medication called bromocriptine, will often restore normal menses and fertility as well as put an end to breast discharge of milk.

Hirsutism. The workup of the woman with excessive body hair is a subject for a whole book, and it involves the use of some of the more esoteric laboratory hormone tests. However, because it is not uncommon, I feel that it is worthwhile to cover the subject, if only lightly.

Actually, excess hair growth is somewhat difficult to define.

How much is really too much? Often the amount of hair present may seem insignificant to the physician, but the patient feels that a complete change in her self-image has occurred and she may even no longer feel sexually attractive. On one hand, women with Mediterranean backgrounds may have a lot of body hair and consider that normal, while on the other hand, Oriental women or women from northern Europe would rarely consider that same amount of hair growth to be normal for them.

Hair growth on the female face, chest, and lower abdomen is "sexual" hair and is dependent upon male hormone. In men, such hair is thick and has been converted from fine hair by the influence of androgens (male hormones). Women, too, have these fine hairs all over their bodies, and because they have a certain amount of circulating male hormone, they may show male-type thickening of their body hair. A recent study stated that "one-third of all normal women college students are reported to have hair extending from the pubic area up the linea alba (center line of the lower abdomen), one-fourth have hair on the face and lip, and 17 percent have chest hair. Three quarters of women over the age of 60 years have chin and lip hair. . . ."[2] For young women, such hair growth may pose a terrible problem in social adjustment, and older women may find it to be yet another blow to their feelings of femininity, along with impending menopause and negative cultural attitudes toward aging and sexuality.

The problem may be due either to abnormal hormone levels or to increased sensitivity of the hair follicle to normal levels of androgen. Most women of Mediterranean origin have the latter condition. Their mothers and sisters usually have similar hair growth patterns. When these women have a hormonal workup, they may find that their hormone levels are normal and the problem is in reality a genetic propensity for increased sensitivity of the hair follicle to androgen.

Nonetheless, the workup should be undertaken, especially if the hair growth has recently appeared, has rapidly increased, or is associated with a decrease or loss of menstrual cycles or more ominous changes such as deepening of the voice, male pattern balding with temporal hair recession, enlargement of the clitoris, decrease in breast size, and male muscle development. The basic tests should be done first, and then, if abnormalities are found, further testing will be necessary for a final diagnosis and proper therapy. The problem may lie in increased androgen production in the ovary or the adrenal gland, but distinguishing the exact site is not simple. If abnormalities are found, then it must be determined if the ovary or adrenal is simply overactive in its androgen output or if a tumor is present.

The first screen that is done in my office, in addition to the usual SMA tests which include those for thyroid function, is a battery of tests for pituitary hormones, FSH, LH, prolactin, and levels of the male hormones DHEAS and testosterone. The results of these tests tell me what further workup is needed. Consultation with a gyn-endocrinologist may be necessary for a complete diagnostic workup.

Thyroid tests. If I polled my patients, I'm sure I'd find the test they are most anxious about is the thyroid test. This is especially true of those who are overweight and have no get-up-and-go. They all pray that they are hypothyroid and then they will be given a little pill that will give them pep and energy and melt all their fat away. Though hypothyroidism is the most common endocrine problem, only the rare woman finds that she has such an excuse. Most fat is due to overeating and underactivity. Nonetheless, thyroid tests are part of my routine screening.

The thyroid gland is a major regulator of the body's metabolic rate. If its function is low, then your body seems to idle along, slowly, whereas if its function is too high, then you race about as if in overdrive. All the body organs are subject to these changes. Heart rate, blood pressure, breathing rate, skin texture, tolerance to heat or cold, energy output, and fat and food metabolism are all under thyroid regulation.

The hypothyroid patient, then, has a slow pulse rate, dry skin, and slight puffiness around her eyes. Her hair seems dull, she has lost hair from the outer parts of her eyebrows, and she reports losing hair from her head, armpits, and pubic areas. She is also constipated.

On the other hand, hyperthyroidism is more common in the perimenopausal woman. The hyperthyroid patient is tense, with increased blood pressure, fast pulse rate, perspiration, increased frequency of bowel movements or diarrhea, and a feeling of being unable to tolerate heat. She may have lots of nervous energy, but as time goes on, she may complain about fatigue. Upon questioning, she may relate that her thighs are weak and tire especially when climbing stairs.

Generalized overactivity of the thyroid gland is called Graves' disease. Such patients are treated with medication, surgery, or radioactive iodine, depending upon their age and a variety of other circumstances. Tumors in the form of hyperactive nodules may also increase thyroid hormone output, as may cancer, though this is rare. In Hashimoto's thyroiditis, an autoimmune disease, for unknown reasons, the body begins to make antibodies against the thyroid. Such patients may first experience hyperthyroidism, only to have it followed by the development of hypothyroidism. Other patients maintain normal thyroid function and have only vague symptoms or thyroid swelling. The problem is twenty times more frequent in women, usually occurring between the ages of thirty and fifty.

Hypothyroidism and hyperthyroidism may be reflected in changes in the blood levels of two main hormones of the thyroid gland, triiodothyronine and thyroxine, known respectively as T3 and T4 for the number of iodine atoms that each molecule of the hormone contains. While T4 is the hormone that is more abundant, it is normally converted in specific quantities to T3, which is believed to be more potent.

The thyroid gland is regulated in turn by the pituitary, which produces thyroid stimulating hormone (TSH), which causes the thyroid to produce its hormones. Thyroid hormone "feeds back" via the bloodstream to the pituitary, which then shuts off TSH production until the thyroid levels fall. TSH can be measured and, in conjunction with T3 and T4 levels, provides information about whether a thyroid problem originates in that gland itself or in the pituitary. Measuring TSH levels is probably one of the best ways to follow a patient who is on thyroid therapy, for they will be within normal range if the amount of thyroid medication is correct. It is also one of the best tests to confirm the diagnosis of hypothyroidism.

For example, let us look at some possible test results to understand how diagnoses are obtained.

Test	Result	Diagnosis
High T4 High T3 uptake High T3 (RIA)	Low TSH	Hyperthyroidism
Low T4 Low T3 uptake Low or normal T3 (RIA)	High TSH	Primary Hypothyroidism
Low T4 Low T3 uptake	Low TSH	Secondary Hypothyroidism*
High T4 Low T3 uptake	Normal TSH	Normal thyroid†
Low T4 High T3 uptake	Normal TSH	Normal thyroid**

*Here the pituitary is incapable of producing sufficient amounts of TSH. Other glands in the body are usually similarly affected by the lack of pituitary drive.

†These divergent values are due to medications such as oral contraceptives, hormone-replacement therapy, pregnancy, or thyroid replacement with thyroxine (T4).

**These values may be obtained in patients on triiodothyronine, (T3 or Cytomel) or on androgen therapy or on certain anticonvulsant drugs such as Dilantin.

Divergent values usually mean that the patient has normal thyroid function but is taking medication that interferes with the hormones or affects the amount of globulin produced that is able to bind the thyroid hormone. More than 99.95 percent of thyroid hormone is carried in the bloodstream bound to proteins called globulins. It is released at a slow rate that is compatible with metabolic needs of the patient. Only the unbound form of the hormone is active. This free hormone can be estimated by the lab when the T4 and T3 uptakes are known.

It is interesting to note that some patients have symptoms of hyperthyroidism such as nervousness, weight loss, increased bowel movements, and the like but have normal T4s. However, it is now known that in its early stage, hyperthyroidism will cause a rise in T3 (which can be determined by RIA, radioactive immune assay) first and then, two to five months later, display the more classic elevated T4.

This little discussion of thyroid function tests was presented simple to demonstrate that though the T4 is a good screening test and is used by most physicians, it alone is not sufficient in a workup of the symptomatic patient who may have thyroid disease.

Iodine is necessary for the manufacture of thyroid hormone. Goiter or swelling of the thyroid caused by insufficient dietary iodine occurs in people living in areas such as the Midwest, where seafood is not a frequent addition to the diet. The thyroid enlarges in an attempt to compensate for this deficiency. Iodine is available in iodized table salt. People in areas where seafood is not available should buy table salt that contains iodine in order to get a sufficient amount of this mineral in their diet.

Also, it is important that your physician be informed of any medication that you might be taking, because medications may alter the results of your laboratory tests. Iodine from cough medicine or that is used in some X-ray studies can interfere with thyroid-hormone measurements. If your doctor is unaware that you are taking thyroid medications, your tests may be falsely interpreted as abnormal. If you are on a birth control pill or on estrogen, the liver's production of proteins that carry the thyroid hormones in the bloodstream is altered. This makes the test results seem abnormal when in reality they are not. Many laboratory tests are available for measuring thyroid hormones, and each measures the hormone in a slightly different form, so that your physician often chooses a series of related tests. This combination of tests allows the physician to interpret your hormone status correctly even if you are on medication.

Thyroid function tests are especially valuable in evaluating women with heavy menstrual flow or with abnormal cycles. It is also important to know whether thyroid function tests are normal before beginning a complicated workup on an infertile woman. In these cases, returning the thyroid function to normal may decrease the menstrual flow, regulate menses, or establish fertility in a previously infertile woman. Hypothyroidism is also associated with habitual abortion (spontaneous abortion that recurs again and again) as well as 2 to 5 percent of cases of galactorrhea (abnormal breast milk production).

ACTH/Cortisol. A feedback mechanism similar to that between the thyroid and the pituitary exists between the adrenal gland and the pituitary. The adrenal secretes hormones that are intimately involved in carbohydrate metabolism and maintenance of salt and water balance. These hormones help the body combat stress and also serve as the bases for manufacture of some of the body's sex hormones. The adrenal's secretion of the hormone cortisol is regulated to a large extent by pituitary secretion of the hormone ACTH (adrenocorticotrophic hormones). Both cortisol and ACTH and a number of related hormones can therefore be measured to determine the functioning of the pituitary-adrenal relationship. Measurements of these hormones are now being used to detect Addison's disease, Cushing's syndrome, and certain types of depression, which are believed to be biochemical in origin.

The dexamethasone suppression test (DST). One of the most interesting tests utilizing cortisol is a test for melancholia, or endogenous depression. Until recently, the diagnosis of depression has been based on the patient's history and on observations that she appears depressed, has lost her appetite, states that she is unable to sleep, has mood swings throughout the day, and is generally withdrawn. Differentiating between patients with melancholia and patients with depression for other reasons is not always easy, but it is important. Patients with endogenous depression respond well to antidepressive medications, whereas patients who have other types of depression do not and are often inappropriately treated with these medications. These patients might be better off with psychotherapy or with other medications such as MAO inhibitors.

Patients with melancholia have a disturbance in brain metabolism which may secondarily affect their adrenal production of cortisol. Cortisol does not cause the depression; rather it seems that various types of depression are associated with inappropriate hormone output.

The test known as a dexamethasone suppression test (DST) came into use in the late seventies. The patient is given one milligram of dexamethasone (a synthetic steroid) at 11 P.M The following day at 4 P.M., a cortisol level is drawn. Normal patients have low cortisol levels, but many patients with melancholia have levels of cortisol greater than 5. Patients with depression secondary to schizophrenia, neurosis, personality disorder, or drug abuse, or who are in mourning will usually not show such an elevation. Also, the DST may become abnormal just before the patient becomes clinically depressed. This allows the physician to treat a patient early, before her condition deteriorates. An abnormal DST tends to return to normal as the patient improves. After treatment, if the DST remains abnormal, then it is likely that the patient needs continuing therapy. The test can be repeated as necessary to monitor the patient, but it is not infallible. While the elevated DST is nearly specific for the diagnosis of melancholia, a substantial minority of such patients have a normal response. In such cases, the usual clinical signs and symptoms of melancholia must be relied upon.

Gonorrhea screening test. There is now a serum test that can detect antibodies to Neisseria gonorrhea, the organism responsible for this venereal disease. Such antibodies exist in the serum of patients who have or have had gonococcal infection. This test is somewhat useful for identifying those asymptomatic female patients who should then be cultured vaginally for gonorrhea.

The test is recommended for women with no clinical history of the disease, particularly those considered at low risk for gonorrhea. It may be especially useful in those situations in which pelvic examinations are not routinely performed. But it should be used only as an aid in selecting those patients who should be cultured for gonorrhea. The actual diagnosis of gonorrhea is based on the results of a gonorrhea culture in conjunction with the patient's history and clinical findings.

The test has many limitations and has never become popular. For example, it is not specific for gonorrhea because there is cross-reaction with other bacteria such as Neisseria meningitidis and Neisseria pharyngis that may exist in the throat. Therefore, many false-positive results are obtained. Also, even if infection is present, the antibodies do not build to detectable levels until two to three weeks after it has begun. By that time, the woman may have already had damage to her organs. A good gonorrhea screening test, as is currently available for syphilis, is urgently needed.

Urine Analysis

Urine analysis, or urinalysis for short, is often underestimated in terms of the importance of the information that it can provide. Although very elaborate studies can be done on the urine and are indicated in certain circumstances, a routine urinalysis is easily done and should be part of a general physical exam; it can reveal change not only in the urinary tract but also in other parts of the body.

A urinalysis should include both a "macroscopic" examination of the physical and chemical properties of the urine and a "microscopic" examination of the cells, crystals, and other components of a sediment that is often formed when a specimen of urine is centrifuged in the laboratory.

The "macroscopic" examination involves evaluation of the color of the urine (which may be altered by the presence of blood, bilirubin, medications, and other chemicals), any unusual odor that is present (such as those produced by certain body chemicals called ketones or by bacterial decomposition of wastes), and "appearance" or clarity of the specimen (which may reflect presence of crystals, cells, bacteria, mucus, etc.). A specific gravity determination is also done. This measure of the number of dissolved particles in the urine reflects the ability of the kidneys to concentrate waste products. The more concentrated the urine, the greater the specific gravity, within a certain normal range. Excess fluid intake, certain endocrine imbalances, and renal disease, as well as sickle cell trait and disease, can all alter the ability of the kidney to concentrate wastes.

The chemicals that are routinely measured (albeit roughly on a routine specimen) include glucose, ketones ("acetone"), protein (albumin), blood, bilirubin, urobilinogen, and nitrite. A pH reading is taken as well.

The most consistent results in routine urine analysis are obtained from the first morning specimen. The reason for this is that the volume of urine produced during the night is normally about one third of that produced during the day. Any substances or formed elements that are present in the urine, therefore, are found in a more concentrated and more easily detectable state. To collect a urine specimen correctly, especially a sterile urine for suspected urinary tract infection, you will be asked to wash your vulva, then rinse the area well. You should then wipe yourself and void the first part of the specimen into the toilet. Then collect the "midstream" portion in the sterile container provided without touching the inside of the container or its cover with your fingers. If there is a delay in returning the specimen to the laboratory, it should be refrigerated.

The urine specimen is first observed for color and clarity. Then a reagent stick is quickly dipped in the specimen, and the resulting color changes are checked against a reference chart. Within a minute, information can be obtained easily and accurately. Abnormalities provide important clues to problems, which may be unsuspected and asymptomatic.

pH. Information on the pH provides clues to urinary tract infection, kidney stones, and acid-base problems. A pH of 7 is neutral; less than 7 indicates acidity, while more than 7 indicates alkalinity. Urine pH for normal adults is usually around 6, but pH measurements fluctuate with diet. Meat, other proteins, and cranberries will make urine more acid, whereas vegetables and citrus fruits make it more alkaline. Very alkaline urine is a clue that infection may be present. This is because some bacteria break down urea, which forms ammonia in the urine.

Urine pH measurement is important to patients with kidney

stones. If the stones are the uric-acid type, the urine should be kept alkaline so stones will be less likely to form. On the other hand, patients with calcium stones should try to keep their urine acid to inhibit their formation.

Glucose. Normally there is no detectable glucose in the urine. Finding glucose in the urine most commonly indicates diabetes mellitus. However, it may also be merely a reflection of a transient disturbance in sugar metabolism, especially following the ingestion of a carbohydrate-rich meal, or may be related to physical and/or mental stress, anesthesia, or altered kidney function. Glucose may occur in the urine during pregnancy, either as a result of altered kidney function or as an early indication of diabetes. Glucose begins to spill into the urine after the blood glucose has reached 160 milligrams per deciliter.

Ketones. Ketones occur in the urine in some forms of diabetes when the blood sugar is not under control. In this instance, ketones reflect the inability of the body to use the glucose because of ineffective insulin secretion. Occasionally ketones occur in the urine of children who have high fevers and high metabolic needs or in patients who are dehydrated due to vomiting or diarrhea. In these cases, as with people who are on carbohydrate-deficient diets, the body can find no glucose and has had to draw on its fat reserves to supply needed energy. Patients on low-calorie diets often check to see whether the diet is working by checking their urine for ketones. Because ketones are by-products of fat breakdown, as body fat is broken down and you lose weight, a certain amount of ketones accumulate in the blood and spill into the urine.

Protein (albumin). Protein is an important sign of kidney disease. Protein, which is primarily albumin, may occur in small amounts in the urine under physiological ("normal") circumstances, such as after exercise, after ingestion of a very high-protein meal, or, in some people, merely as a result of standing. This phenomenon is called orthostatic or postural proteinuria and can be tested by having the patient sample the urine immediately after about eight hours reclining, and then again after a short period of standing erect. Proteinuria due to postural factors will be absent from the specimen taken following the long period of reclining.

Any persistent finding of the protein in the urine may indicate a significant problem. There may be damage to the kidney membranes which filter these materials. When this occurs, the protein particles are lost from the body and pass into the urine. Infection, high fever, and diseases that cause kidney damage such as high blood pressure, diabetes, collagen diseases, or autoimmune diseases may also cause persistent proteinuria.

Blood (hemoglobin). Blood or hemoglobin in the urine is a signal of infection, kidney disease, or tumor of the urinary tract. It may also be present because cells have broken down in the circulation. However, generally it indicates infection, inflammation, or irritation of the kidneys or urinary tract. There may be symptoms of urinary bladder infection, various forms of nephritis, the presence of kidney stones, or kidney tumors. An indication of blood on the dipstick should be followed by microscopic examination for the presence and number of red blood cells and of other formed elements that may provide clues to the nature of the problem. Red cells and other changes can be seen under the microscope long before a patient would notice any color change in her urine. When the microscope shows red cells accompanied by an excessive number of white cells, infection is usually the cause.

Bilirubin. Normally no bilirubin is detectable in the urine. The breakdown product of red cell hemoglobin, bilirubin, becomes detectable in the urine when the outflow of bile from the liver is obstructed by stones or other problems in the bile duct system or in liver disease. Bilirubinuria also occurs in hepatitis, cirrhosis, cancer of the pancreas, or exposure to liver toxins. A positive urine test must be followed up by blood tests to determine the cause of the problem.

Urobilinogen. Urobilinogen is often the earliest sign of liver disease or red blood cell breakdown. Urobilinogen is an indirect product of hemoglobin breakdown. It is a pigmented substance produced from bilirubin-related materials in the intestine by bacteria that normally inhabit the intestinal tract and is responsible in part for the color of urine and feces. Obstruction of the bile ducts will diminish the amount of bile entering the intestine and, consequently, the amount of urobilinogen produced. Absence of urine urobilinogen is due to complete bile duct obstruction. Increases occur primarily in liver disease such as hepatitis, cirrhosis, and sometimes hemolytic disease, in which excess hemoglobin breakdown occurs secondary to increased rupture of red blood cells.

Nitrites. Nitrites are produced by bacteria acting upon other nitrogen-containing compounds in the urine and are therefore indicative of bacterial infection. Urine is normally sterile when it is produced in the kidneys and flows through the urinary tract. If an infection is present, however, large numbers of bacteria produce nitrites, and a foul ammonialike odor is present in the urine. Finding nitrites alerts the doctor that significant infection is present and that culture and sensitivity testing should be done.

Microscopic Examination

The dipstick tests should be followed by a microscopic examination. The urine should be spun for a few minutes in a centrifuge, the top portion poured off, and the urine sediment poured onto a slide and looked at under the microscope.

The following are some of the formed elements that are frequently encountered in the urine.

Epithelial cells. Epithelial cells cover the surface of the bladder, urethra, and vagina and are often shed into the urine. Irritation or infection of any of these sites may lead to increased numbers of these cells in the urine. In female urine, they are usually contaminants from the vagina, especially when the woman has vaginitis.

White blood cells. White blood cells coming from the vagina are often similarly found as contaminants in female urine. This is why obtaining a clean-catch, mid-stream urine is so important. Bladder, kidney, or urethral infections produce increased numbers of white blood cells. However, if your urine stands for long periods of time at room temperature, the white blood cells might break down and be missed. Excess numbers of white blood cells are probably the most important indication that infection of the urinary tract is present.

Red blood cells. Red blood cells, as mentioned, generally reflect urinary tract disorder, although they may be present again as "contaminants" when a woman is menstruating. Though they are most likely to be associated with infection, they may also be caused by kidney injury, tumors, stones, or poisons. A red or red-brown smoky color to the urine may indicate the presence of blood.

Casts. Casts are molds of the kidney tubules formed by the deposit of protein within them. These structures are usually seen only in fresh urine. Casts may also contain red or white blood cells or crystals. Although they may be present in tiny numbers in healthy people, particularly after strenuous exercise, large numbers or certain types of casts indicate serious kidney problems.

Crystals. The crystals found in the urine reflect the type and concentration of substances present in the bloodstream and urine. People who are predisposed to forming urinary-tract stones may show large quantities of crystals of the substance of which those particular stones are formed. People who have gout or problems with high uric acid concentrations may show uric-acid crystals in the urine. The types of crystals that precipitate are dependent upon the acidity or alkalinity of the urine. However, normal urine may contain urate, oxalate, phosphate, carbonate, or uric-acid crystals. Sulfa drugs also may produce crystals, and that is why patients are advised to drink large amounts of water to prevent problems when on sulfa medications.

Bacteria. Normally urine is sterile, and no bacteria should be seen on a freshly voided specimen. However, as urine sits, bacteria that might be present multiply rapidly in it. Therefore, if the physician is interested in observing whether or not there are bacteria in the urine, he or she should do so on a fresh specimen or one that has been refrigerated. It follows, too, that urine should be cultured or refrigerated soon after voiding to prevent bacterial overgrowth.

All pregnant women should be screened for urinary-tract

infection at their first prenatal visit. Infection in pregnancy is especially dangerous and must be prevented. Approximately 4 to 10 percent of pregnant women have urinary-tract infections but are asymptomatic. As many as 40 percent of them later develop symptoms of urinary-tract infection, usually kidney infection, if they are not treated.

Detecting and treating asymptomatic infection early in pregnancy will prevent the development of pyelonephritis (kidney infection), which is one of the most frequent causes of hospitalization during pregnancy. Pyelonephritis usually develops during the third trimester of pregnancy. Permanent kidney damage has been reported in 18 to 51 percent of infected women studied after delivery. Pregnancies complicated by urinary-tract infection are potentially dangerous because they are associated with increased infant death rates and more frequent preterm deliveries. Prevention is easy and will prevent harm to mother and child alike. Therefore, if you or your daughter is pregnant, make sure that a complete urinalysis, including a microscopic examination of the urine, is done at the first prenatal visit. Then make sure that a culture is also obtained.

Pregnancy Testing

There are a number of blood or urine tests available to determine whether pregnancy has begun. They differ in sensitivity, that is, in how early they can diagnose the pregnancy. For example, the slide tests on urine that physicians use in their offices give an answer in a couple of minutes, but these tests are often the least sensitive and the woman must be at least ten to fourteen days late with her period for the test to be certain. Then there are urine tube tests that detect pregnancy six to nine days after the missed period.

Most of the over-the-counter home pregnancy test kits use tube tests that are similar to those physicians use in their offices. I think that it is very nice to do the test at home and "be the first to know," but I also think that the tests are much too expensive and that most women are better off bringing their urine to a lab or physician's office, where the test will be done accurately and interpreted correctly. In my experience, women often spend money on the home test kit, run the test, are not sure if they have done the test correctly or if they can believe the test results, and then bring a second specimen to the office anyway for confirmation.

Pregnancy tests should be done on a concentrated, first-morning urine specimen. Use of a diluted specimen taken at another time of the day is a frequent cause of false negative pregnancy tests, especially in the early stages of a pregnancy when high levels of hormone have not yet built up. So if you do use one of the over-the-counter kits, be certain that you do the test on your first morning specimen and that you drink no fluids after supper the night before.

All these urine tests detect human chorionic gonadotropin (HCG), a hormone produced during pregnancy. As you would suspect, early in pregnancy, the levels are very low. As pregnancy advances, more and more hormone is manufactured and detection becomes easier. Recently, new urine tests have become available for use in physicians' offices and labs. They can detect a pregnancy even before the period is missed. Possibly the most sensitive test is a blood serum test for pregnancy. There are situations in which using such a test is urgent.

One is when the woman is suspected of having an ectopic pregnancy (a pregnancy occurring outside the womb, usually in a fallopian tube). Because of the danger of sudden rupture of the tube with resultant hemorrhage and possible death, early diagnosis is essential. Ectopic pregnancy should be suspected in women of childbearing age who have symptoms of abdominal pain, especially in the area of the ovaries, and who have had a change in their bleeding patterns or lack of menstruation.

Unfortunately a urine test is not sensitive enough to rule out ectopic pregnancy. About one half of women with proven ectopic pregnancies have negative urine pregnancy test results. Ectopic pregnancies generally produce lower levels of hormone than normal pregnancies, so urine tests should not be used to rule out this problem.

The most sensitive and specific lab test for the detection of pregnancy is the serum radioimmunoassary (RIA) for the beta subunit of the HCG hormone. This test can diagnose pregnancy eight days after conception, several days *before* the next period is due. If the test for the beta subunit is negative, then the woman can be assumed *not* to be pregnant and is spared the operative procedures and general anesthesia associated with alternative means of diagnosing ectopic pregnancy. However, if the test is positive, then the woman must be placed in the highest risk category, for she probably has an ectopic pregnancy or is having a spontaneous abortion. She then must be very carefully observed or have surgery, as indicated.

For women who want to become pregnant but cannot, the beta-subunit test has also proved to be a valuable diagnostic tool. It is now realized that there are some women who conceive yet because of a poor progesterone response are unable to "hold" the pregnancy. By diagnosing a pregnancy early and giving supplemental progesterone (even before the missed period has occurred), some women can be carried to the point in their pregnancy where their own production of progesterone becomes normal. By this means, many women have finally had their wishes of motherhood fulfilled. The beta-subunit test has become an important tool for the physician who is trying to aid the infertile woman as well as in helping to diagnose patients having abdominal pain who might have an ectopic pregnancy.

Stool Test for Stomach or Intestinal Cancer

Finding microscopic traces of blood in the stool is often one of the earliest signs of cancer of the stomach or intestines, and several tests that reveal the presence of blood in the stool have been devised for detecting asymptomatic gastrointestinal cancer. They are known by a variety of commercial names such as Hemoccult, Hematest, Hemacheck, and Fecatest. The patient usually does the test at home, smearing tiny amounts of stool on a specimen card with an applicator stick. She then mails or brings the card to the physician's office for testing as soon as possible. In order not to confuse the results, no red meat, beets, turnips, or horseradish should be eaten, and for two days prior to testing, vitamin C and aspirin or aspirin-type drugs must also be avoided. A high-roughage diet with plenty of fruits and vegetables is recommended, however.

A positive test alerts the physician that further workup of the patient may be in order.

If you have plowed through this entire chapter, you probably have some medical background—if not, you deserve special congratulations. It wasn't easy, was it? Most women will use this chapter for reference, looking up what they need when they need it. But it can also be a guide to what should be done to help solve diagnostic problems.

Familiarity with lab tests can be very helpful in that it can make medical jargon a little less foreign...a little more meaningful. Use the chapter well. Ask your doctor to show you your lab reports. I always share them with any patient who requests them. I often offer the extra copies from the lab even when they don't want them just to help clear out some of the papers from their chart. Some of the women who have been overwhelmed by the amount of tests on the sheets can now be referred to this chapter as a sort of homework assignment to better understand their own results.

Good luck with your testing. Make an active effort to integrate it with your new knowledge about your body. Hopefully you will now be able to actively pursue medical care that will be comprehensive as well as comprehensible. In this way you should get the best of all possible care for *you*.

Notes

1. NATURAL HORMONE REPLACEMENT THERAPY, OR NO MORE SCARE STORIES ABOUT MENOPAUSAL THERAPY

1. Robert W. Kistner, "The Menopause," *The Female Patient* (September 1979): 31–37.

2. Ibid.

3. Penny W. Budoff and Sheldon C. Sommers, "Estrogen-Progesterone Therapy in Perimenopausal Women," *Journal of Reproductive Medicine* 22 (May 1979): 241–247.

4. G. Virginia Upton, "The Perimenopause," *Journal of Reproductive Medicine* 27 (January 1982): 9–10.

5. C. Ann Mashchak et al., "Comparison of Pharmacodynamic Properties of Various Estrogen Formulations," *American Journal of Obstetrics and Gynecology* 144 (Nov. 1, 1982).

6. Ibid.

2. NO MORE HOT FLASHES—GOOD NEWS!

1. A. M. Voda, "Climacteric Hot Flash," *Maturitas* 3 (1981): 73.

2. James P. Semmens and Gorm Wagner, "Estrogen Deprivation and Vaginal Function in Postmenopausal Women," *Journal of the American Medical Association* 248 (July 23–30): 445–448.

3. P. L. Martin, S.S.C. Yen, A. M. Burnier, and H. Herrman, "Systemic Absorption and Sustained Effects of Vaginal Estrogen Creams," *Journal of the American Medical Association* 242 (December 14, 1979): 2699–2700.

4. Sidney Rosenberg, *American Journal of Obstetrics and Gynecology* 139 (1981): 47.

5. Merete Sanvig Christensen et al., "Dose-response Evaluation of Cyclic Estrogen/Gestagen in Postmenopausal Women: Placebo

Controlled Trial of its Gynecologic and Metabolic Action," *American Journal of Obstetrics and Gynecology* 144 (1982); 873–879.

6. C. Christiansen et al, "Effects of Natural Estrogen/Gestagen and Thiazide on Coronary Risk Factors in Normal Postmenopausal Women: A Two-Year Double-blind Placebo Study," *Acta Obstet. Gynecol. Scand. (Supplement)* 88 (1979): 83.

7. Ronald K. Ross et al., "Menopausal Oestrogen Therapy and Protection from Death from Ischemic Heart Disease," *The Lancet* (April 18, 1981): 858–860.

8. Trudy L. Bush et al., "Estrogen Use and All-Cause Mortality," *Journal of the American Medical Association* 249 (1983): 903–911.

9. Erkki Hirvonen et al., "Effects of Different Progestogens on Lipoproteins During Postmenopausal Replacement Therapy," *New England Journal of Medicine* 304 (1981): 560–562.

10. Wulf H. Utian, "The Mental Tonic Effect of Estrogens Administered to Oophorectomized Females," *South African Medical Journal* 46 (1972): 1079.

11. M. Aylward, "Plasma Tryptophan Levels and Mental Depression in Postmenopausal Subjects," *International Research Communications System Medical Science* 1 (1973): 30.

12. Robert B. Greenblatt, D. H. Bruneteau, and J. Merchandani, "Menopausal Migraine," in *The Menopausal Syndrome*, eds. R. B. Greenblatt, V. B. Mahesh and P. G. McDonough (New York: Medcom Press, 1974) p. 102.

13. R. Don Gembrell, "The Menopause: Benefits and Risks of Estrogen-Progestogen Replacement Therapy," *Fertility and Sterility* 37 (April 1982): 457–474.

14. Rogerio A. Lobo and William Gibbons, "The Role of Progestin Therapy in Breast Disease and Central Nervous System Function," *The Journal of Reproductive Medicine* 27 (1982): 515.

15. Ibid., 517.

16. Charles B. Hammond and Wayne S. Maxson, "Current Status of Estrogen Therapy for the Menopause," *Fertility and Sterility* 37, (January 1982): 15.

17. Barbara S. Hulka, Lloyd E. Chambless, David C. Deubner, and William E. Wilkinson, "Breast Cancer and Estrogen Replacement Therapy," *American Journal of Obstetrics and Gynecology* 143 (1982): 638–644.

18. Charles B. Hammond and Wayne S. Maxson, *op cit.*

19. R. Don Gambrell, "Clinical Use of Progestins in the Meno-

pausal Patient," *Journal of Reproductive Medicine* 27, (Supplement, August 1982): 535.

3. OSTEOPOROSIS: PREVENTING THIS SILENT KILLER

1. Elmer E. Specht, "Hip Fracture, Skeletal Fragility, Osteoporosis and Hormonal Deprivation in Elderly Women," *Western Journal of Medicine* 133 (October 1980): 297–303.
2. R. Don Gambrell, "The Menopause," *Fertility and Sterility* 37, (April 1982): 457–474.
3. Lila E. Nachtigall, Richard H. Nachtigall, Robert D. Nachtigall, and E. Mark Beckman, "Estrogen Therapy I: A 10-year Prospective Study in the Relationship to Osteoporosis," *Obstetrics and Gynecology* 53 (March 1979): 277–280.
4. M. V. Krause and L. K. Mahan, *Food, Nutrition and Diet Therapy* (Philadelphia: W. B. Saunders Co., 1979), p. 890.
5. Everett L. Smith, "Exercise for Prevention of Osteoporosis: A Review," *The Physician and Sportsmedicine* 10 (1982): 72–83.
6. Ibid.
7. Ibid.

4. NO MORE MASTECTOMIES

1. J. S. Stehlin, Jr., R. A. Evans, A. C. Gutierrez, J. Cowles, P. D. Delpolyi, and P. J. Gruf, "Treatment of Carcinoma of the Breast," *Surgery in Gynecology and Obstetrics* 149 (1979): 912-922.
2. Maurice D. Steinberg, Leslie Wise, and Mary Ann Juliano, "Psychological Outcome of Lumpectomy Compared to Mastectomy in the Treatment of Breast Cancer," Unpublished paper presented at the World Congress of Psychosomatic Medicine, Montreal, Canada, September 1981.

5. NO MORE UNNECESSARY HYSTERECTOMIES

1. Philip Cole and Joyce Berlin, "Elective Hysterectomy," *American Journal of Obstetrics and Gynecology* 129 (1977): 117–123.
2. Dinh and Woodruff, *American Journal of Obstetrics and Gynecology* 144 (December 1, 1982).
3. Barbara Bolsen, "Study Suggests Vaginal Hysterectomy is Safer," *Journal of the American Medical Association* 247 (1982): 13–19.

9. No More Unwanted Pregnancy at Age 40 . . . or 43 . . . or 45 . . .

1. Christopher Tietze, *Induced Abortion: 1979*, third edition (New York: The Population Council).

2. R. A. Hatcher, G. K. Stewart, F. Guest, N. Josephs, and J. Dale, *Contraceptive Technology 1982–1983*, eleventh edition, (New York: Irvington Publishers).

3. J. H. Johnson, "Tubal Sterilization and Hysterectomy," *Family Planning Perspectives* 14 (1982): 28–30.

4. Ibid.

5. R. A. Hatcher, op. cit, p. 7.

6. Ibid.

10. Medical Laboratory Tests

1. Thomas H. Maugh, "A New Marker for Diabetes," *Science* 215 (February 1982): 5.

2. Lewis B. Morrow, "Hirsutism," *Primary Care* 4 (1977): 128.

Index

321

PENNY WISE BUDOFF, M.D.

is in private practice on Long Island and is clinical associate professor of family medicine at the State University of New York at Stony Brook. She lectures widely to physicians as well as lay audiences, and has frequently appeared on television to talk about new developments in women's medicine. In addition to her previous book, *No More Menstrual Cramps and Other Good News,* she has published many research articles in prominent medical journals.

———————————

Dr. Budoff has created Vitamins for Women to fill the need for a comprehensive vitamin and mineral supplement containing, among other important ingredients, sufficient calcium to help prevent osteoporosis. Originally available only to her patients, they now can be obtained through mail order. If you would like more information about Vitamins for Women, use the coupon below.

By the year 2000, 2 out of 3 Americans could be illiterate.

It's true.

Today, 75 million adults... about one American in three, can't read adequately. And by the year 2000, U.S. News & World Report envisions an America with a literacy rate of only 30%.

Before that America comes to be, you can stop it... by joining the fight against illiteracy today.

Call the Coalition for Literacy at toll-free **1-800-228-8813** and volunteer.

Volunteer Against Illiteracy. The only degree you need is a degree of caring.

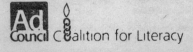

Ad Council   Coalition for Literacy

Warner Books is proud to be an active supporter of the Coalition for Literacy.